Dear Laurence

Keep the faith.

[signature]

P XXVI

"Ilo's effort to provide a 'creative appropriation of Catholic social ethics' in dealing with the challenges facing Africa today is impressive both in his review of Catholic Social Teaching and in his grasp of so much of the literature of contemporary socio-economic analysis of Africa. The breadth of coverage of topics is notable and makes the book a helpful *vade mecum* for those of us engaged in development work in Africa (and wider)."

—Peter J. Henriot
Former Director Jesuit Centre for Theological Reflection (JCTR), Lusaka, Zambia

"In *The Church and Development in Africa* . . . Prof Stan Chu Ilo has done wonderful research and produced a creative and critical analysis of the role of faith-based organizations (FBOs) in changing Africa's troubling social context. It is a well packaged and riveting 'road map,' so to speak, of how best the Churches and aid organizations can reach out in friendship, solidarity and charity to the problem-ridden and poverty-stricken countries of the African sub-region. This is a serious, significant and welcome contribution to that on-going social dialogue. Very few works in the subject area match this work in depth and clarity."

—Reverend Felix Nwatu
Academic Dean (Theology) and Professor of Systematic Theology, Bigard Memorial Seminary, Enugu, Nigeria

"What an epic book! This is a profound and important book. Prof Stan Chu Ilo take us on a powerful journey through Catholic theology to Africa, its history and the development challenges of today. It is a book full of both personal passion and systematic rigor. It interweaves personal story, deep theological reflection, and robust academic analysis to reach workable and practical principles for aid today. It brings a fresh, African and Catholic perspective to an aid literature, populated largely by defunct Western prescriptions."

—Rich James
Principal Consultant, International NGO Training and Research Center, Oxford, co-author *Capacity-Building for NGOs: Making it Work*

"A fascinating blend of Catholic social theory, cultural criticism, and practical guidelines for integral human development in Africa. By interpreting Pope Benedict's *Charity in Truth*, Professor Stan casts a refreshing light into the so-called 'Dark Continent.' This is must read for anyone interested in Africa or the current controversy over foreign aid. The hope permeating this book will stir any human heart!"

—Most Reverend Richard Grecco
Bishop of Charlottetown, Prince Edward Island, Canada, Chair Episcopal Commission on Justice, Conference of Canadian Catholic Bishops

"Stan Chu Ilo provides an important contribution to an important topic. His thorough analysis and his thoughtful insight make this a must read for anyone involved with and interested in development work. His perspective as an African-Canadian theologian provides a fresh approach that will help us all engage in international development with greater respect and integrity."

—**WILLARD METZGER**
General Secretary Mennonite Church of Canada, Former Director Church Relations, World Vision Canada

"In this book, Fr. Ilo has harvested from two sure sources—Catholic Social Teaching and Pope Benedict's recent encyclical, *Caritas in Veritate* (Charity in Truth). The many documents that comprise Catholic Social Teaching both provide an incisive examination of the economic, political, social, and technological practices that affect human culture as well as an incomparable guide for remedying the attendant ills. With intelligence and insight, Fr. Ilo carefully explores these sources and draws from his own experiences as an African and a humanitarian to offer both guidance and encouragement. He reminds us that development, in all of its forms, has moral and spiritual dimensions, not just economic, political, social and technological aspects; and we are diminished when we neglect the moral and spiritual dimensions of our analysis and actions. We need a moral compass to discover our authentic self and the right relationships that inform it, and this book serves as a good and trustworthy companion for that journey."

—**DENNIS PATRICK O'HARA**
Associate Professor of Ethics and Eco-Theology; Director, Elliott Allen Institute for Theology and Ecology, Faculty of Theology, University of St. Michael's College

"*The Church and Development in Africa* poses the fundamental question of whether, and how, we can conceive sustainable development through an 'African reflection' governed by a reimagined Catholic social ethics. The author of the book, Dr. Stan Chu Ilo, troubles the mind and stirs the heart with an overwhelmingly positive analysis anchored in first hand data collected in the course of numerous journeys across Africa. This is a timely and important book that will appeal equally to all students of Africa, especially those fascinated by the confluence of aid, charity, the ethics of development, and political spiritualities."

—**EBENEZER OBADARE**
Associate Professor of Sociology, University of Kansas, U.S.A.

The Church and Development in Africa

African Christian Studies Series (AFRICS)

This series will make available significant works in the field of African Christian studies, taking into account the many forms of Christianity across the whole continent of Africa. African Christian studies is defined here as any scholarship that relates to themes and issues on the history, nature, identity, character, and place of African Christianity in world Christianity. It also refers to topics that address the continuing search for abundant life for Africans through multiple appeals to African religions and African Christianity in a challenging social context. The books in this series are expected to make significant contributions in historicizing trends in African Christian studies, while shifting the contemporary discourse in these areas from narrow theological concerns to a broader inter-disciplinary engagement with African religio-cultural traditions and Africa's challenging social context.

The series will cater to scholarly and educational texts in the areas of religious studies, theology, mission studies, biblical studies, philosophy, social justice, and other diverse issues current in African Christianity. We define these studies broadly and specifically as primarily focused on new voices, fresh perspectives, new approaches, and historical and cultural analyses that are emerging because of the significant place of African Christianity and African religio-cultural traditions in world Christianity. The series intends to continually fill a gap in African scholarship, especially in the areas of social analysis in African Christian studies, African philosophies, new biblical and narrative hermeneutical approaches to African theologies, and the challenges facing African women in today's Africa and within African Christianity. Other diverse themes in African Traditional Religions; African ecology; African ecclesiology; inter-cultural, inter-ethnic, and inter-religious dialogue; ecumenism; creative inculturation; African theologies of development, reconciliation, globalization, and poverty reduction will also be covered in this series.

SERIES EDITORS

Dr Stan Chu Ilo (St Michael's College, University of Toronto)

Dr Philomena Njeri Mwaura (Kenyatta University, Nairobi, Kenya)

Dr Afe Adogame (University of Edinburgh)

The Church and Development in Africa

Aid and Development from the Perspective of Catholic Social Ethics

∾

Stan Chu Ilo

⌖PICKWICK *Publications* · Eugene, Oregon

THE CHURCH AND DEVELOPMENT IN AFRICA
Aid and Development from the Perspective of Catholic Social Ethics

African Christian Studies Series 2

Pickwick Publications
A Division of Wipf and Stock Publishers
199 W. 8th Ave., Suite 3
Eugene, OR 97401

www.wipfandstock.com

ISBN 13: 978-1-60899-779-4

Cataloging-in-Publication data:

Ilo, Stan Chu.

The church and development in Africa : aid and development from the perspective of Catholic social ethics / Stan Chu Ilo.

African Christian Studies Series 2

X + Y p. ; 23 cm. Includes bibliographical references and Index.

ISBN 13: 978-1-60899-779-4

1. Social problems—Africa. 2. Church and social problems—Africa. 3. Benedict XVI, Pope, 1927–. 4. Catholic Church—Doctrines. I. Title. II. Series.

BL2462.5 I46 2011

Manufactured in the U.S.A.

All royalties for this book will be donated to the author's development projects in Africa through *Canadian Samaritans for Africa*: www.canadiansamaritansforafrica.org.

This work is dedicated to the loving memory of

Maren L. Somers

February 19, 1984—June 20, 2010

You left too soon, but you touched many lives in all the five continents where you worked for the Engineers Without Borders-USA. The light you lit in my community and in my heart is still burning. You taught us all how to do charity in truth, and the value of a common humanity in a common planet.

Contents

Foreword

WORKING IN ZAMBIA FOR a faith-based organization involved in promoting integral development, I have been greatly impressed and encouraged by the relevance of the Church's Social Teaching (CST). During the past twenty years I have seen that the values and ethics of CST have implications for the direction that development should take if it is to be truly people-oriented, just and sustainable.

Whether offering alternatives to the harsh dictates of Structural Adjustment Programs, or critiquing national budget priorities and implementation strategies, or advocating for trade policies that promote local products, or struggling to find responses to climate change consequences affecting the lives of millions of people, our team at the Jesuit Centre for Theological Reflection (JCTR) has been directly and indirectly influenced by CST options and orientations.

We have taken seriously that the Church's social teaching provides a value-added dimension to the debates and decisions influencing the future of Zambia and our wider African world. This has meant shaping our policy interventions—for example, scholarly reports, parliamentary testimonies, media campaigns, personal stances—under the influence of the body of social wisdom we refer as the social teaching. It has not meant simply quoting papal documents or bishops' pastoral letters. It has required translating the values and ethics into the language of political strategies and economic plans.

I have seen the power of the CST in focusing our attention on the most important elements in debates and in clarifying priorities. It is a focus on the centrality of humanity, of rights and duties, of community and sustainability, of the priority for the poor. As a consequence, it has meant that our work, at its best, has been distinct from the usual social analysis found in both governmental and non-governmental documents and pronouncements. (I say "at its best" because we may not always have done all the good things I speak of here!)

PRACTICAL APPLICATION

You can appreciate, therefore, the eagerness I experienced when I received a draft of the book you now hold in your hands. A book with such an attractive title: *The Church and Development in Africa: Aid and Development from the Perspective of Catholic Social Ethics.* I looked forward to being enlightened and enriched by Professor Stan Chu Ilo's application of CST to the many challenges of contemporary Africa. In particular I was hopeful to see a practical application of the most recent major contribution to the body of CST, Pope Benedict XVI's *Caritas in Veritate, Charity in Truth.*

I was not disappointed in reading Stan Chu Ilo's book. His effort to provide a "creative appropriation of Catholic social ethics" in dealing with the challenges facing Africa today is impressive both in his review of CST and in his grasp of so much of the literature of contemporary socio-economic analysis of Africa. The breadth of coverage of topics is notable and makes the book a helpful *vade mecum* for those of us engaged in development work in Africa (and wider).

Of many points that I could briefly take up in dialogue with Father Ilo, let me mention here three that touch very much my own work in Zambia: politics, social teaching and African Synod.

ENGAGEMENT IN POLITICS

The first is the interaction between Church and State in the controversial area of politics. The Bishops Conference of Zambia, cooperating with other Church bodies here, has been consistent in raising up issues of justice and peace. When this has in many instances meant challenging the Government's activities, the charge has often been raised against the Church of "interfering in politics." The response of the Bishops has been that the positions they take are indeed "political" in the sense of engagement in the real life of society, but are not "partisan" in the sense of supporting any particular political party position.

I believe that Father Ilo's discussion of "Render to Caesar—Render to God" is particularly insightful in this matter. He clearly rejects an "other-worldly" approach to Christian life, an approach that would disengage the faithful Christian from the day-to-day struggles in the political order. He writes, "Christian faith professed only within the walls of the Church and which is not lived outside the Church precincts through credible life styles, and acts of love and defended in the public domain is empty." Defence in the public domain necessarily will engage us in the politics of our time, be it at local, national, or international levels. But we will not be explicitly partisan.

RELEVANCE OF CST

In holding to this position, he is in my view in line with Pope Benedict's thought in *Caritas in Veritate*. And this brings up the second point for dialogue with Father Ilo's book. He makes a significant contribution to understanding and appreciating *Caritas in Veritate* by shining its light on contemporary African issues. Or, to make this point in even a more relevant fashion, by letting the African issues raise questions with Benedict's exposition of CST. That is, the author grounds his analysis of CST in its relevance to the stories that he can tell of Africa's potentials and problems, joys and sorrows.

I found this approach particularly useful. For many years I lectured for CST courses in seminaries in Zambia and elsewhere in Africa. I would never begin my classes with expositions of what I understood to be the doctrine of CST. Rather I would ask the students to identify from their personal experience the challenges and difficulties facing Africa today in attempts to improve the overall development picture. Then within this context, we would together try to draw out from the CST the lessons that might be helpful in responding to these challenges and difficulties.

Father Ilo utilizes this approach in a manner that comes alive with stories from his own experience and from insights of writers on the contemporary African scene. It is true that he spends considerable time at the beginning of this book in a very heavy theological and philosophical grounding of *Caritas in Veritate*. Readers not particularly drawn to such discussion could, I believe, lightly skip over this section and move to the more practical discussions that make Benedict's thought particularly relevant to current discussions.

AFRICAN SYNOD

The third point for dialogue with Father Ilo is to express joy at his attempt to engage the message of *Charity in Truth* with the lessons and calls of the First and Second African Synods. These extremely important meetings touched on so many of the issues that he so clearly and cogently discusses. The First African Synod (1994) took up the theme of *evangelization* in its fullest sense. The Second African Synod (2009) dealt with the broad issues of *reconciliation, justice, and peace.* Both Synods were prepared for by wide consultation. The Second Synod is now in process of implementation, with calls that echo very strongly Father Ilo's priorities.

I had the wonderful opportunity to be involved in the Second Synod, as an advisor for the bishops of the AMECEA region (eastern and south-central Africa). After reading Father Ilo's book now, I can say that I wish he had been present at that Synod to sharpen the Bishops' theological discourse with his keen appreciation of the need for "a creative appropriation of Catholic social ethics." Again and again, I heard calls for putting CST into practice as the Church in Africa strives to be in service of reconciliation, justice, and peace. And there was frequent expression of disappointment that this CST was so little known and so unpracticed in the lives of Catholics in key political leadership roles throughout the Continent.

So I suppose that this book is now all the more relevant as a help for the necessary steps to implement the Synod. I know that I will rely upon it as a very substantive aid in the work that our JCTR does in Zambia, and I will encourage others to probe into its riches.

—Peter J. Henriot, S.J.
  Director
  Jesuit Centre for Theological Reflection (JCTR)
  Lusaka, Zambia

Preface

THIS BOOK GREW OUT of a conversation I had in the summer of 2009 with my spiritual mentor, Rev. Gen Emekaekwue, the retired director of the Nigerian Military Chaplaincy. When Pope Benedict XVI's encyclical, *Charity in Truth*, was released in June, 2009, it signified a renewal of the commitment of the Catholic Church to global conversation, advocacy, and collaborative efforts for a better and just world order. Unfortunately, there were no sustained intellectual, pastoral, and theological conversations on the message of the encyclical and on how to creatively apply it to diverse contexts. This was particularly worrying because the economic crisis of 2008 reminded the world of the dangers to an economy and a society which is run without ethically driven gospel values. A Christian voice and a Christian activism are called for always to offer a guiding light in the often-complex movement of history. It was while discussing the message of the encyclical and how the world could be improved through the practice of charity that my mentor challenged me to articulate our conversation in a book form. So I got to work. This book, therefore, was born from a conversation between friends and is intended simply as an invitation to people, especially Christians, to an ongoing dialogue on how Christians and men and women of goodwill can commit to the cause of changing the world through the practice of charity.

At a very personal level, I am convinced more than ever that charity is the most important virtue to change the world. I have also seen the redeeming and transformative impact of charity on people's lives. Growing up after the Civil War in Nigeria, which wiped away many people from my family, I often heard my parents talking about how *Caritas* (the charitable arm of the Catholic Church) and other

Christian and humanitarian agencies saved millions of Easterners including my own family members. These people could have starved to death without humanitarian intervention. There are so many people who are condemned to die by poverty, wars, injustice, and broken social, economic, and political systems. Their futures lie in the hand of charitable men and women who can make the individual sacrifices for the common good. We see around us how little acts of kindness can change people's fortune and future. However, charity shines through not only in life-or-death situations. It is manifest when we reach out to members of our families who need our help; when we visit someone who is sick or who is in jail; when we listen to the hidden pains of the other, and when we reach out to the poor and the lonely in our neighborhoods or in far-flung places in the world. Charity is sharing our gifts with others; telling the truth to others in love, and in making constant daily efforts to wipe away tears from the eyes of the sorrowful, and give strength to the weary and hope for the forlorn lonely traveler on the path of life. Charity is saying, "I am sorry" in order to end conflict even when we feel we are right. It manifests itself in every human act that overcomes selfishness, greed, pride, and prejudice, and plants a flower of love in another human heart. Charity is the constant need in a world of change and is the very seed needed to transform the world into a garden of joy, peace, and justice, where God is found.

Because I fervently believe that the power of charity is the redemptive grace needed for our times, I decided to work on this book, not knowing how it would proceed and end. This uncertainty influenced my writing style. In some sections of the book, I adopt a personal narrative; in others I attempt rational arguments to convince readers of the need for Christian charity and Christian social activism in our world. This work is meant to be a conversation addressed both to the intellect and to the heart. I use tools of social analysis in sociocultural studies as well as theological, philosophical, and exegetical tools to illumine my arguments and ground my stories as well as to justify the principles and practices that I am proposing.

I have been enriched by the kindness and generosity of so many people in Europe, North America, and Africa. Without the kindness of so many, beginning with my parents and family, I do not think that I would be alive today. We all can feel the saving reality of charity in the very bones of our being. We have all received from our families, our churches, our nations, and our particular communities much that has made us who we are. We have received especially from God the gift of our being, our world, and everything around us. This realization that everything we have and are comes from God and from the world around us, within us, and beyond us, should inspire us all to reach out to others and make our imperfect lives a full offering to God and to our neighbors. However, charity is not simply reaching out to the poor; it is the giving of ourselves as well. Any act of charity without sacrifice is empty, and any act of kindness without pain to the giver is nothing—mere vanity. Charity should stem from a deliberate movement of the heart and the will, and a willingness to deny ourselves something of value to bring about the happiness and wellbeing of another.

Also, charity is linked to justice in an intimate way. Charitable people must ask why poverty continues to spread, how we can play a part in destroying the citadels of injustice and build the city of God here on earth. Doing charity in concert with working for justice demands concerted and joint efforts by Christians to eradicate the structures of injustice that allow poverty, inequity, suffering, and social evils to fester in the world. This is an essential element of authentic Christianity and a necessary step in advancing the kingdom of God. Every time we reject injustice and selfishness; every time we sacrifice something of value to improve another's life, every time we show an act of kindness and compassion by reaching out to the vulnerable, every time we stand up to defend the rights of the poor, minorities and people on the margins, and every time we take a positive step to reduce our ecological footprints or to save and heal our planet, every time we do any of these we are bringing about the kingdom of God.

Being a Christian is much more than going to church on Sunday or looking up to heaven while closing our eyes to the suffering and pain of our wounded neighbors and our bleeding earth. Thus, this book is a Christian manifesto for social reconstruction and social transformation. Charity brings social transformation through the conversion of human hearts from self-centeredness to other-centeredness, and through the grace of solidarity, compassion, and care. It inspires advocacy for the weak and for a better ordering of society. Christian activism spawns social reconstruction through the transformation of individual and social conscience, and by influencing political and public squares to conform to God's plan and become instruments for building God's kingdom here on earth. This requires a new ethical framework that can radically change global politics and the suffocating policies of globalization that debauch the autonomy and the flourishing of small units, while stifling the voices of the weak and the vulnerable. This means that morality must be activated in terms of making choices that further the common good and enhance prosperity and well-being of everyone on the planet, as preparation for the fulfillment of all things in Christ.

This book was also inspired by the first and second synods on Africa. They both called for a new evangelization in Africa and for concrete steps towards making Africa a place of reconciliation and peace where justice and divine light guide the ordering of the cultural, political, social, and economic life of nations. This work, therefore, addresses Africa's social context in a special way and actually shows how the social gospel being proposed here could help change the African condition and thus fulfill the dreams of African peoples, nations, and churches. The book also offers a critique of ongoing humanitarian and aid initiatives in Africa, a topic broached briefly in my previous work, *The Face of Africa: Looking Beyond the Shadows*. My argument in this work is that there is an art to Christian charity and working for justice. This art was shown to us when the Lord Jesus Christ came to earth and made a tent with us. He could have remained in heaven, but he became one with us, identified with our human conditions, and felt our pains. Thus he was able to save us from the forces of sin, evil, selfishness, and pride all of which harm the social order. That same kind of participatory practice is proposed in Christian engagement with the African social context. An armchair, top-down approach to Christian charity is the bane of our times. Christian charity demands sharing in the lot of the poor, by bridging the long-distance charity of disengagement characterized by random acts often triggered off by crisis of different kinds in Africa. Christian charity, in addition, should not be driven by self-projection. The poor are not a means to the advancement of the rich and the powerful. They are subjects of a loving relationship and not objects to feed the passion, fads, and fancies of the more privileged members of society. This calls for cultural proficiency in dealing with Africans, a proficiency that requires a vulnerable mission that includes immersion in, and understanding of the African context with all its beauty, diversity, complexity, and ambiguity. At the end of the book, I introduce the ten commandments on doing charity in Africa. While there are no negative consequences for violating these commandments on the part of the giver, I am convinced that if charities, especially Christian groups, followed my ten commandments, their imperfect offering will bring so much joy to them and to their African brothers and sisters. These ten commandments show how we all can embrace the participatory practice needed in all authentic Christian charity and development initiatives. This is an important step, in my thinking, through which we—Africans and non-Africans who believe in the future of Africa—can change the face of Africa. Changing the face of Africa and the face of the earth is the vocation of all Christians; it is the invitation that I extend to all through this book. It is, interestingly, the desire which all Christians express when they pray the Lord's Prayer: thy will be done on earth as it is done in heaven.

Acknowledgments

As I was completing the writing of this book, our charitable community was devastated in June 2010 by the sudden death of Maren Somers, who was the project director of our charitable projects in Nigeria, a joint partnership between the Engineers without Borders-USA at University of Illinois Champaign-Urbana, the Luke 4 Foundation, and Canadian Samaritans for Africa. Maren's death at twenty-six reminded me of the true meaning of life. We do not choose when we die or the circumstances that will bring us to the end; we can only choose how we live. The choices we make define our lives and the lives of many. How wonderful to know that the decisions I make today can bring beauty to God's universe, and also illumine my heart and the inner recesses of my life with the light of glory and joy! How encouraging it is to know that my choices can bring happiness to many others whose living condition presently makes happiness a distant reality! The choices Maren Somers made for the poor and for international development brought joy and happiness to many people across the globe. As the Holy Writ says, "Length of days is not what makes life worthwhile." It is the choices that we make which define the meaning of our lives. Maren in her short life had travelled to more than thirteen countries reaching out to the poor, the vulnerable, women, and children. She applied her engineering skills to serve the interest of others. I have dedicated this book to her memory. But she is only one of many others who have touched me profoundly and have changed me permanently. The members of the Board of Directors of our charity, Canadian Samaritans for Africa have been also sources of inspiration. I want to thank especially, Brigitte Kurowski-Wilson who embodies authentic Christian charity and kindness in many ways.

The families of Paul and Mary Marrocco as well as Loretto Lane have embraced me as one of their own and together have given me a home away from home. Together too we continue to work hard on how to make the world a better place for many Africans.

I reserve a special thanks to Ellen MacAdam, who sponsored my graduate studies, and continues to support my priestly ministry and to reach out in charity and kindness to a number of women co-operative and micro-credit unions in Africa. My special thanks go to Bishop Nicola De Angelis of Peterborough for his fatherly support and to the clergy, religious, and faithful of the diocese whose faith and kindness continue to be sources of joy and inspiration.

I express a special thanks to Dr Peter Henriot, S.J for reading through this work and writing the foreword. This work has gained from my interaction and friendship with the following friends and colleagues: Prof. Dennis O'Hara, Prof. Mario D´Souza, Prof. Anne Anderson, Prof. Michael Vertin, Prof. Obiora Ike, Prof. Anekwe Oborji, Prof. Bruce Lietchfield, Prof. Paulinus Odozor, Prof. John Dadosky, Prof. Jesse Mugambi, Prof. Benezet Bujo, Prof. Alex Ojacor, Prof. Agbonkhianmeghe Orobator, S.J, Prof. Uche Ugwueze and Prof. Laurenti Magesa. My special thanks and appreciation go to Rev. Dr. Joseph Ogbonnaya, Rev. Joachim Nnanna, Rev. Beke Utieteng, Rev. Barry Eneh, Rev. Basil Okeke, Rev. Charles Enyinnaya, Rev. Cosmas Ajawara, Rev. Dr Emeka Obiezu OSA, Rev. Anthony Ezeonwueme, Rev. Stephen Akujo, Rev. Maurice Okolie, Rev. Jude Iloghalu, Sr. Bride Ogiri, Sr. Dr Ebere Amakwe, Sr. Josephine Odowuike, Rev. Lukasi Amousou, SJ, and Rev. Charles Awotwi among others who have been very supportive all the way. This work has benefited from the editorial comments of Rev. Ernest Okonkwo, Dr. Paul Marrocco, Fezi and Nkrumah Mauncho, Jim O'Leary, Linda Ncube, John Sagen and Fr. Peter Selvaraj. Special thanks to my parishioners both in Hastings and Courtice, Ontario, Canada, and my secretaries and their families, Barry and Elizabeth Mackinlay, Mike and Teresa Janiga, Paul and Bernadette Spicer, and Lyn Carson. The Sisters of St Mary of Leuca in Courtice and the Sisters of St Joseph Peterborough have been very special and supportive to our charities.

My special thanks go to Cardinal Anthony Okojie, Archbishop A. J. V. Obinna, Archbishop John Onaiyekan, Bishop John Okoye, Bishop Michael Mulhall, and Bishop Richard Greco, my spiritual mentors and friends. I am also grateful to Chief Mrs. Francesca Emmanuel, Bishop Matthew Hassan Kukah, Rev. Dr. George Ehusani, Rev. Dr. Willy Ojukwu, Christy Okoye, Shirley Connell, Debbie Ford, Granville Anderson, John Mackle, Mary Anne Greco, Mary Armstrong, Ted and Yvonne Majoor, Dr. Wilfred Mamah, Athan Nweke, Marie Moser, Louise Houston, Dr. Jim Profit S.J, and Dr. Willard Metzger, Mike Udom, Ruffino Ezema, Fr. Clair Hickson, Jennifer Kolz, Sr. Helen Russell, Sr. Dr Mary Rowell, Sr. Dr Joan Cronin, and Sr. Dr Margaret Myatt for their contribution to this work and to my personal, intellectual, and spiritual development.

My parents, His Royal Highness Igwe and Lolo Vincent and Rose Ilo, and my siblings Ebubedike Vinmartin and Ijeoma Ilo, Dr Cajetan and Onyinye Ilo, Princess Onyinye and Martin Ude, Barrister Jude and Nkem Ilo remain my greatest guide and inspiration, and to them I offer my deepest gratitude more than words can ever express. My special appreciation goes to Pickwick Publications for embracing this book project and for their editorial guidance and ongoing support. I am grateful to all my students, to the staff, and faculty of St Michael's College, Toronto where I have found an intellectual home like no other.

Introduction

You eat to excess; Christ eats not what he needs. You eat a variety of cakes; he eats not even a piece of dried bread. You drink fine Thracian wine; but on him you have not bestowed so much as a cup of cold water. You lie on a soft and embroidered bed; but he is perishing in the cold . . . You live in luxury on things that properly belong to him. Why, were you the guardian of a child and, having taken control of his estate, you neglected him in his extreme need, you would have ten thousand accusers and you would suffer the punishment set by law. At the moment, you have taken possession of the resources that belong to Christ and you consume them aimlessly. Don't you realize that you are going to be held accountable?

—John Chrysostom

I am convinced that together we can eradicate hunger from our planet, but we must move from words to actions. Let us do it for a more prosperous, more just, more equitable and more peaceful world. But above all, let us do it quickly because the poor and the hungry cannot wait.

—FAO Director-General Jacques Diouf at the End of the
World Summit on Food Security, Rome, Nov 18, 2009

EVERY PERSON HAS A story to tell: the story of their lives, or the story of other people's lives or the story of people, events, and things which touched them or impacted their lives for better or for worse. The power of stories cannot be over estimated. I learnt early in life about the power of stories. I come from a wonderful community of Adu Achi in Eastern Nigeria, which like many Igbo societies has a story-telling tradition. Every moral or spiritual truth was captured in stories and proverbs; every event in life was explained by relating it to folklores and legends that have been handed over from one generation to the next.

For many cultures, civilizations, and religions, stories are the best means for communicating moral, religious, and ethical truths. Many biblical narratives, for instance, continue to have lasting impact on millions of lives. Most Christians will remember easily the parables of the Good Samaritan, or the Widow's mite, or the Prodigal Son to mention but a few. They all leave powerful and lasting images and spiritual imprints on the mind and soul. Stories can lift us to the highest peak of human fulfillment and transcendence; they can also sink us to the lowest depths of human pain and anguish. Sometimes, stories leave us simply serene, numb, indifferent, or tepid; they can energize, empower, and challenge us. The story of our world sometimes lifts one's spirit when we see the beauty and ingenuity of people. We are amazed when we see men and women of different races, religions, and ideological divides unite as one and join hands of friendship in the pursuit of authentic human freedom, and the defense of human rights. We are lifted by a sense of common humanity, which has stimulated present concern to combat climate change and environmental pollution, as well as common charitable concerns and advocacy for the poor, the suffering and the marginalized.

On the other hand, when we see the rising incidents of violence, intolerance, hate crimes, neglect of the poor, the weak, and the elderly; when one experiences the effects of corruption, sexual abuse, and exploitation of vulnerable people, or when we see the effects of selfishness, greed, and frauds which have devastated the global economy one is shocked at the loss of a sense of authentic humanity, and ethico-social conscience. Thus, the story of our world continues to amaze and baffle many of us, but it is not a finished story nor do we understand fully our part in the story or how the story will unfold. Creation is a continuing story and every man and woman must find how he or she fits into the story and how to play his or her part in enriching our common story.

This book is an invitation to look at the story of our world, and how each of us fits into that story and what we can do to make the world a better place. I tell the story from the point of view of the African social context, using the social and ethical compass of the social gospel of the Catholic Church. This book is about how the social conditions of Sub-Saharan Africa fit into the wider story of our world when we look at the global and African stories through the lenses of faith and social ethics. It is also about how we can see the global story as one rich and complex interconnected chain that must be strengthened through the practice of charity in truth. It is about understanding human and cosmic development as a regenerative ethics of communion, friendship, love, solidarity, and mutuality.

Sometime in 2009, I was driving an elderly lady from our parish church in Hastings to see her sick husband in a hospital in Peterborough, Ontario, Canada. As we drove along, a very interesting conversation developed as we reflected on the meaning of suffering, death, and the power of love. There was an event in her life that she shared with me, which repeatedly came up in my mind as I worked on this book. It also shows in a very simple but profound way the power of love, on one hand, and how poverty affects our lives and limits our being in many ways. This lady lost her faith early in life as a result of a sad experience. When she was in elementary school she could not take part in the yearly Christmas pageant because her family could not afford to pay for her costume. This was during the time of the Great Depression. She had always dreamt of playing the role of Mary, the Mother of Jesus Christ in the pageant. Unfortunately, in those days things were so hard and the economy so bad that her poor parents could not afford to make a costume for her. She thought to herself then that the parish should be able to get her a costume or at least permit her to act without a special costume, but she did not have the courage to seek such a concession from the nun who was in charge of the Christmas pageant.

She felt so ashamed and sad every Christmas seeing most of the other children from rich families playing the roles of the Holy Family, and that of the animals, the wise men, and the shepherds. These events happened more than seventy years ago, but this lady still carries the scar and the burden, even in her old age. Poverty robs people of their freedom, and limits their abilities to become who they are meant to be. Poverty robs people of joy, it makes people voiceless and powerless. Our failure sometimes to care for the poor, to be the voice of those who are condemned to live and walk in the shadows of death because of poverty; and the failure to even notice such people among us is perhaps one of the greatest tragedies in human history.

As this lady's husband lay dying in the hospital, she found herself again asking other questions about the meaning of life, sickness, suffering and death: Why should my husband lose his memory? Why should one person suffer so many health complications? What did he do to merit these? This lovely lady was blaming God for the suffering of her husband, and was blaming God for the suffering of the Great Depression. Like many seniors in Canada and other developed countries, she had lost a lot of money during the economic recession of 2008–2009, and she saw all these things as the direct consequence of a divine positive act. If God allowed these things to happen, there is no need to believe in God. She thought perhaps that the Bible maybe was not a true account of how God operated in creation. Interestingly, she agreed with me that her love for her husband was stronger than her husband's suffering, and that her courage to work hard in life to overcome the poverty of her family was more meaningful to her than the humiliation she suffered as an eight year old at not being part of a Christmas pageant. In the power of her love, she found the meaning of her suffering and poverty. But that was not the only lesson she found in her personal story. She began to realize, she reflected, that her love for her husband was not simply meaningful to her alone, it also brought much joy and meaning into the life of her husband. Even though her love was not able to prevent her husband's death, it helped to bring a great deal of strength, grace, and happiness into the whole situation for all the members of the family, including her dying husband.

The stories we hear from ordinary encounters in life reflect the complexities of human life. They are real stories of real people: the stories of our family, our communities, professional groups, our schools, and our ethnic, racial, and religious groups. In the story of any human being, the perceptive mind finds a narrative of his or her own history because we are all connected more profoundly than we can ever imagine. I remember the amazing grace and generosity of Monica and Dennis, and their five children. I was travelling by road in the summer of 2007 from Kampala to Nairobi, when our bus broke down near Eldoret, some 350 kilometers away from Nairobi. This happened around 6pm, and it was raining heavily. The *Akamba* bus carrying us was leaking water from all sides and it was better staying in the rain than inside the bus as we were all getting soaked. I did not know anybody in the area and the mobile phone I had borrowed from a friend for the journey had no credit in it and the shops around were all closed. The driver told us that there is no way the bus could be repaired that night under such a heavy rain and that everyone has the choice of either sleeping inside the bus or finding a place of lodging for the night in the sleepy town some 20 km to Eldoret. My heart was pacing rather rapidly because I was travelling alone and was feeling a little afraid because in those days leading up to the much-disputed 2007 elections in Kenya, there was a significant rise in violent crimes. The *Mungiki* gang was the most notorious and had attacked a number of buses inside the cities and on the outskirts as well. Meanwhile, a number of passengers were leaving the bus after strong worded exchanges between them and the driver and his bus conductor. I did not know what to do.

Sitting by my side since the stopover at the Uganda-Kenyan border town of Malaba was a woman who had five children, one a nursing baby and a child of two who also was sharing the row seat meant for two. Her other three children were sitting right behind us. Throughout the two hours' journey from Malaba to Eldoret, I was glued to my book, and was really regretting choosing that particular spot because I could neither communicate with Monica who spoke little English nor could I communicate with her little child. But as the bus was getting emptied of passengers, Monica was busy on the phone with Dennis, her husband who drives a cab operated by "a big man" in Eldoret. Her husband spoke good English and when he arrived to pick his family, I opened up to him about my predicament. He asked for my identity, which I happily obliged him. He offered to host me for the night, but told me that he was afraid that I might find it hard sleeping in a two-room apartment fully loaded with sundry items, household goods, without any space and lacking any comfort and without mosquito gauze or nets, and with little ventilation. He suggested that he could drive me down to the nearby Anglican Church where I might find hospitality. However, with the heavy rain, and the fact that Dennis had to return the car to the "big man" to make returns for the day, I simply wanted a place I could call home for that night. That night was the most pleasant for me because this family accepted me with so much love. They were willing to give up their lone bed for me which I declined as I was enjoying my conversation with their older kids who were in elementary schools and could communicate in English with some limitations. They were happy that they could teach me some Swahili words in exchange for some English words, which I taught them. We ate together, laughed together, and prayed together. Dennis told me the story of his family, the struggles of raising five children without much income, and the debilitating sickness that had incapacitated his wife so that she could not contribute financially to the upkeep of his family. I also shared my own stories with them. As the night wore on, I dosed off in the couch with some discomfort and anxiety, but grateful that I found love among total strangers.

By 6.00am in the morning I was woken up by Dennis who had to leave early for work. He was so gracious and kind to give me a ride to the park in Eldoret to continue my journey. What surprised me most was that when I offered Dennis some money in gratitude, he declined it and gave me a very long-winded advice on the meaning of life. What remained with me was one line which he spoke with so much pride: *"We are poor as you could see but we have not lost what makes us humans, which is love."* I was shocked by the fact that he refused my offer because I saw for myself that they needed the money more than I did. I knew also that it is rare for a poor and needy person to refuse help or reject financial gift. But this was a deep lesson for me on what it means to be human. Maybe Dennis was richer than I thought, and maybe I was the one who was poor. I knew that before I accepted to sleep in their home, I was very afraid and many thoughts were going through my mind: maybe they will rob me at night. Maybe they will kill me and use my passport to travel to Europe or North America. I should have travelled by air instead of taking the risk of travelling by road. I should have remained in the bus etc., etc. My fear impoverished me more than their lack of means impoverished them; and their generosity enriched me more than my doubts and anxiety. At the end of the day, I saw the generosity and graciousness of a simple Kenyan family, who taught me some important lessons about life, by their own story and generosity. By their dignity and self-respect even in their poverty the true sum of their wealth was evident. Thus, in every story of a family, I find my own family story as well as the story of our human family as creatures of God.

In a sense, this book grew out of the many stories that have become part of me through my faith, academic life, pastoral ministry, and involvement in a number of charitable projects and causes in Africa and North America. It is also part of a continuing reflection on the bigger stories and wider picture of life, community, social ethics, and their implications for a more just and healthy world, where everyone is loved and accepted as a human being. This book is my attempt to remind myself and my fellow travelers on this planet that we are held together in care by the loving hand of God, and that we are all connected in a global community in which the intersection between humans and the environment, and among human beings themselves have become tighter and more intimate.

It is a book that reminds people of the need to listen to each others stories, and become part of each others stories because we share a common origin in God and must embrace each other if we are to find our way together to our home. Everyone has a story or stories to tell, we are each the result of many events which all add up to create a good or bad narrative depending on how one interprets the interaction of these events. The stories of each person, each culture, civilization, and the global community are not set on stone. It is always evolving, availing itself of new insights, new shades, new intersections, and new creation.

The challenge of the modern world is the imprisonment to one narrative: seeing myself as the beginning and end of all things makes me a slave to myself and robs me of the thrill and expansive grace of stepping into the stories and worlds of others. If a nation closes itself to other nations, it becomes a slave to its own ideologies, its own limitations, and the pretensions of self-sufficiency, thereby losing the measuring rod and corrective and creative expansion that it could have gained from other nations. If a religion makes an idol of herself, she becomes a false god to herself and loses the true splendor of God who is constantly stretching us beyond the limited horizon of human possibilities and religious faith. But limiting other people's narrative could also be external and imposed, that is why it is often said that history is written by the victors. However, at the end of the day it is humanity as such that suffers when we do not enter into other people's world, when we distort their histories, or when we close the door to the possibilities in other people's world by our own prior conclusion of who they are. This is so often the case with people on the margins. How many wrong conclusions we have drawn about the indigenous peoples and nations of North America? How many false judgments have been made about people from Africa, or of the migrants and refugees in many Western countries and of the poor people in our societies? How many false conclusions have been drawn about certain religious traditions, people with different sexual orientation, certain racial groups, and certain nations and cultures? We are all victims of the blinders and blinkers we have inherited or acquired from reading other people's stories as a single narrative based on prejudice or abbreviated history. The same wrong conclusion could be reversed: many people in Africa think that all is well with every person from Canada or the USA and that there is so much prosperity in these countries that everyone here lives in flowing abundance. I was shocked myself the first time I travelled outside Africa to Rome when I saw beggars in St Peter's Square and noticed that some of these beggars were Europeans! We need to enter into other people's story and see that in every story of any man or woman is a bit of my own story.

When I finished reading Pope Benedict XVI's social encyclical, *Charity in Truth*, what struck me immediately was the clarity and depth of his vision. This vision and insight came out clearly in the link he makes between charity and truth, which was an invitation for us to see the whole story and not parts of it. It is this total picture approach that can give us an integrated vision of life, love, human destiny, and the golden path we all must walk in creating a more charitable world. However, a better world is not something we can invent. Rather, it is something that we have received as a gift from God, because it is written into the story of the universe by God. We can discover this gift if we become attuned to the hymn of the universe and see clearly the echo of divine presence and the intimations of transcendence hidden in the human heart and in the heart of the created world. In the cry of the poor widow, in the anxiety of the rich aristocrat, in the depression of the mega rich over a broken marriage, or the pain of an African woman for healing for her bareness, we can sense the deepest hunger of the human heart for meaning, happiness, and transcendence. This is written into the very structure of our human history whose ultimate term is found in God. Bringing God into the whole picture becomes not an add-on but the very condition of possibility for finding the authentic direction of human history and the ethical impulses and spiritual forces that will direct our steps. Seeing the whole picture is, therefore, in my thinking, the hermeneutics for reading *Charity in Truth*, and for discovering the authentic path for doing charity. Doing charity to anyone will demand our knowing the person's story and becoming part of that story. The story of every human person has a connection to my own story because we share a common identity of being made in the image and likeness of God. Charity is, therefore, to be done from the whole story of the human person, from the whole perspective of our human destiny, but also from the whole story of creation which Pope Benedict calls "our home."

Understanding the origin and destiny of all things draws us to adopt a moral and spiritual vision to development. The lack of this kind of vision, leads to a narrow economic dialectics that sometimes fuels human greed and selfishness. Such a lack has many negative consequences as recent history has shown: economic downturns, poverty, injustice, wars, violence, protectionism, terrorism, and other allied evils. The good news here is that there is a better path towards human fulfillment on earth, which is the vision Pope Benedict develops in his encyclical. He draws wisdom from the rich treasures of nature, the Christian socio-ethical vision, biblical tradition, and insights from philosophers and theologians alike. From these, he proceeds to advance a social ethics for dealing with the challenges of globalization and the moral, social, political, and economic problems that it brings. This is why this social encyclical speaks to many other audiences beyond the Catholic community. The challenges to which the pope draws our attention are faced by everyone. They are challenges which impact our world in a profound way irrespective of our religious or ideological persuasions. In addition, the boundaries of discourse is shifting in many ways, and conversation about how to build a new world is one that is now being carried on across religious, political, cultural, national and economic frontiers. This is why the social encyclical is an invitation to a wider global dialogue on how to build a better world. Furthermore, the social gospel uses social and economic data which are drawn from the joy and pastiche of life as basis for appropriating the gospel fruits. It is therefore, important to read the encyclical as part of a renewed appeal for humanity to see the whole picture, to see the interaction needed between different voices for a better world, and to find our place in the whole picture of the created universe.

The first selfish statement we find in the Old Testament was the response that Cain gave to God's question when he killed his brother, Abel, out of envy and resentment. When God asked Cain, "Where is your brother?," Cain's answer was; "Am I my brother's keeper?" Here we see a selfish tendency which the world should reject. Am I my sister's keeper? Why should I see my story in the story of the suffering of millions of people because of the earthquake in Haiti or the Asian Tsunami? Why should a Canadian see the poverty of Africa as impoverishing his or her life? Why should the rise in HIV/AIDS infection in Russia concern my own health and well being in Sweden? Why is the melting of the Antarctica a concern to me in the safe comfort of a Safari walk in Tanzania? Why should the ecological disaster caused by gas flaring in the Niger Delta region of Nigeria cause me anxiety in the safe beaches of Lake Ontario? I think the encyclical calls our attention to who our neighbors are and our moral responsibilities to them.

The encyclical is also an attempt to make humanity to ponder again: Where is my brother earth or my sister sea? Where is the poor in our midst? Where are our neighbors? If I see the sea as part of my story, and the poor as part of who I am; if I know and enter into the story of others, I will suffer with them as well. This encyclical does not seek to enunciate principles alone; it shows how to apply them. It is a bold cry from the heart of the Church that we cannot continue to allow the world to run on the logic of economics, or the power of dominion. It is a call that humanity should return to the path of justice and peace through a renewed commitment to sacrifice and selflessness for the good of the other. We also need to make a return to the moral and spiritual vision of life, community, human destiny, and integral development that helps to give us the true story of reality as such and show us our place in it.

My attempt in this book is to draw out the fundamental message of this encyclical within the wider social gospel tradition, and apply this message to Africa's social context. While reading this book should not be a substitute to reading the encyclical itself, the work offers a summary of the encyclical and draws out the intelligibilities in all the principles of Catholic social teaching which are found in this encyclical. The book gives a comprehensive and systematic presentation of the thinking of the Catholic Church on the social questions of the day. The book shows how the social questions of the day impact on African development, aid, and charitable initiatives. It further engages the principles and practice of charity in truth and their implications for the development of Africa, the only continent that has witnessed gradual and steady decline in all the indices of human development within the last decade. It is also the only continent that, according to statistics, will not be able to meet the Millennium Development Goals (MDGs) by 2015. If the principles of the social order advanced by Pope Benedict are true, their validity can best be tested through critically appropriating them in the continent which is being changed and affected most profoundly by the social, economic and political forces of the global economy and neo-liberal globalization.

In chapter 1 and 2, I will offer a summary of the main teaching of the encyclical within the wider social gospel tradition of the Catholic Church. I will follow a thematic approach in this chapter showing how the encyclical continues the central message of Catholic social teaching on the principles of solidarity, subsidiarity, and participation, ecological ethics, human rights, natural law foundation for human dignity and rights, social ethics, and the moral framework which should govern the market forces. I will also analyze in depth the new principle of gratuitousness introduced by Pope Benedict as the force and flowering of charity. Pope Benedict identifies the central social issue of our time as globalization. In the light of this, I will devote substantial space to a critical appraisal of how the Pope interprets globalization. I will conclude the chapter with an exploratory proposition on the meaning of development when conceived through the lenses of the wider human and cosmic story in their various layers and tapestry.

In chapter 3, I will explore the rich and diverse stories of Sub-Saharan Africa. The goal of the chapter is to show that a total picture approach to understanding African history helps one to be in a better position to do charity in truth in Africa. I will explore the dreams and despair of Africa, the homelessness of Africans as the conceptualization of the African condition, and some of the crises facing the continent, namely, HIV/AIDS, poverty, health, globalization, ecological crisis, water crisis, food crisis, the challenges of education and cultural development, among others. I will also explore the strengths and weaknesses of present donor and development initiatives in

Africa and expose the secondary motives that have governed some of these charitable initiatives. The chapter shows how entering into the stories of Africa will enrich the world, and bring solidarity and support for the various local and international efforts to stimulate African development.

This chapter also seeks to create a better analytical framework for understanding the diversity of the African continent, which often hampers development. Many people outside Africa often wrongly read Africa as a single story with common problems and identity. Africa is a construct of many layers and not a reality with a univocal referent. This wrong reading has often inspired most non-African driven charities and development initiatives. The chapter concludes with an argument on the link between poverty and human rights, showing that the existence of poverty in many parts of the world, especially in Africa is a serious abuse of human rights. Doing charity, therefore, is both a moral and humanistic obligation. However, in doing charity in Africa efforts should be made to build on the assets of the people and not simply attend to the needs in Africa, which most often sustains an ever-revolving chain of dependency.

In chapter 4 and 5, I will apply the principles developed in chapter 1 and 2, and the integrated and fuller reading of African history in chapter 3, to the practice of charity in truth in general and in Africa in particular. I will explore how three groups (Christians, Christian international charities working in Africa, and Catholic charities) should operate in Africa if they desire to have lasting and significant impacts in Africa. I will devote a considerable space to developing what I call a vulnerable approach to social ministry that will demand an immersion in other people's story, and a direct and immediate identification with their condition. Charity, I will argue, is not a social welfare initiative. On the contrary, using a Christian ethical framework, charity should be a way of life essential to Christian identity. Thus, I will demonstrate how doing charity is relevant for a total ecclesiology against a binary notion of faith and Christian life that creates a gulf between the secular and the sacred, and the demands of justice and the obligation of charity. There is also an attempt in this chapter to develop an African theology of development. Such a theology is an integrated reflection on faith in its engagement with history; it proceeds through a critical analysis of African social context. It seeks to show that integral development is already the beginning of the eschatological harvest of God's kingdom. A theology of development will be concerned with how to justify the practice of charity in truth. The practice of charity—which embraces the whole story of peoples especially those on the margins of society—will begin with a thorough cultural hermeneutical theology through which we enter into other people's world. The chapter concludes with proposing how churches in Africa can practice charity in truth through an instrumental, prophetic, critical, practical, and credible way of being which is presented as being both mission and praxis. I will also develop the notion of civilization of love that chimes into the ethical vision of Pope Benedict for the social reconstruction of our world, and makes possible the practice of charity. I will make a conscious effort to show how each of the different dimensions of the civilization of love relates to the African social context.

This work is a call for a renewed ethical and moral consciousness in our world, and for a new theological understanding of integral development. It has a universal message, but its phenomenological referent is drawn from the African condition and contemporary history. It drew its sources from the heritage of Catholic social teaching, as well as from the social sciences, philosophy, theology especially social ethics, and the growing data on the ethics of ecological and environmental consciousness. It is hoped that anyone who reads this book will be filled with a new sense of hope about the possibility of a better world especially for the poor people in the world and more specifically the struggling peoples of Africa. This hope is within the range of our human possibility, if we stretch ourselves beyond the limits of our human horizon to touch the margins of God. The wisdom of bringing morality and spirituality into the picture is what is often lacking in our world, and Pope Benedict's social encyclical shows how we can make the transition from a purely humanistic philanthropy, to a social ethics that is rooted in a theistic anthropology and leads to authentic human fulfillment and cosmic peace and harmony. Our attempt here is to say that Pope Benedict's vision is not an illusion, nor is it an ideological or doctrinal generalization or posturing. On the contrary, it is a truth that we can discover in our world, in our personal stories, and through listening to the stories of others, and by listening to God. However, we must all move out of our comfort zones, and embrace our own stories and integrate them within the new stories, possibilities, and limitations of the many peoples, religions, races, and non-human members of this rich and infinite universe. This is obviously an ongoing conversation, which this book seeks to advance from my faith as an African who believes in the God of our Lord Jesus Christ and the God of my ancestors.

1

The Message of Pope Benedict XVI's Social Encyclical and Catholic Social Ethics

THE LINK BETWEEN CHARITY AND TRUTH

CHARITY IN TRUTH (*CIV*) is an invitation to Christians, as well as men and women of goodwill who are not Christians, to apply a spiritual vision to addressing the pressing economic, ecological, social, political, and moral challenges facing humanity today. Its message is closely connected to the two previous encyclicals of Pope Benedict XVI, forming, as Stratford Caldecott commented, a triptych on the Christian faith in both its theoretical and practical dimension, namely love, hope, and faith grounded in truth.

Thus, the primary thesis of the encyclical is that authentic development requires the establishment of the correct scale of value on the human person who is both the primary actor and the focus of development. This development must occur within the broader goal of attuning our actions to realizing the divine purpose of creation. Development initiatives carried out solely on the bases of economics, production, profit, technical progress, and technological determinism will continue to fail to serve the person and thereby society. These initiatives must take into account the sacredness of human life, the

1

dignity of every human person, the dignity and importance of family life and the wisdom of respecting the right order of things, justice in our treatment of each other, and our relationship with nature. In addition, the common good is interpreted by Pope Benedict as a common concern that cuts across nations, races, and, one could add, other life forms. The promotion, preservation, and protection of the common good, therefore, requires action and solicitude by all Christians and people of goodwill at both interpersonal levels, as well as in political organizations and institutions (CIV, 7).

The human condition is essential to the Church's mission of building God's kingdom on earth. Her mission draws both from the Lord's mandate of reconciling all things in Christ as well as from the prophetic tradition of being immersed in and engaged with the living condition of God's people at all times. The Pope begins his reflection by noting that "charity in truth, to which Jesus Christ bore witness by his earthly life and especially by his death and resurrection, is the principal driving force behind the authentic development of every person and of all humanity" (CIV, 1). The introduction to the encyclical establishes the main grounds for the Church's teaching on the primacy of love and the origin and goal of all authentic human love. The correspondence of love and truth is found in Christ, who is the Truth and the Incarnation of divine love. Love is also the heart of God. This is because trinitarian communion is the union of love, friendship, community, solidarity, and divinity in the three divine persons and from the Trinity to humanity and the created universe. "Charity is love received and given. It is 'grace' (*charis*). Its source is the wellspring of the Father's love for the Son, in the Holy Spirit. Love comes down to us from the Son. It is creative love, through which we have our being; it is redemptive love, through which we are recreated. Love is revealed and made present by Christ (cf. John 13:1) and 'poured into our hearts through the Holy Spirit' (Rom 5:5). As recipients of God's love, men and women are subjects of charity, and thus they are called to make themselves instruments of grace, so as to pour forth God's charity and weave networks of charity" (CIV, 5) This union is the origin of all things, such that we can conclude that creation and everything in it are the fruits of the creative love of God the Father, the saving love of Jesus Christ, and the sanctifying love of the Holy Spirit. Love is, therefore, to be seen by all Christians and all men and women of goodwill as central to who we are. Thus, the proper locus for Christian operation and ecclesial life *ad intra* and *ad extra* is a loving relationship built around the Holy Trinity. Charity is thus the basis of the Church's social teaching (CIV, 2).

The question one may ask is: Why does Pope Benedict make a link between charity and truth? He wishes to accentuate this link because, "charity has been and continues to be misconstrued and emptied of meaning, with the consequent risk of being misinterpreted, detached from ethical living and, in any event, undervalued" (CIV, 2). This is an all too common experience from everyday living in contemporary society. We often do not see the whole picture of reality nor do we appreciate enough the diversity and extensiveness of creation. Truth grounds and directs the end proper to every human action. Truth, according to St Thomas Aquinas, is the highest of values, the indispensable source of authentic love and moral virtue that can flow only from a true knowledge of self, world, and God.[1]

The Incarnate Logos is the Truth: "For this I was born and for this I came into the world, to testify to the truth" (John 18:37). This meaning of truth is found in his farewell discourse in John when the Lord teaches in John chapter 14 that he is the Way, the Truth, and the Life. Here, we see that truth relates to the things about God, which have been revealed to human beings through Christ. The things about God relate not only to the divine essence or the identity of the Christian God as Trinity, but also they relate to us human persons, in our origin and ultimate destiny. The truth about God relates to creation and the goal and destiny of creation. It concerns also human action, and the

---

1. Ashley, "Introduction," 3. Aquinas goes on in the first ten chapters of *Summa Contra Gentiles* to give a preliminary understanding of truth, "The ultimate end of the universe must, therefore, be the good of the intellect. This good is truth. Truth must consequently be the ultimate end of the whole universe, and the consideration of the wise man aims principally at truth. So it is that, according to His own statement, divine Wisdom testifies that He has assumed flesh and come into the world in order to make the truth known" (Aquinas, *Gentiles*, 1/1:2). Truth is identified as wisdom by Aquinas, a concept which he began to develop in his commentary on Aristotle's Metaphysics. We can admit this for now that when we speak of truth it refers to the highest aspiration of the human intellect, which finds its fulfilment in contemplation, in embracing the source of all truth the Incarnate Logos. It is this alone which organizes all things, and gives meaning to all things, and draws all things together. Thus charity in truth is the most appropriate way of showing the intimate connection between the two highest aspirations of the human person, that of the intellect (truth), and that of the heart (charity).

ultimate goal of the moral demand that should govern our actions and their true end. It inevitably relates to the human, cosmic, and cultural development and to the transcendent values which govern them.

Apprehending the truth, and the content and splendor of truth, guides the practical action that is proper to charity. It is not "charity and truth" but rather "charity in truth," which means that charity inheres in the truth. It is thus directed to the end proper to the human person, which is found in the truth of things as such. Being and truth are prior to practical action and practical moral choices. Thus, the pursuit of the good must be directed primarily by the true end of both the human person and all creation. This end we apprehend through our intellect and faith as defined by God. Steven A. Long captures this insight very well when he writes, "The speculative horizon of all ethical choice together with the order of ends implicit in any and every ethical decision provides the fragrance of genuine grandeur in moral philosophy, enabling it to rise to the contemplation of the nature of the good life. It is precisely this genuinely philosophic character that is lost to moral thought by its absorption in a praxis separated from truth. But contemplating the true of the good is not servile, and authentic freedom does not reside in liberty from the need to conform one's mind to the order of being. "[2]

Humanity is often a slave to one narrative, we do not see the other side of the coin nor do we stretch our gaze beyond the human horizon or the limitations and thrill of the present moment. How many marriages, relationships, and social or business pacts have fallen apart because the promise of love, honesty, and fidelity made at the beginning, was not kept together consistent with the truth of our humanity including its limitations and weaknesses? There are all forms of humanitarian activities in hidden alleys in many communities across the globe, and new initiatives for African development which are often driven by parochial motives or some self-serving ideologies or isolated economic and political goals. Notably, these initiatives sometimes proceed from a single narrative of Africa as a poor continent without an immersion in the diverse and rich stories of the continent, which go beyond poverty and suffering. They, therefore, proceed from a lack of the fullness of truth of the reality of Africans.

2. Long, "Law or Reason," 176.

The link between charity and truth is rooted on both theistic and anthropological foundations. Charity is not simply an act or disposition of benevolence towards another, or social welfare, or mere philanthropy. It has a divine and transcendent meaning. It is the effusion of that which God has made available to us in Christ for our own good, now directed towards the good of another. Charity is not a mere sentiment or a feeling of good will even though these do work together to enhance the splendor of Christian charity. For Pope Benedict, charity is truth, love, and word. These are deeds that flow from the truth. Seeing this link demands the wisdom that comes from both reason and more importantly from faith.

As Serge Thomas Bonino argues very lucidly, divine revelation brings about three realities to the human search for truth: the perfection of the intellect—it ripens, heals, purifies, and fulfills the intellect; it also brings a union between the intellect and the object of faith, God. Faith unites the knowing subject with the object of faith and the first truth, God. "The order of grace comes from a more profound gift of God: it consist on the one hand in the objective revelation of the mystery, received in faith, and on the other hand in the dynamism of charity as participation in the love with which God loves himself and loves his spiritual creatures. In relation to nature, grace is irruption and newness: It opens 'new horizons' to human existence."[3] Faith's object as the First Truth is the full completion of the dynamism for perfection rooted in human knowing, beyond which none can go and outside whose structure one can have the possibility of falsehood. This foregrounds all moral praxis, social theories, and the ethos of salvation and integral liberation. What is clear using Aquinas's explication of faith and truth is that both the formal and material objects of faith cohere in such a way that the human subject is led through the material objects to the formal object, the First Truth. The relation between charity and truth can only be seen through the eyes of faith which orders all our human actions and our existence, as well as our relations with one another and the world of nature in the direction of God. Herein lies the need to see the whole story of creation, and our lives in an integrated narrative with many different but related layers. Charity is not a one-dimensional human aspiration; it is part of the whole reality of human identity, human community, cosmic harmony,

3. Bonino, "Nature and Grace," 233–34

and ultimate human destiny with all the moral and spiritual implications therein.

Charity, according to the Pope is a value that has a specific meaning. Thus, we cannot infinitely extend the meaning of charity, but its meaning is specified by the truth about God, the human person, human destiny, the divine governance of the world, morality, and the social order. It is obvious from the foregoing that discussion about charity and the social doctrine of the Church will demand an integrated vision unified by truth. According to the Holy Father, the dynamic and specific nature of charity is what gives rise to the social teaching of the Church as *caritas in veritas in re sociali*: the proclamation of the truth of Christ's love in society (CIV, 5). In order to make this connection clearer, I will look at the distinction between a theistic anthropology, which is the basis of the Church's social teaching, and norma normata for human rights against some secular anthropological positions.

Theistic Anthropology as Basis for Charity in Truth

Theological anthropology is the proper starting point in discovering the purpose for which the human person was created by God. Thus, fidelity to the human person requires fidelity to the truth that alone guarantees freedom and integral development. The social question, according to CIV is radically an anthropological question that centers on the inviolable dignity of the human person and the transcendent value of natural moral norms. Beginning with this foundational relationship, it becomes necessary to resolve the complexities around the social questions of the day (CIV, 45–46). Thus, full understanding of these foundational precepts for a theistic anthropology is necessary in order to appreciate this link between charity and truth, the dimensions of which Pope Benedict's social encyclical brings out clearly in order to enrich the treasure of the Church's social teaching.

The mystery of the human person cannot be grasped apart from the mystery of God. Christianity upholds as a fundamental belief that the human person is created in the image and likeness of God. This understanding is the most permanent, ontological ground and establishes the foundation for understanding Christian anthropology. This theme is seen as the key to the biblical understanding of human nature and to all the affirmations of biblical anthropology in both the Old and New Testaments. Many other religions such as Islam and African

Traditional Religions, for example, understand God as the creator of man and woman, but they do not have the idea that God made the human person in the image and likeness of God.

Christian understandings of "image and likeness" tend to fall into three main groups in classical Christian thought: First, a theological branch which interprets the image as God's self-manifestation, on one hand, and which has an anthropological interpretation of the image of God as who the human person is in relation to God, on the other hand. Both trajectories of interpretation could be found in the writings of the early fathers like Origen, Tertullian, and Irenaeus. J. Richard Middleton establishes the richness of the idea of the *imago dei* for a correct Christian anthropology. He argues that some Christian theologians have a substantialistic understanding of the image of God in man. Such theologians from Augustine to Aquinas conceive of the image of God as rational substantial soul mirroring its divine archetype. This is the effect of the pervasive influence of Platonism on Christian theology supplemented in the Latin West by notions such as conscience, spirituality, immortality, freedom, and personhood.[4]

Second, a group of Christian theologians who conceive of the image of God in the human person in a dynamic, relational mode in which the image is the ethical conformity or obedient response to God's love. The third group conceives of the image as a functional mediation of power from God to the human person to become king and steward of creation both for the human and non-human world. These represent three strands of interpretation that date back to Irenaeus for whom imago refers to that which is ontologically constitutive of humanness (rationality and freedom), while likeness (*similitudo*) designates the ethical similitude which had been lost by the Fall and is restored in Christ.

These theological reflections on Imago Dei are based on the creation account of Genesis. The creation accounts in Genesis (1:1—2:3; 1:26–27) designate two imprecise words *tselem* (image) and *demut* (likeness) for the image and likeness of God. *Tselem* occurs seventeen times in the Old Testament meaning in some instances a concrete and physical representation, image, statue, picture (Gen 1:26; 5:3; Ps 39:6), identity, and, in other cases, it has a more abstract sense interpreted as shadow or dream (Ps 73:20). *Demut*, on the other, is the noun of

---

4. Middleton, Liberating Image, 19.

an abstract verb, *dama,* which means "to be like," a more general resemblance. *Demut,* therefore, explicates the fact that if the human person is created in the image and likeness of God there cannot be a substantial identity. Created in the image and likeness of God, the human person is not God: he is God's creature and depends on God. This identity of God and the human person is not a similarity in the physical order. This resemblance means that the human person is like God and is the only one (person) among earth's creatures that God speaks to and who answers God (Gen 1:28–30; 2:7). [5] The semantic range of meaning is very wide and beyond the scope of this book. But it is important to note as Edward Curtis observes; "There seems to be nothing in the biblical understanding of the images that would give content to the meaning of the image of God beyond that which the context of the passages suggests, and it appears that the basis for any further understanding of the image of God will have to be found outside the biblical material. This even raises the possibility that this is an idea that Israel borrowed from another culture."[6] The image of God idea appears then to have originated from the royal ideology of ancient Near Eastern peoples. This may be attributed among other reasons to the fact that the idea of making or reproducing God's image as such is foreign to ancient Israel. Thus, image and likeness are to be understood in terms of capacities, intelligence, and other qualities more than physical resemblance between God and the human person. According to Preuss, the LXX usually renders *demut* by *homoioma* (likeness), form, appearance (fourteen times); but we find *homoiosis* (likeness, resemblance) five times, *eikon* (image, likeness) once (Gen 5:1), while the Latin Vulgate translates it as *similitudo* (likeness) nineteen times.[7] While the use of "image" connotes a physical resemblance in terms of the face of a king on a coin or ownership in terms of orientation towards which the image belongs; "likeness" conveys a less physical and mathematical quality. Image and likeness thus have more to do with function and position in the created order than with form and appearance.[8]

5. See Kooy, "Image," 682.

6. Curtis, "Image of God," 390.

7. Botterweck and Helmer, Theological Dictionary of the Old Testament, 257.

8. Curtis, "Image of God," 391.

It is obvious, however, that the terms "image" and "likeness" in the Old Testament have a wide range of meanings, including the following realities: the human person is the climax of God's creative act and has a preeminent place in the created order; the human person is a being like God but he or she is not God; he or she is the only one that is created in the image and likeness of God and he or she is to have dominion over the whole of creation. The human person, or more properly, the human race (adam), (that is humanity as a whole, every human being irrespective of sex, age, condition or status in society) is placed at the centre of creation, and the image of the potter, used by the Yahwist author of Genesis, expresses very well God's solicitude in man's regard (Gen 2:7). It also suggests that the human person is the primary place where God manifests God's self, and that humanity stands in a special relationship with God, and should function both like God and on God's behalf. All the created things were placed at the service of the human person. Responsible stewardship is required of the human person. I shall return to this analysis of human stewardship in my treatment of Pope Benedict's ecological prescription for development.

I must add, however, that anthropocentric ecological concerns which center the whole of reality and the created world on the human person can be a very limiting approach and is open to misinterpretation. This Judeo-Christian notion, amplified in Western philosophic and theological traditions needs to be enriched by non-Western Christian thinking as found for example in African ontology. The autonomy of the human person, and the limitless exercise of a presumed absolute human freedom and human rationality presaged in the Enlightenment and which has become the lightning rod of postmodernism appears to delegitimize divine governance of the world. God becomes an obstacle to the free exercise of human reason and human creativity in making and unmaking the world. The ecological crisis that we face in today's world should be properly seen as an anthropological crisis. There is a common consensus that the human person of all the members of the ecosystem is the one most to be blamed for the ecological crisis of the day. However, an African ontology in which "to be" is to "to have life or vital force" introduces an idea of mutuality, exchange, co-dependence among all the members of the ecosystem. Each has a "vital force" to give to the other, and all of them receive this "vital force" from a higher Being, who is within and beyond creation. Existence is, therefore, a participation in the common vitality of every member of the universe, and all share in a common life from God, which can either be increased or diminished according to how we respect the law, harmony, sacredness, and autonomy constitutive of the very being of every reality. I shall propose a more extended interpretation of natural law and Christian anthropology in the later part of this chapter and the next.

The relationship of the human person to the rest of earthly creation, of which God constitutes him the ruler, does not exhaust his vocation. His place in this world is established basically on his situation in the sight of God. Being drawn from the earth, the human person is weak, mere flesh, and earthy, and by himself, he can but go back to the earth (6:3). If he lives, it is because God has endowed him with life that makes him a living being: "then the Lord God formed man of dust from the ground, and breathed into his nostrils the breath of life; and man became a living being" (2:7). The human person's existence is dependent on the spirit of life that comes from God; it depends likewise on his or her obedience to the Word of him who created the universe and everything in it. If he does not observe the command of his Creator, he will die (2:17), that is to say that the life that made him to be will return to God, its source, while man will go back to the earth from which he was drawn (Gen 3:19; Job 10:9–12; Wis 15:7–11).[9]

The priestly account of creation (Gen 1), speaks more of the love of God for the human person, of the human person's dominion over the fish of the sea, and over the birds of the air and over the cattle and over the earth and over every creeping thing that creeps upon the earth. "So God created (*bara'*) man in his own image, in the Image of God he created him; male and female he created them" (Gen 1:26–28). The emphasis here is on the beauty and importance of human creation; the male and female as constitutive of what it means to be human. The human person enjoys a special dignity among all creatures because he or she resembles God. Anyone who will shed man's blood will impair God's image (Gen 9:6).

Accordingly, the human person is the most beautiful of all creatures because he or she is God's partner and bears the divine likeness which sin will not be able to efface and which he will transmit to his

9. Ibid.

descendants (Gen 9:6; 5:1–3). The dignity of the human person stands out in answering God and in carrying out faithfully his or her mission on earth. By giving life, he or she imitates God who gives life to all things; and together male and female will fill the earth. By subjugating all, the human person will imitate God, the Lord of heaven and earth. Summarizing the anthropology of the Old Testament as found in the creation accounts in Genesis, Gerhard von Rad writes,

> On the topmost step of this pyramid stands man, and there is nothing between him and God: indeed, the world, which was in fact made for him, has in him alone its most absolute immediacy to God. Also, unlike the rest of Creation, he was not created by the word; but in creating him God was actuated by a unique, solemn resolve in the depths of his heart. And in particular, God took the pattern for this, his last work of Creation, from the heavenly world above. In no other work of creation is everything referred to very immediately to God himself as in this.[10]

The deeper meaning of the image and likeness of God in the human person is brought out in a special way in the New Testament. The New Testament's constant reference to the image of God is rooted in the christological basis of the image of God in us. In a certain sense, we can juxtapose *imago dei* and *imago Christi* if we did a correct interpretation of the NT texts that refer to the image of God, following the tradition of the fathers as also reflected in various magisterial documents. In this regard, Joseph Ratzinger writes, "Christ is the eschatological Adam to whom the first Adam already pointed; as the true image of God that transforms man once more into the likeness to God."[11] This interpretation is found in the whole of the NT. Christ is presented in the NT as the unique perfect image of God the Father. As the perfect Imago Dei, Jesus Christ alone is the image of God. In that sense, he is equal to the Father, and to the Holy Spirit. The deformed image (of God) is found in all human beings by virtue of creation and the Fall. All human beings like Adam are made in the image and likeness of God and retain the wound of Sin. The restored image is given by virtue of God's free gift in Christ through baptism and the grace of justification: "the ones he chose specially long ago and intended to

---

10. Von Rad, Old Testament Theology, 146.

11. See Vorgrimler, Documents of Vatican, 159.

become true image of his Son, so that his Son might be the eldest of many brothers" (Rom 8:29, *Catechism of the Catholic Church*, 1701).

We see particularly in the Pauline writings, that the restoration of the image of God in the human person is universal, "All baptized in Christ, you have clothed yourself in Christ, and there are no more distinctions between Jew and Greek, slave and free, male and female, but you all are one in Christ Jesus" (Gal 3:27–29). We can summarize a christocentric Christian anthropology as found in the NT by noting: (1) the true nature of the human person: human nature and dignity arise from the fact that the human was made in the image and likeness of God at the time of creation, and is ordained towards the realization of the perfect image through redemption and salvation in Christ. The mysteries of creation and redemption in Christ are central to a proper understanding of the human person. (2) Following from the preceding point, the understanding of human destiny, human dignity, human rights, development, climate change, environmental pollution, and the unmitigated exploitation of the earth, and the riddle of human life and its destiny must embody a theistic anthropology that recognizes that human fulfillment and religious and beatific consummation are intimately connected. (3) The mystery of the human person is best understood in the mystery of Christ, the Perfect Image of God (Heb 1:1–4). By becoming man, the incarnate logos became the image of the invisible God. Through his Paschal Mystery, Jesus restores the image and likeness of God to the human person and actually brings it to perfection. Being the exemplar or archetypical man, in whose image we are made, he exemplifies in himself the image of God. Since it is Christ himself who is the perfect image of God (2 Cor 4:4; Col 1:15; Heb 1:3), the human person must be conformed to him (Rom 8:29) in order to become son or daughter of the Father through the power of the Holy Spirit (Rom 8:23). To become the image of God requires an active participation on the part of the human person to enable him or her to be transformed according to the pattern of the image of the Son (Col 3:10) who manifests his identity by the historical movement from his incarnation to his glory. According to this pattern set by Christ, the image of God in each person is constituted by his own historical passage from creation, through conversion from sin, to salvation and to his or her consummation. According to the *Catechism of the Catholic Church*:

Disfigured by sin and death, man remains "in the image of God" in the image of the Son, but deprived "of the glory of God" of his "likeness." The promise made to Abraham inaugurates the economy of salvation, at the culmination of which the Son himself will assume that "image" and restore it in the Father's "likeness" by giving it again its glory, the Spirit who is "the giver of life."[12]

In summarizing the insights from Scripture and the writings of the church fathers, one sees the higher foundation for human rights and integral development as rooted in the truth of Christian anthropology. The Old and New Testaments reveal that in Christian humanism, persons are intrinsically relational and objectively valued and dignified, being created in the image and likeness of God. Development is, therefore, built around Christian humanism, but the human person is also called to create cultures, society, and conditions for a healthy environment. However, if the truth about the human person is distorted, the whole edifice crumbles. Since the truth about charity which is urgently needed in the world today is rooted in the truth of God, one can conclude with Pope Benedict that theological anthropology must build such a foundation through locating the truth about the human person in the truth about God with a value discourse and social theory which should naturally flow from this connection. John Paul II summarizes the position as follows: "Truly, one must recognize that, with an unstoppable crescendo from the Old to the New Testament, there is manifested in Christianity the authentic conception of man as a person and no longer merely as an individual. If an individual perishes, the species remains unaltered: in the logic established by Christianity, however, when a person dies, something unique and unrepeatable is lost."[13]

Theistic Anthropology: Some Important Theological and Philosophical Voices

A theistic anthropology, as we have pointed out, proposes that there is a human nature, that the human person has a transcendental origin and destiny, that human freedom is directed to doing God's will be-

---

12. International Theological Commission, "Communion and Stewardship," 11–12.

13. Filibeck, Theme of Violence, 52.

cause his dignity lies in responding to God in love. This anthropology presupposes that the human person is sacred, that the human person is intrinsically social and oriented to God. We are born to communion and relationality. Rights are, therefore, lodged in the ontology of human dignity; rights cannot be dehistoricized or disembodied as separate from the experiences of human beings who are creatures related to others.[14] Authentic and integral development must draw its foundation from this basic truth. Charity is sustained by this basic truth about being as such. This is against any form of individualism that sees rights as absolute claims of the individual as such, and separates rights and human and cultural development from the full integration of the human person in terms of his or her vocation in life, the goal of the human society, the created world, and communion with the Trinity.

In addition, a theistic anthropology answers with deep conviction the question of the existence of a human soul, the human body, sexual differentiation, marriage, moral choices, sacredness of human life and issues of the goal of the created world in general, the created universe and the place of the human person in it. It will give answer to the ultimate purpose of the moral demand and of human destiny. This thought has evolved in its expressions but the main core of a Christian humanism could be found in the writings of many Christian writers across the ages.

Augustine for instance writes:

> It [the soul] is therefore called immortal, because it never ceases to live with some life or other, even when it is most miserable, so . . . the human soul is never anything safe rational or intellectual; and hence, if it is made after the image of God in respect to this that it is able to use reason and intellect in order to understand and behold God, then from the moment when that nature so marvelous and so great began to be whether this image is so worn out as to be almost none at all, or whether it be obscure or defaced, or bright and beautiful, certainly it always is.[15]

The central theme of Augustine's *De Trinitate* is the divine Trinity not the Imago Dei, which comes up later in the second half of this work, as Augustine searches for the created mirror within

14. Elshtain, Who are we?, 57.

15. Augustine, Trinity, 117–18.

which he shall catch a glimpse of the Trinity that he knows by faith.[16] Basing his writing on his doctrine of the Trinity, Augustine presented a personalistic, psychological, and existential account of the image of God in the human person. He is described by Leonard A. Kennedy, as the philosopher of the person, the philosopher of the will, and the philosopher of freedom.[17] For Augustine, the image of God in us has a trinitarian structure, reflecting either the tripartite structure of the human soul (spirit, self-consciousness, and love) or the threefold aspect of the psyche (memory, intelligence, and will). According to Augustine, the image of God in us orients us to God in vocation, knowledge, and love.[18] Augustine fully articulates the notion of the human will, because he understood and "became aware of the existence of the will, of its freedom, and of its power. He faced up courageously to the recognition and admission that he was responsible for his actions and even for the existence and power of the habits he had cultivated but later deplored."[19]

In Aquinas, the image of God does not possess a static and ahistorical quality, he rejects the substantialist understanding of the mind and adopts an Aristotelian ontology of the powers (See ST. Questions 75 and 93; as well as *De Veritate*, Questions 1–10).[20] Imago Dei in Aquinas is fundamentally dynamic, active, and has a historical character, since it passes through three stages: the *imago creationis* (*naturae*), the *imago recreationis* (*gratiae*) and the *similtudines* (*gloriae*).[21] This movement is that of *exitus-reditus*, rooted in divine purposes in creation and redemption, and inscribed in the created order by the very finalities of human nature.[22] The image of God is realized prin-

16. O'Callaghan, "Imago Dei," 101.

17. Kennedy et al., Images, 114.

18. See Augustine's Confessions, 1/1:1.

19. Kennedy et al., Images, 115.

20. Aristotelian ontology of powers is interpreted by Aquinas as the powers of the soul in relation with the habits which perfects the soul. The image of God is found in these powers and the habits of the soul are secondary. By willing and knowing God people not only imitate divine action, on which their knowing and willing is patterned, but they come closer to the God to whom they aspire. For the three ways of interpreting *imago dei* in Aquinas find the fine synthesis in Wawrykow, Westminster Handbook to Aquinas, 73–75.

21. Aquinas, Theologiae, 1/93:4.

22. See Di Noia, "Imago," 276.

cipally in an act of contemplation in the intellect.[23] It is in the act of knowledge and love of God through faith, hope, and charity that the imaging of God is realized. Contemplating God is the ultimate good and happiness of the human subject "The perfection of the rational creature consists not only in what belongs to it in respect of its nature, but also in that which it acquires through a supernatural participation of Divine goodness" (I–II, 3, 8). Using physical creatures as the starting point, because they are closer to us in our perception of reality, Aquinas argues thus: Each being has a natural inclination towards its own good, his own perfection, whether it is to acquire its own perfection (if it does not already exist) or to rejoice in it (if it already exists). This is clearly evident to us from looking at the appetitives like food, drinks, etc. If one is hungry, one gains satisfaction from eating food for example. Aquinas discerns in each being another inclination: the tendency to communicate its own good, to have others participate in its own perfection. Thus, if this kind of inclination exists in natural things, how much more will it exist in a supreme manner in God to communicate his likeness or good to human creatures as much as human being are open to receive it (ST, 1,19, a. 2). "Human beings must be active in the grace-enabled actualization of the image of God within them. Coming from God, they are active participants in the movement of their return to him. What draws them is their pursuit of the good of human life that is continually revealed as the Good beyond life." [24]

J. Augustine Di Noia argues that St. Thomas arrives at the culmination of the theology of the *imago dei* when he shows how Christ the perfect image of the Father is the principle and pattern of the restoration of the perfect image of God in us. All the mysteries of Christ's life, especially his passion, death, and resurrection, bring about the work of transformation in us by which the image of God, damaged by original sin and our personal sins, can be restored and perfected. Configured and transfigured in the *imago Christi* by the power of the Holy Spirit, we return to the Father, and come to enjoy the communion of the Trinitarian life, which is the essence of the beatitude. This conception can be distinguished from that of Bonaventure, for whom the image is realized chiefly through the will in the religious act of the

23. Aquinas, Theologiae, 1/93:4–7.
24. Di Noia, "Imago," 276–77.

human person. For Aquinas, the human being created in the image of God is by the very fact of his human nature and from the very first moment of his existence directed towards God as his ultimate end. For Aquinas the human person is that which is most perfect in all of nature. Person and being are not incompatible in philosophy but rather essential to each other.

Exploring the depth of Thomistic anthropology which grounds later developments in Christian anthropology in such writings as that of Hans urs von Balthasar, Jacques Maritain, and Pope John Paul II will take us beyond the limited scope of this book. Let me underlie some of the basic elements in Thomistic anthropology which have helped shape the foundations of the social teaching of the Church which are so evident in Pope Benedict's social encyclical and other magisterial documents on Catholic social teaching: (1) The human person belongs to the order of being. This is an order that is real and true for all time and for all peoples independent of their knowing it. In effect, we can discuss the transcendental attributes of being, which relate to the substantial ontological structure of beings in general and of specific natures (human, animal, etc.) in that order of being. Essence and existence are two primary principles of being. Essence answers the "whatness" of something, while existence answers the "thatness" of something. As a thing is so it acts, hence human nature proceeds from who a human person is.

Nature is the term used for the essence of living beings, and human nature is the defining principle that all human beings have in common. It is the basis of the uniqueness and inviolability of human life, human rights, integral development, ecological advocacy, the building of democratic institutions, the fight against poverty and injustice, human capacities and powers, and human potential. Human nature is not merely the sum of the person's physical and biological elements or his bodily capacities, it refers to that which is natural to human beings (thinking, loving, willing, understanding, sleeping, praying, and eating etc.). We can see immediately that a human person is more than a speck on the earth; he has an essential nature, which, though constitutive ontologically, is not static. This is so because the human person has a dynamic principle, which as Jacques Maritain writes, is the individuating principle, which makes each person different from another person, and evolving in his or her fulfillment towards fullness of being and ultimate human destiny. Jacques Maritain, in this regard writes:

> To say that a man is a person is to say that in his depth of his being he is more a whole than a part and more independent than servile. It is to say that he is a minute fragment of matter that is at the same time a universe, a beggar who participates in the absolute being, mortal flesh whose value is eternal, and a bit of straw into which heaven enters. It is this metaphysical mystery that religious thought designates when it says that person is the image of God.[25]

(2) The understanding of the human person must embody four permanent ontological relations. They are fundamental for our understanding of every human person and are also the bases for universal rights and for human activities in the world. This is why the *Catechism of the Catholic Church* as a Compendium of Catholic doctrine affirms and confirms the unity of the human person as such, the unity of faith and ultimately, the unity of truth for all time and all peoples. The relations are the ontological constituents of the person, that is, of his or her very being, which are disturbed by sin but not destroyed by sin. These four relations are: (i) the ontological relation between God and the human person, that is, that the human person is created; he or she is created in the image and likeness of God. (ii) The ontological relation of the human person within himself or herself, the relation of body to soul, or that which is material to that which is spiritual. The central dogmas of the Christian faith imply that the body is an intrinsic part of the human person and thus participates in his or her being created in the image of God. Hence St. Paul will write: "Glorify God in your body" (1 Cor 6:20).[26]

Catholic anthropology holds that it is because of the spiritual soul that the body made of matter becomes a living human body; it is the rational principle in the human person and the source of all his natural inclinations. Spirit and matter in the human person are not two natures but are united; their union forms a single nature (CCC. 365). (iii) The human person's relation to the whole created world. Men and women are the summit of the work of creation and there is a solidarity and harmony between the human person and the works

---

25. Quoted in Gallagher, Maritain Reader, 131.
26. See Radcliffe, "Sexual Ethic," 306.

of creation. Development of any kind will begin with embracing this whole truth about the human person (iv) The relation between man and woman. In the creation of man as male and female, man discovers woman as another "I" sharing the same humanity (CCC. 371). The divine image shines through in the communion of persons, in the likeness of the union of the divine persons among themselves.

Prudence Allen has shown that many of the great fathers like Augustine and St. Thomas have varying interpretations of the complementarity of the sexes[27]. She proposes an integral sex complementarity (different from sex polarity, reverse sex polarity, and fractional sex complementarity or sex unity), which considers man and woman as whole and self-defining individuals, more like integers than fractions.[28] Her insight draws from recent developments in Christian anthropology in terms of the dignity of the human body and existential personalism that holds that a person actively creates his or her identity by the gift of his or her life to another.

Christian anthropology is clearly synthesised in *Gaudium et Spes* and in the writings of successive popes down to Pope Benedict XVI. Lawrence J. Welch's article "*Gaudium et Spes*, the Divine Image, and the Synthesis of Veritatis Splendor" provides a good summary of the anthropology of this important conciliar document and how John Paul II developed the teachings of that great document. Imago Dei consists in the human person's fundamental orientation to God, which is the basis of his or her human dignity, his or her existence in society and the inalienable rights of the human person. Because every human person is an image of God, he or she cannot be subservient to any this worldly system or finality. His sovereignty within the cosmos, his capacity for social existence, and his knowledge and love of the Creator are all rooted in his being made in the image and likeness of God.

Gaudium et Spes takes the person of Christ as the clear criterion for its statements that Christ is "the key, the center, and the purpose of man's history." This principle is clearly explicated in no. 22; "In fact, the mystery of man is revealed only in the light of the mystery of the incarnate Word." Article 12 presents the image as a capacity to know and love the Creator, it also presents the image as male and female.

27. See Allen. "Complementarity," 251–362.

28. Allen, Woman, 540.

Implicit in this, is the constitutive human relationality of communion, which mirrors the divine communion of the Trinity. Article 17 presents freedom as the exceptional sign of the image of God within the human person. Article 22 shows what it means to be created in the image and likeness of God as conformed in the image of Christ. Every human being is touched by the event of the Incarnation, for Christ unites himself in some fashion to every child of God. This unity is not an ahistorical pure form; it has a concrete base: the cross. *Gaudium et spes* also teaches that human creativity manifests divine creativity as its model (GS 34), and must be directed to justice, human fellowship and the establishment of one human family (GS 24).

Gaudium et spes, however, does not specify or explain the precise meaning of freedom vis-à-vis Christ, nor does it define the relationship between freedom and communion in the divine imaging. The relation between the sincere gift of self and freedom is left unexplained. It is not also clear how the cross is related to the restoration of our freedom and how it makes us capable of communion. These are aspects of Christian anthropology, which according to Lawrence J. Welch, John Paul II addresses in his many encyclicals. An essential dimension of this is brought out in the theological anthropology of Benedict's *Caritas in Veritate*. Welch summarizes this anthropology this way: "Christ through his Cross had made it possible to exist in freedom and communion and thus image God, who is a communion of divine persons. Christ, the new Adam, re-forges the divine image in his sacrifice for the sake of his bride, the Second Eve. Our appropriation of this re-forged image lies in our following of Christ in his one sacrifice. In this way, Pope John Paul II proclaims that Christ reveals the truth about God and at the same time the whole truth about the human person."[29]

In the classical period, it was iconoclasm that charged that the image of God in the human person is a kind of anthropomorphism, which fostered idolatry. One of the best responses to this is the magisterial work of Christoph Schonborn, *God's Human Face: The Christ Icon*.[30] In the modern and contemporary period, there are renewed attempts to dislodge the theological framework that sustained a Christian anthropology of human nature as made in the image and

---

29. Welch, "Gaudium," 814.
30. See Schonborn, *God's Human Face*.

likeness of God. The theme was regarded as ill advised to experience by empiricists like David Hume and Jean Paul Sartre who denied the ontology of human nature. Theistic thinkers like Descartes reduced human nature to mere rationality and came out with ambiguous conception of the human person as a thinking thought. There are also some reductionist thinkers who devalued the human body or reduced the human person to the sum of his or her parts. But it is secular humanism and existentialism that deny that religious aspirations have any validity or relevance to human and moral fulfillment. These cast a thudding blow against Christian anthropology.

Atheistic thinkers who deny theistic anthropology exalt the psychological over the physical, consciousness over the body. The presuppositions of these non-theistic thinking are worth underlying. In the first place, a denial of human nature (Jean Paul Sartre and Hume) means a denial of any essence. Existentialism, which holds that existence precedes essence hence making the human person the author and finisher of his or her destiny and succumbing to the myth of human sufficiency, can only lead to a blind alley where there is no normative principle, no standard, since nothing is fixed. The human person is then left on his or her own on a journey that has no clear destination. Existential thinking has apotheosized human subjectivity hence the constant cry of the existentialists is the angst and despair of a being abandoned in the complexities and inexorable fate of the human person's ploys and self-defined ends.

Ludwig Feuerbach, Karl Marx, and Sigmund Freud, all following Kant, conceived the human person as a self-constituting autonomous subject apart from any relationship with God. It is not the human person who is made in the image and likeness of God, rather it is God who is made in the image and likeness of the human person; God is nothing else than an image projected by the person. In the end, atheism appeared to be required if the human subject was to be self-constituting. The human person is the object of the God he or she proposes as the image in him or her. He or she is the predicate of the very substance he or she mirrors as his or her image. God is the human person's creature and not the Creator of all things. This is similar to the analogy Archbishop Thomas Collins of Toronto made in a recent discourse. He notes that in the past many Christians used to say: "Speak Lord you servant is listening," but in today's world where many

Christians and non-Christians face the challenge of seeing God as an obstacle to their claims for an unfettered freedom many people now say to God: "Listen Lord, your servant is speaking." God becomes our servant or a dead God who cannot speak to us anymore because we have drowned his voice through the works of our own hands, which in our limited thinking will grant us infinite progress. In the words of Feuerbach, "If man makes himself a predicate of his predicate, then in the self-abasement of this abstraction he is untrue both to his dignity and to his bodily nature; he regards and treats himself together with nature, to which he belongs, as something inferior, in order to gain a supposedly more valuable spirituality."[31]

There are many consequences of holding a non-theistic anthropological position. I, however, add that not all non-theistic anthropology denies human nature, but we are concerned here in showing that a non-theistic anthropology always diminishes the full truth about the human person and hence his or her human dignity and rights, and the cause of integral development which charity in truth demands. In the first place, denial of human nature or human essence is to deny finality to human life. Nothing will have any meaning and enduring value for the human person, or any ultimate destiny beyond the grave. In addition, human freedom will be exalted and the real purpose of freedom minimized or lost totally as each man or woman is left to his or her own judgment. This is the root of a secular mentality that makes individual preferences the ultimate norm for moral judgment.

Jacques Maritain provides the most critical response to this kind of non-theistic anthropology, which offers us some insight for evaluation. According to Maritain, the person is a substance whose substantial form is a spiritual soul; person is a substance, who lives a life that is not merely biological and instinctive, but is also a life of intellect and will. It is a very simple-minded error, Maritain argues, to believe that subjectivity possesses no intelligible structure on the ground that it is an inexhaustible depth; and to conceive of it as being without any nature whatsoever for the purpose of making it an absurd abyss of pure and formless liberty. Non-theistic anthropology misunderstands the basis of personality, interiority, and subjectivity:

> They remain lightheartedly ignorant of the personality, meta-
> physically considered, being the subsistence of the spiritual

31. Cited in Gallagher, Maritain Reader, 223.

soul communicated to the human composite, and enabling the latter to possess its existence, to perfect itself and to give itself freely, bears witness in us to the generosity of expansivity of being which, in an incarnate spirit, proceeds from the spirit and which constitutes, in the secret springs of ontological structure, a source of dynamic unity and unification within . . . They do not see that, even before the exercise of free choice, and in order to make free choice possible, the most deeply rooted need of the person is to communicate with the other by the union of intelligence, and with others by the affective union. Their subjectivity is not a self, because it is wholly phenomenal.[32]

These philosophical and theological explorations thus far are aimed at demonstrating that Pope Benedict XVI's teaching draws from the theological anthropological tradition of the Catholic Church best described as Christian humanism. The principle of charity needs to be based on faith in the God who brought all things into being and to whom all things will return; development has to be based on a right scale of value in which God has priority and in which human dignity is prized and not priced. The human person has to be understood as both a child of God whose hope and future is in God, and also as both steward of creation and held in care by creation at the same time. Charity in truth is, therefore, not a creation of the Pope, but it is a principle that he discovers in the constant teaching of the Church, the practice of the faith of God's people, natural law, and the living moral tradition of the Church and especially of the saints. Questions about the common good, human rights, ecology, and sustainable development, social advocacy for the poor, democratic reforms, and the requirements of justice and charity all draw from charity in truth. Truth about reality as such.

Charity demands justice both at the inter-personal levels and among communities, nations, and in religious institutions and organizations. In CIV 6–7 the Holy Father shows how people can practice charity in truth with regard to justice and the promotion, preservation, and protection of the common good, which deals with the good that is linked with life in society. In the first place, the call of charity goes beyond the requirements of justice. If we love people we strive to be just and fair to them. Charity demands that we treat people with

32. Ibid., 175–76.

dignity, respect, and reverence; that we do not cheat others, that we relate with people out of truth and due regard to the moral requirements of justice. However, charity has a surplus value beyond the often legalistic and contractual demands of justice. This is what the Pope calls the logic of giving and forgiving (CIV, 6), which goes beyond the logic of justice. He teaches further: "The earthly city is promoted not merely by relationship of rights and duties, but to an even greater and more fundamental extent by the relationships of gratuitousness, mercy and communion. Charity always manifests God's love in human relationships. It also gives theological and salvific value to all commitment to justice in the world" (CIV, 6).

The same principle applies to the common good. The Pope continues the teaching of the Church on the vocation of every Christian to work towards a better society, through the promotion of the common good. However, he calls for proper discernment. Every Christian according to his or her gifts is called to the service of the political and social community to which they belong to bring the light of Christ to illumine the public square. However, the goal is not to build a world that is perfected without God but a world that enables every human person to attain to God through the human earthly pilgrimage. He concludes by teaching that, "Man's earthly activity, when inspired and sustained by charity, contributes to the building of the universal city of God, which is the goal of the history of the human family. In an increasingly globalized society, the common good and the effort to obtain it cannot fail to assume the dimensions of the whole human family, that is to say, the community of peoples and nations, in such a way as to shape the earthly city in unity and peace, rendering it to some degree an anticipation and a prefiguration of the undivided city of God" (CIV, 7).

FROM *POPULORUM PROGRESSIO* TO *CARITAS IN VERITATE*

Caritas in Veritate comes more than forty years after the publication of Pope Paul VI's great social encyclical, *Populorum Progressio* on integral human development. There have been some commentators who deny the continuity between Benedict's social teaching and that of both Paul VI and John Paul II. This is far from the truth. In an address to the Roman Curia on December 22, 2005[33] Pope Benedict makes a distinction between "a hermeneutic of discontinuity and rupture" and "a hermeneutic of reform, renewal, and continuity" in interpretation of Vatican II's document and subsequent documents. While *Populorum Progressio*[34] is itself not a Vatican II document, Pope Benedict's social encyclical is germane here for understanding the continuity in his social encyclical and other papal social encyclicals going back especially to Paul VI's. The hermeneutic of discontinuity has become very loud in today's Church especially in the West wherein every statement of the Pope has been parsed ad absurdum. Such a hermeneutic feeds on popular secular cultural imagination that wishes to deconstruct truth and enthrone the dictatorship of relativism. It is buoyed by a secular media and some theological trends that lack any metaphysical range. Such a hermeneutics of discontinuity sees each and every papal document as the product of compromises and alliances, texts are exegeted to discover which camp produced them so as to hermetically enclose them into a certain theological framework. This creates confusion, and undue contestations and leaves the wheel of ecclesial life stymied by unhelpful theological categorizations.

The hermeneutic of continuity and renewal, on the other hand, is one that is well expressed by Pope John XXIII in his speech inaugurating the Second Vatican Council on October 11, 1962, when he spoke of the need for renewal of the teaching of the Church to meet changing times while at the same time transmitting the doctrine "pure and integral, without any attenuation or distortion."[35] Pope Paul VI makes this explicit when he teaches: "The substance of ancient deposit is one thing, and the way in which it is presented is another, retaining nonetheless the same meaning and message."[36] Thus, Pope Benedict XVI teaches that commitment to a specific truth in a new way demands a new reflection on this truth and a new vital relationship with it. It is also clear, he notes, that new words can only develop if they come from an informed understanding of the truth expressed, and on the other

33. Acta Apostolicae Sedis, 40–53.

34. In no. 3–5 of *Populorum Progressio*, Pope Paul VI points out that the encyclical was inspired by Vatican II.

35. See Benedict XVI, "Hermeneutic," xii.

36. Paul VI, Constitutiones, 863–65.

hand, that a reflection on faith also requires that this faith be lived.[37] He continued this teaching on the hermeneutics of continuity in no. 12 of CIV when he points out that it is misleading to create an extraneous division in magisterial teaching especially in the case in question on the social doctrine wherein two typologies of social doctrine are proposed one that is pre-conciliar and another that is post-conciliar. On the contrary, he points out that his social teaching is in continuity with the previous teaching just like that of previous popes including Pope Paul VI's, form one single deposit; "there is a single teaching, consistent and at the same time ever new. It is one thing to draw attention to the particular characteristics of one encyclical or doctrinal corpus. Coherence does not mean a closed system: on the contrary, it means dynamic faithfulness to a light received. The Church's social doctrine illuminates with an unchanging light the new problems that are constantly emerging. This safeguards the permanent and historical character of the doctrinal patrimony" (CIV, 12). The social doctrines draw from Scripture, the writings of the fathers, the living tradition of the Church, especially her moral and social life with regard to those on the margins of society, the lives of the saints, the witness of faith, and the continuing reflection of the Church guided by the Holy Spirit on the application of unchanging truth of faith to changing social situations. Thus, Pope Paul's encyclical underlined the indispensable importance of the gospel for building a society according to freedom and justice, in the ideal and historical perspective of a civilization animated by love. He understood development in both Christian and human terms: "Development cannot be limited to mere economic growth. In order to be authentic, it must be complete: integral, that is, it has to promote the good of every man and the whole man. As an eminent specialist has very rightly and emphatically declared: 'We do not believe in separating the economic from the human, nor development from the civilizations in which it exists. What we hold important is man, each man and each group of men, and we even include the whole of humanity.'"[38]

Populorum Progressio was indeed very decisive and had far reaching effects in the Church's social ministry. It not only offered a Christian vision of development and the goal of human society, it also

37. Ibid.
38. Paul VI, Populorum, 14.

offered an economic interpretation of the causes of war and argued for economic justice as the surest road to peace. The pope rejected unequivocally many of the basic precepts of capitalism including unrestricted private ownership of means of production, the uncontrolled desire for profit to the detriment of the poor, and the rough edges of free trade. He also drew attention to unequal development for people in the developing countries, the scourge of poverty and imperialism, which continued to hold many peoples and nations in chains.[39] The encyclical gave new impetus to the work of the newly constituted Pontifical Commission for Justice and Peace (Created in January 1967 by Pope Paul VI as an ecclesial initiative and structure authorized by Vatican II). In addition, this commission fostered a global Catholic movement that became like a sentinel leading to a more active involvement of the Catholic Church in worldwide causes for justice and peace. It helped to deepen global Catholic conversation on the role of the Church in the world, and creation of justice and peace commissions in parishes, dioceses, and Episcopal conference offices, Vatican offices and nunciatures among others.[40] It moved the Church's social justice concerns beyond laying down principles to active involvement in the transformation of the social sphere.

The social encyclicals of the popes are not isolated from the whole doctrine of the Church. This is why one cannot separate one encyclical's message from other body of teachings of the Church or from those of a particular pope. The social teaching is part of the good news that the Church carries to the ends of the earth. It deals with principles that should both animate and govern the social order based on the truth, as well as the practical steps towards bringing this about in very direct and meaningful ways. The Church's social teaching advances the truth that we cannot separate development from liberation from sin and from social structures, from tyranny or oppressive and exploitative economic and political structures. We cannot separate evangelization from advocacy for the transformation of the social sphere, from the reconciliation of peoples, or from the common search and work for peace; nor can we sever the links between social ethics and life ethics. The social doctrine of the Church draws from faith and leads to faith.

---

39. See O'Brien and Shannon, Catholic Social Thought, 238–39.

40 For a more detailed discussion of the worldwide Catholic movement for justice and peace, see Gremillion, "Justice and Peace," 188–90.

Here again we see the strong link between charity and truth, the call to love one's neighbor is not simply a social concern, it is also a Christian call and draws from the experience of faith. This faith is the truth of our Christian being which shows our origin and ultimate destiny, and the goal of our earthly journey. Pope Benedict points out that Pope Paul's social encyclicals are intimately and integrally linked to the whole body of magisterial teaching of Paul's papacy, but more importantly it shows the *nexus mysteriorium* (the intimate linkage) of doctrines. One cannot separate *Populorum Progressio* from *Evangelii Nutiandi* or from *Evangelium Vitae* of Pope John Paul II. All of them speak to the fundamental place of the gospel in integral development, and the advancement of peoples. Thus, the vocation and freedom of the human person must be located within the general corpus of truth about Christian humanism. One must underlie this truth for a proper hermeneutic of Benedict's social encyclical and as a way of appreciating the limited insight of many critics of this social treasure of teaching. Summarizing *Populorum Progressio*, Benedict writes:

> The truth of development consists in its completeness: if it does not involve the whole man and every man, it is not true development. This is the central message of *Populorum Progressio*, valid for today and for all time. Integral human development on the natural plane, as a response to a vocation from God the Creator, demands self-fulfillment in a "transcendent humanism which gives him greatest possible perfection: this is the highest goal of personal development." The Christian vocation to this development therefore applies to both the natural plane and the supernatural plane; which is why, "when God is eclipsed our ability to recognize the natural order, purpose and the good begins to wane" (CIV, 15).

We can now apply the principle of the hermeneutic of reform, renewal, and continuity to Benedict XVI's social encyclical. We immediately see as the Pope himself observed that he is standing on the shoulders of the previous popes, and shedding new light to an old truth in the face of the new challenges we face in a globalized world. Four new realities are immediately observed by the Pope in CIV 9: (1) The inter-dependence of people is not matched by ethical interaction of consciences and minds that would give rise to a true human development. (2) Development today is lacking human and humanizing values in many cases; (3) Charity needs to be illumined by the light of faith and reason; (4) The distinctive quality of Christian charity as rooted in some transcendental values about the origin and destiny of creation is something that is beyond the immediate calculus of technical progress. Under-development is not primarily a material order (CIV, 19). Paul VI located the cause of under-development in (1) the human will which neglects the duties of solidarity, (2) in ways of thinking which does not always give proper direction to the will, and (3) the lack of brotherhood among individuals and people which are often seen in racism, the rejection of migrants, new forms of selfishness at individual, inter-subjective and international levels. It is obvious that a new way of thinking, willing, and seeing is required in the discourse about development. This requires a new worldview that is built on truth. This is what Pope Benedict XVI sets out to demonstrate as the missing link in the changing world of today.

Herein lies the need for truth to be brought to the fore in the consideration of charity in today's world. Thus, the encyclical could be summarized as a reflection on the splendor of charity animated by the wisdom of truth as they work together to aid the development of peoples, nations, economies, and the ecology for a globalized world. The Pope shows how the sapiential dimension of divine love can illumine the social sphere and inspire Christians to social consciousness through an informed social conscience and commitment to truth. This was not brought out in previous encyclicals and Pope Benedict calls on the contemporary world to integrate these values in development for the good of the world. He concludes on the need for truth by teaching:

> fidelity to the truth, which alone is the guarantee of freedom (cf. John 8:32) and of the possibility of integral human development. For this reason the Church searches for truth, proclaims it tirelessly, and recognizes it wherever it is manifested. This mission of truth is something that the Church can never renounce. Her social doctrine is a particular dimension of this proclamation: it is a service to the truth that set us free. Open to the truth, from whichever branch of knowledge it comes, the Church's social doctrine receives it, assembles into a unity the fragments in which it is often found, and mediates it within the constantly changing life-patterns of the society of peoples and nations (CIV, 9).

Two important factors according to Pope Benedict XVI had influenced Pope Paul VI's *Populorum Progressio* with regard to charity and truth, namely, that the whole Church in all her being and acting-when she proclaims the gospel, when she celebrates the liturgy, and when she performs works of charity, is engaged in promoting integral human development. The second is that authentic human development concerns the whole of the person in every single dimension. Thus, "without the perspective of eternal life, human progress in this world is denied breathing-space. Enclosed within history, it runs the risk of being reduced to the mere accumulation of wealth; humanity thus loses the courage to be at the service of higher goods, at the service of the great and disinterested initiatives called forth by universal charity" (CIV 11). We can see clearly the hermeneutic of reform, renewal, and continuity in CIV with regard to the meaning of development, the proper origin and direction of the social mission of Christians and the Church, and the end proper to the social mission which is the procurement of abundant life for all the members of the cosmos. Already, there is a gradual development in Pope Benedict's social gospel in the effort to move Catholic social teaching to a more integrated understanding of development beyond an anthropocentric viewpoint. But his anthropocentric theological foundation for charity is located within the broader horizon of truth, which places the moral acts proper to realizing the common good of all within a divine horizon within which the human person and the rest of creation has a differentiated but related roles.

HUMAN DEVELOPMENT IN CHANGING TIMES: THE CHALLENGE OF GLOBALIZATION

I shall now proceed to highlight the significant teachings of Pope Benedict's social encyclical. Two points will be discussed in this section: globalization, and the causes of global economic crises, while the other issues ecological questions of our times, and principles for sustainable development will be taken up in chapter 2.

A. Globalization

Development is a very complex term that is open to many interpretations. Since the endorsement of the Millennium Development Goals by the UN in 2000, which set the global development agenda until 2015, discussion of development has taken front burner in global politics and discourse. In many cases, discussion has often focused on economic development and economic progress. The moral, intellectual, spiritual, and ecological dimensions of development, which define integrated and sustainable development, are at best trivialized, and often ignored in the global political discourse on development. On the contrary, Pope Paul VI had pointed out that development should be about the human person, and securing them primarily from hunger, deprivation, endemic diseases, and ignorance. Application of this emphasis would involve the restructuring of political, economic, and social life in such a way that people would gain the freedom to pursue their ordered ends and have equal access to the common good. A widened moral perception is necessary to the understanding of the changing contexts of discourse about development today. This is the challenge posed by CIV for the Church first and through the Church to the world.

The phenomenon of globalization, a term with Pope Benedict uses twenty-seven times in CIV has become the drama of our times. Indeed, in CIV 33 he writes very conclusively that "the principal new feature has been the explosion of worldwide interdependence, commonly known as globalization . . . It has been the principal driving force behind the emergence from underdevelopment of whole regions, and in itself it represents a great opportunity. Nevertheless, without the guidance of charity in truth, this global force could cause unprecedented damage and create new divisions within the human family." This message has been central to the advocacy of Pope Benedict for poverty eradication. His New Year (2009) Message for the celebration of the World Day of Peace was devoted solely to how the global fight against poverty should proceed. He argued in that message that fighting poverty requires attentive consideration of the complex phenomenon of globalization. This is important both from a methodological standpoint, but especially for understanding poverty from a wider moral perspective. Through the application of the tools of the social sciences and of economics, globalization can be seen to be a phenomenon within an immense complexity with both economic benefits and threats to peoples.

Globalization must be evaluated from the moral point of view, in order to alert humanity of its moral and spiritual implications including poverty, inequality, and injustice which are rapidly spreading among peoples in developing countries, and are increasingly contributing to the marginalization of the vulnerable and minorities even within wealthy societies. Essential in this discourse then is that to measure globalization is not simply a matter of quantitative data, it calls for other non-material considerations which will throw more light on social justice issues, and the affective, moral, and spiritual poverty seen in people whose interior lives are disoriented and who experience all kinds of malaise despite their economic prosperity. Pope Benedict does not say Yes or No to globalization. On the contrary, he calls attention to the centrality of God and through God, the moral and spiritual governance of the world and the transcendence of the human person, as the guiding light with which we look at globalization. Indeed, in his 2008 New Year message, he condemned any economic system which degrades human dignity through poverty and inexcusable suffering brought about by unjust structures; "It remains true however, that every form of externally imposed poverty has at its root a lack of respect for the transcendent dignity of the human person. When man is not considered within the total context of his vocation, and when the demands of a true 'human ecology' are not respected, the cruel forces of poverty are unleashed, as is evident in certain specific areas."[41] Some of the features of this phenomenon identified by the Pope include:

- Economic crisis caused by failed human systems. These failed systems require profound cultural renewal. To effect this renewal, it is necessary to begin with fundamental values and upon these foundations to modify those systems in order to build a better future.

- A wasteful and consumerist culture that has continued to harden the lines between the rich and poor in both developed and developing countries.

- Excessive protectionism and trade barriers with regard to intel-

41. Benedict XVI, "Fighting Poverty to Build Peace," 2.

lectual property in health care, and other cultural models, and social forms which promote inequality and hinder the progress of peoples and nations especially those on the margins of life.

- The collapsing systems of social security in developed countries caused by greed and corruption as well as the absence of such social securities in many poor countries.

- The increasing difficulties of trade unions and organizations to secure the rights of workers as a result of social and economic factors.

- The increasing mobility of labor and deregulation causing the loss of previously attendant benefits and the danger of unregulated working conditions, psychological instability, and social dislocation which endangers social harmony and family stability (CIV, 25).

- The cultural crisis caused by the shrinking of spaces and the increasing cultural exchanges among people which could lead to cultural eclecticism and cultural leveling: "What eclecticism and cultural leveling have in common is the separation of culture from human nature. Thus, cultures can no longer define themselves within a nature that transcends them, and man ends up being reduced to a mere cultural statistic. When this happens, humanity runs new risks of enslavement and manipulation" (CIV, 26). Authentic dialogue in order to help to overcome these two extremes (each of which could lead to cultural relativism) is needed especially so that people can get to the deeper layers of cultural life and discover the presence of God through these cultural traditions. In CIV 29 the Holy Father calls for more interaction at the level of human knowledge in order to promote authentic development of peoples. Human knowledge here refers to the understanding of the origin and goal of human life. This call should inspire a better appreciation of the kind of development that is required to create a better world. Many different cultural traditions have rich, unique values about the dignity of the human person, respect for the environment, and the divine origin and destiny of the human person. These values all contribute to the human knowledge referred to by the Holy Father. Were all of them to be brought together, the world would be greatly enriched. This would immediately counter any mono-cultural model that could be promoted by globalization, and thereby prevent the further impoverishment of the weak and further suppression of minorities.

- Globalization has produced unequal development. There is increasing hunger, poverty, food shortage and lack of other basic necessities of life especially water in many poor countries of the world. The solution to the global economic crisis should not be pursued in isolation by developed countries. Pope Benedict points out that the right to water is actually a human right. This is a bold statement. It will be especially significant for many people in Africa for whom the absence of clean drinking water is often the difference between life and death (CIV, 27).

- Globalization has often led to all forms of cultural and moral problems. There are the contagion of abortion and anti-life mentality which has placed contraception as the only answer to over population, the spread of HIV/AIDS etc. The redefinition of marriage to include same-sex relations in many countries in the West continues to pose challenges to Christian families and undermine the primary good of family in its openness to life. Many development agencies and nations in the Global North have often placed acceptance of abortion, and contraception as the condition to be fulfilled by African nations and organizations before they can receive aid, undermining the gratuitousness of charity. The Pope teaches that openness to life is at the centre of all authentic development (CIV, 28).

- Religious freedom is often threatened in the world today by religious fundamentalism, religious intolerance, and suppression of the rights of people in many countries to freedom of religion. This threat surfaces in different forms in many African countries. In some regions, Christians are not allowed to build churches or to evangelize. Political leaders threaten religious leaders because they are uncomfortable with their prophetic voices. In some other countries especially in the West, the whole idea of separation of Church and state have worked against the cause of the gospel as Christianity is becoming less visible in the public square, while those Christians who wish to live their faith publicly are coming under increasing persecution. Aspect of globalization have made this possible by the dispersal of such messages of intolerance easily and by the mutual exchange and influence which anti-Christian and secular worldviews could have across different cultural and political frontiers.

- Technological determinism is another shifting boundary in the globalization discourse to which the encyclical draws attention. This happens in different ways: (1) The placing of absolute trust in the works of human hand even when we increasingly see the failures of such works to save us. (2) The exclusion of anything technological from moral evaluation. Hence the Pope calls for an inter-disciplinary approach to technology (CIV, 31) that would allow faith, theology, metaphysics, and science to come together in a collaborative effort in the service of humanity. (3) The lack of wisdom in the use of scientific works. Many influential people who embrace this mode believe that science and technology have their own inbuilt rationality: that if it is possible to "progress" technologically, then that is something which should be pursued regardless of moral and other concerns.

- Globalization has also led to migration of peoples on a very large scale. This has heightened the need for a new moral sensibility to address the conditions of many migrants and the root causes of the greater movement of people from poor countries to rich countries. In many cases, these migrants remain an underclass, poorer and profoundly so in their new country, a living condition worse in many cases than they experienced in their home countries.

- According to Pope Benedict, there are also the dangers of unregulated financial markets that have remained largely speculative and prone to abuse, exploitation, and extortion in which the weak and the poor are most at risk. This reliance on market forces has also affected the unregulated exploitation of the earth's resources, and the lack of an ecological morality. Thus while the wealth of the world is growing in an absolute sense, inequality is on the increase as new forms of poverty and suffering continue to manifest themselves in the changing context of a globalized world.

- In CIV 33, the Pope writes about the African condition even though nearly completely avoided pointing a finger to any particular nation throughout the entire encyclical. What he does write relates specifically to Africa. He points out that living conditions in many countries have not changed since 1967 when Pope Paul VI published *Populorum Progressio*. Why has this been the case? One reason he gives is that new forms of colonialism have arisen in many countries which were under colonialism at the time of Pope Paul or were then in the process of gaining their independence at that time. These countries are unfortunately held in internal slavery by their leaders, as well as held in thralldom by the stifling network of globalization which makes it impossible for them to be equal players in the neo-liberal capitalist market of a globalized world. The unbroken chain of dependency in Africa continues to imperil the lives of many and spread poverty like a wild fire. In a sense, many Africans view globalization in fatalistic terms (cf. CIV, 42).

- Globalization is in need of new solutions which involve a new economic logic to curb the increasing social inequality within and between nations. Solutions should also bring about a deeper reflection on the meaning and goal of the economy (CIV, 32) and profound and far-sighted revision of the current model of development so as to correct its dysfunctions and deviations. It will above all require embracing of the full truth about the human person, recognition of the sovereignty of the divine in governance of the world, and the vision of faith on the ultimate destiny of all things. This sharpened moral sense will direct the course of world economy and politics along a path that leads to God and to authentic human, cultural, ecological, and sustainable development. Therefore, we need to broaden the scope of reason and make it capable of knowing and directing these powerful new forces, animating them within the perspective of the civilization of love whose seed God has planted in every people and in every culture (CIV, 33). Pope Benedict, however, advises that globalization should not be evaluated deterministically since it is the product of merely human and cultural forces. Globalization like all cultural products of humanity is open to redemption and transformation to promote human good. How can this be done? This good is to be realized through a people-based and community-oriented cultural process of worldwide integration that is open to transcendence (CIV, 42). We shall apply this proposal when we evaluate the concrete effects of globalization in Africa in the present world economic and cultural settings in chapter 3.

THE PRINCIPLE OF GRATUITOUSNESS

In this encyclical, Pope Benedict introduces a new principle in Catholic social teaching. This is what he calls the principle of gratuitousness as an expression of fraternity (CIV, 34). This principle was first used in the *Compendium of the Social Doctrine of the Church* (2005) in showing that God's universal plan of love for humanity began through God's liberating action in the history of Israel (20–27). Creation is God's free act of love. God creates in order to save; and he remains in history to freely restore creation and lead history beyond its own limits to himself. In God's act of creating, we see the fruitfulness of an unconditional gratuitous love. The same is true of his Covenant. His divine initiative is always accompanied by giving life to all things, blessing them, and granting them what they need to bear fruit. Indeed, divine mercy, justice, righteousness, goodness, and governance are all the result of the inner principle of gratuitousness. This comes to its consummation in the sending of the Son, as free gift; the gift of the Holy Spirit, and the gift of grace that grants us divine life.

Divine gratuitousness comes with moral precepts for humanity because God wishes that this same manner of being should be replicated in human moral actions. "Man and woman created in his image and likeness (cf. Gen 1:26–27), are for that very reason called to be the visible sign and the effective instrument of divine gratuitousness in the garden where God has placed them as cultivators and custodians of the goods of creation" (*Compendium*, 27).

Pope Benedict shows the full human dimension of divine gratuitousness by illustrating that this principle is fundamental in Catholic social teaching, especially in living charity in truth. This principle is both anthropological and theological. Again, we must repeat that a proper theistic theological anthropology is the proper starting point for discovering the link that the Holy Father makes between charity and truth. We all experience our lives as a gift. The gift is given by God. We can take an example from the life in the family and another from the life in the Church. We received our lives from our parents. We received our nourishment, our education, and our identity through the first interaction within our families, in the environment and via the inter-subjective elements that helped to shape our lives. There is no one who can deny that inbuilt in our existence is the reality of gratuitousness that St. Paul summarizes when he writes: "Is there anything you have which you did not receive?" (1 Cor 4:7; also see Jas 1:16–18).

The same can be said of our relationship with the Church. We who have been received into the Church were given the grace of membership as a gift. At significant stages of our lives, from the cradle to the grave the Church constantly brought to us the gift of divine life. Through the sacraments, the Church has opened to us the doors to the sacred even before we fully knew the meaning and content of the faith. We can apply this to all aspects of human living, especially within the context of societal living in communities, and nations. We enter into other people's service and we are all indebted to our families, the Church, our ethnic groups, nations, and various institutions for the gift of who we are. The social dimension of our humanity is a gift from God for it draws from the communion of the Trinity, thus we are gifts from God for God and our neighbors.

Selfishness is the very antithesis of the principle of gratuitousness and wars against the liberality and total availability of charity. The Pope calls for fraternity and friendship to build up the foundation for economic development. However, there is also the need for robust civil society and third sectors animated by the principle of charity, which could draw richly from the very heart of the Christian faith. We learn from our Christian faith that we are made as gifts from God and that our lives have their most significant meaning when they have been sacrificed for the sake of the other. This is also true at the individual level. However, the Church becomes the more trinitarian when she celebrates and incarnates charity in truth in her actions, animated by the principle of gratuitousness. The Christian is in union with the Trinity when he or she incarnates the very character of love as free gift. One can summarize the ailment of the world today as selfishness, pride and an exaggerated false sense of security and self-sufficiency. The hardening of the self, and the claims to self and group triumph, shown in the absolute trust placed on market forces, on technical progress, national security, and personal investment are the drama of the times. These can lead to false hope and security, and may even mask some deep-seated angst and insecurity which all show the blighting at the subjective and social sphere of the truth about who we are.

Here the anthropological and theological bases of the principle of gratuitousness shine through: we are created for gift and it is in going beyond ourselves to reach out to others that we assume the distinctive quality of being oriented to divine transcendence. Going beyond ourselves overcomes the primordial evil of our being imprisoned to the self, an evil conquered for once and for all time by the Lord Jesus on the cross. Theological anthropology centered on the Trinity demonstrates that gratuitousness is something we have received both as part of our being and is also inseparable from our vocation. "Gift by its nature goes beyond merit, its rule is that of superabundance. It takes the primary place in our souls as a sign of God's presence in us, a sign of what he expect from us. Truth—which is itself a gift, in the same way as charity—is greater than we are, as Saint Augustine teachers" (CIV, 34). In reaching out to others, we are indeed reaching up to God who is found in the least of the brethren. We are also building trust, which is the basis for friendship, community, and communion. Without trust and belief in love we cannot properly build any market economy nor establish a common good to which all individual actions will be directed.

The principle of gratuitousness is also the basis of trust but especially gives new tenor to social ethical principles such as transparency, honesty, and responsibility, as well as giving new force to the formation of moral consciences in personal and social responsibility.

Market forces, and the forces of globalization require the principle of gratuitousness to govern the inner social conscience and sensitize the moral choices of the human agents who are behind these forces. This should lead them to be compassionate, kind, and just by living charity in truth. Thus, economic and commercial logic are not sufficient unto themselves. Neither are the appeals to commutative, distributive, and social justice enough for the task because love is not contractual, love always seeks to do more so as to be more. Gratuity goes beyond the requirements of laws and beyond the equalization terms and relations of demand and supply, or winner takes all, or the logic of giving in order to acquire (the logic of exchange) and also giving through duty alone (the logic of public obligation) (CIV, 39).

The demands of charity do not in any way reduce the urgency of advocacy and activism to change the structures that promote injustice, inequality, and social dysfunction in society. On the contrary, they accentuate the need to change those structures of sin that make poverty and injustice prevalent in contemporary society. The Pope alludes to this in writing about the emancipation of the poor: "The poor are not to be considered a 'burden,' but a resource, even from the purely economic point of view. It is nevertheless erroneous to hold that the market economy has an inbuilt need for a quota of poverty and underdevelopment in order to function at its best. It is in the interest of the market to promote emancipation, but in order to do so effectively, it cannot rely only on itself, because it is not able to produce by itself something that lies outside its competence. It must draw its moral energies from other subjects that are capable of generating them" (CIV, 35). Truly emancipating the poor is mandatory, not simply to provide succor to those suffering, but to do everything to change the very structures which make people poor and powerless, and drain them of their hope.

The Holy Father concludes chapter 4 with an extended treatment of the ways through which the market should properly function for the common good. Against the binary model of development which sees the state and the market as two autonomous entities, he calls for multi-layered interaction among the three subjects identified by Pope John Paul II in *Centesimus Annus*: the market, the state, and the civil society. What does the Pope teach with regard to the market?

In the first place, one must note that the Church does not claim expertise in economic matters; she is a teacher of the faith, and uses the principles and truths drawn from faith to form the conscience of Christians and men and women of goodwill toward authentic charitable living. Thus, the question of whether the Pope is a socialist or a capitalist does not arise here. In addressing the question of the market economy, which all but collapsed in the Fall of 2008 in the industrialized world, the Pope wishes to cast sacred light on the process of civilizing the market through charity and truth governed by the unconditional principle of gratuitousness.

Secondly, the Pope's foray into altering some tenets of market economy is governed by the principle of gratuitousness, a concept previously proposed by him. Thus, when private enterprises place profit over people (CIV, 40); and when the state shirks its responsibility of regulating the market and safeguarding the common good, they leave the market, the economy, and the common good open to exploitation unjust, inhuman, faceless, and unregulated market forces. The same is true for economic activities within nations and between nations. There is an urgent need for stronger regulatory framework to safeguard the common good, and to enable the emancipation of the poor, while respecting the individual's application of his or her genius for economic enterprise. The principle underpinning the Church's social doctrine remains the same: justice must be applied to every sphere of the economy. The economic market should not remain deterministic but should be regulated through the proper use of human freedom, and be based on the protection of the common good, and the protection of the weak. It is especially these, the downtrodden who are vulnerable to the blind forces of the market economy.

The Pope calls for the articulation of political authority at the local, national, and international levels so as to give direction to the process of globalization. What is obvious is that the increasing poverty in places like Africa, is the result of many factors of which globalization is one. According to the Pope, nations of the world need to strengthen their democratic institutions, work towards a more just and ethical frameworks. In addition, new models of statecraft should be worked out to regulate the economy to serve the cause of the common good and diffuse world wide prosperity which has remained limited to the developed countries. The building of relationships, friendship, compassion, care, and concern for the others which the principle of gratuitousness strengthens will help wean the negative growth of individualism and utilitarian ethics in the market economy, in states, international organizations and aid agencies, and in personal relations in communities. This comprehensive re-organization and the Pope's proposed change in emphasis will help to create communion, friendship, a spirit of sharing, the deeper appreciation of the common origin and destiny of the human race, and promote the ethical and spiritual energy to love others without counting the cost.

STEPS TOWARDS MEETING THE SOCIO-ECONOMIC CHALLENGES OF OUR TIMES

Many people the world over are concerned about how to meet the socio-economic challenges of our times. Globally, there are more regulation of the financial market, bailouts of collapsing banks and financial houses, companies, and conglomerates. There is however, a fundamental challenge facing the world that goes beyond the limits of the regulatory practices that are often firmly imposed in many countries and internationally. Development of peoples demands charity in truth, which draws from a proper scale of values based on the origin and destiny of the human person and the purpose of creation as a whole. In chapters 4 and 5, Pope Benedict points out how specific challenges facing the contemporary world could be met. He draws together in this analysis all the basic principles which under gird Catholic social teaching: integral development, the link between rights and duties, solidarity, subsidiarity, the common good, the recognition that the human race is one family, the right to work with fair wages, the recognition of the family as a basic good, the respect for life from conception to natural death, the ultimate purpose of human life, the protection and respect of the environment, and human nature as both gift and responsibility, and the principle of gratuitousness, among others. While I do not wish to further define all these principles that I have already touched on, I do wish to highlight some of the socio-economic challenges relating to the fundamental principles of Catholic social teaching which the Pope has identified and his proposals for their resolution:

Rights and Duties

There is a universal consensus that human rights are a common global heritage that must be defended at all times and at all cost. There is a need for Christian engagement with secular voices and other religious traditions in promoting and defending the rights of people. The social gospel advances a situation where these rights are protected through the moral and spiritual transformation of individuals and societies that will remove those negative conditions that lead to abuse of human rights. Indeed, enumerating these rights does not make sense if they are not respected and upheld as sacred trust of our common humanity. Human rights remain important for theological ethics and

Christian practice of charity because, according to George Newland, in the twenty-first century large numbers of people continue to be abused, tortured, and murdered. Large number of peoples continues to die of hunger and diseases when the resources to prevent them are present. Large numbers suffer from all kinds of discrimination to a degree that is serious enough to damage their lives in quite unnecessary ways. Despite giant strides made in human progress, descent into barbarism seems as easy in our current century as it has ever been.[42]

There are still millions of people in many parts of the world especially in places like Africa, Asia, Eastern Europe, and Latin America whose right to life are threatened by poverty, and whose human freedom are stifled by dictatorship. There are increasing incidence of abuse of religious freedom in many countries, and new forms of religious intolerance in the Middle East, North Africa, Northern Nigeria, and in North America and Europe. This intolerance is particularly egregious in formerly strong Christian societies in the West where the freedom to live in a Christian environment is being subtly denied because of the so-called separation of church and state. It is important to understand clearly the foundation of human rights. Benedict argues that there is a normative philosophical and metaphysical order which undergirds and makes possible any human rights logic. A short history is necessary to set our discussion in perspective.

Human rights, as we understand the concept today, emerged as part of a process of evolution. The *Magna Carta* had already been signed in England in 1215; the Petition of Rights followed four centuries later in 1628, and after the Glorious Revolution came the Bill of Rights in 1689. Almost a hundred years later, in 1791, came the Bill of Rights of the United States Constitution, making America the first state to be in submission to a constitution defining human rights as the bases and foundation of government. It was preceded in 1789 by the French Declaration of the Rights of Man and citizen.[43] There were series of other national declarations of human rights, but eventually the horrors perpetrated by the Nazi and Fascist governments in the twentieth century made obvious the need for a joint effort by the international community to protect the rights of the human person. This was what gave rise to the Universal Declaration of Human Rights

42. Newland, Human Rights, 7.
43. Villa-Vicencio, Reconstruction, 98.

(1948) and the two international covenants that followed it in 1966 (International Covenant on Economic, Social and Cultural rights and the International Covenant on civil and Political Rights). These international declarations and covenants and their different variants in national constitutions did not define what human rights mean, but rather specified what the rights are in and of themselves. John Finnis emphasizes difficulties inherent in defining rights thus: "In short the modern vocabulary and grammar of rights is a many-faceted instrument for reporting and asserting the requirements or other implications of a relationship of justice from the point of view of the person(s) who benefit(s) from that relationship. It provides a way of talking about 'what is just' from a special angle, the view point of the 'other(s)' to whom something (including inter alia, freedom of choice) is owed or due, and who would be wronged if denied something."[44]

Finnis points out that the modern grammar of rights provides a way of expressing virtually all the requirements of practical reasonableness between the most general principles and the moral norms in those whose wisdom or prudentia has not been supplanted by vice. Rights, according to him, are extensive and supple in their reach but that the structures are not properly understood. There is accordingly much misunderstanding about the nature of rights, their meaning, and the duties and responsibilities that go with them. This conflict arises because our concepts of rights today are derived largely from jurists, legislators, and lawyers. Rights then—whether natural or moral, civic or economic—are framed within juridical and actionable terms and the resolution of claims of right demands a clearly articulated value system based on an integral understanding of the human person. Here importantly, the Catholic teaching on the dignity and rights of the human person provides vital insight.

Between 1891 and 1961, Catholic social teaching developed into a fairly coherent doctrine within which human rights were systematically articulated.[45] The concept of person in Christian anthropology refers to the uniqueness, unrepeatability, absolute value, and sacredness of the individual. The elaboration of the rights of the human person is tied to the moral thinking about human destiny and the place of the human person in society. The *Compendium of the Social Doctrine*

44. Finnis, Law and Rights, 205
45. Dorr, Option for the Poor, 255.

of the Church in chapter 3, "The Human Person and Human Rights," begins the discussion of human rights by stating that the human person is the living image of God himself (n.105). It further recognizes and affirms the centrality of the human person in every sector and expression of society (n.106) and that the human person can never be a passive element of social life but its subject, foundation, and goal. Any reflection on human rights must begin with an understanding of who the human person is, the common good and the principles of justice. This is central to the teaching of Pope John XXIII in *Mater et Magistra* as follows; "Individual human beings are the foundation, the cause and the end of every social institution . . . On this principles, which guarantees the sacred dignity of the individual, the Church constructs the whole of her social teaching" (*Mater et Magistra*, 219–20).

Whether human rights are claims, powers in us, laws (jus), social convention, legal instruments or human capacities, the elaboration of these rights will demand an understanding of the human person. However, the global rights revolution took place during the time when the Catholic understanding of human rights was being discussed and elaborated following the publication of *Pacem in Terris* and the Second Vatican Council. Michael Ignatieff, however, opines that rights could be discussed even outside of those expressed in religious institutions' terms as such, and can be an expression of the will of the people. He goes forward to explicate the meaning of human rights: "Rights are not just instruments of the law, they are expressions of our moral identity as a people. When we see justice done—for example, when an unjustly imprisoned person walks free, when a person long crushed by oppression stands up and demands her right to be heard—we feel a deep emotion rise within us. That emotion is the longing to live in a fair world. Rights may be precise, legalist, and dry, but they are the chief means by which human beings express this longing."[46]

Modern Catholic thinking on the nature and foundation of human rights could best be described in John XXIII's statement in 1961 that the modern tradition of the Church is "dominated by one basic theme-an unshakable affirmation and vigorous defence of the dignity and rights of the human person."[47] John A. Coleman argues following A. Gewirth that appeal to human dignity is not a sufficient foundation

46. Ignatieff, *Revolution*, 2–3.

47. Hollenbach, *Claims*, 42.

for human rights. This is because appeal to human dignity as foundation for rights fails to specify the precise nexus between human dignity as an evocative quality and a particular alleged object of a right claim. In addition, the argument for rights based on inherent dignity does not satisfy the requirements of non-circularity. Furthermore, appeals to human dignity as the foundation of human rights could also promote individualism and legitimize a liberal political philosophy that could be at odds with the Catholic social theory (Gregory Baum).[48] He argues further that rights should be grounded on the necessary conditions of human actions because rights are the condition for the realization of human worth in action. One will add that the necessary condition for human actions arises primarily from a metaphysical apprehension of who the person is; the priority of the essence over the act, of being over action should be upheld. Thus, human dignity as foundation for human rights simply admits that one is a person and should be respected and granted these rights independent of what he or she undertakes, or his or her status.

It seems to me that Coleman's critique of human dignity as foundation for human rights diminishes the priority of a theistic anthropology and of the truth of being over the moral and political actions of the state or practical deeds of individuals. It also will limit the rights of poor people, minorities, physically, or mentally challenged people and others who do not have the freedom for enacting the constitutive actions that Coleman proposes. Rights are not simply powers to do, but simply the intrinsic value and higher gift to exist, to simply be. In addition, the rights of individuals are rights within a community; it is essential to understand that our actions and our freedoms are to be directed to the free exercise of our moral and spiritual choices with a view to contributing to the common good. Individual rights are not exclusive claims, and should not be in contradiction with the common good, or with the life of the community and the end of human life as such. However, more acceptable is Coleman's call for sacramentalizing human rights through icons like Archbishop Romero of El Salvador, or Archbishop of Desmond Tutu of South Africa, and Pope John Paul II all of whom through their resistance to dictatorship have became icons for Christians in the human rights struggle.

48. See Coleman, "Theory," 349–55.

There are various positions on the nature of the rights themselves. One idea of human rights is the contractual theory. According to this view, rights depends upon the state and some form of social contract between the ruler and the ruled which imposes certain obligations on the legislator. This theory is principally associated with the French philosopher Jean-Jacques Rousseau, who posits that making some metaphorical contract between citizen and state is the basis on which states should be governed. He, like John Locke, and Thomas Hobbes had the idea of the state of nature governed by the rule of the jungle, but with the emergence of government the rights and freedom of citizens are better protected and the common good is promoted. As Michael Zuckert writes, "The state of nature, according to Hobbes, is the home of the right of nature (*jus naturale*), or the right of all men to everything, including one another's bodies and for Locke in the state of nature human beings possess a title to perfect freedom and uncontrolled enjoyment of the rights and privileges of the law of nature."[49]

A fundamental weakness of the contractual theory of rights is that it is based upon an assumption that over time people have come to accept; that the state has certain powers and that citizens may expect certain things from their government. Even though national constitutions are formulated through long processes of negotiation and eventual agreement, the very fact of these rights being specified in national constitutions and international law does not mean that they are mere products and achievement of human and social conventions. Again enshrining rights in national constitutions does not mean that states and parties will respect and guarantee these rights to their citizens. Worldwide we repeatedly see the abuse of human rights in many countries, and by many countries. Many poor people globally have been denied their rights to live in social conditions where their human fulfillment could be realized. In many cases these abuses are defended through various appeals to national security. The contractual theory fails to show how the abuse of rights could be defended and how a moral vision could be brought in the appreciation and respect of the rights and dignity of every human being on earth. It fails to show how people could accept the truth that if the rights of any person is abused especially the poor, the vulnerable, minorities, etc., that my humanity is also diminished.

---

49. Zuckert, Rights and Republicanism, 343.

Contractual theory of rights could also give rise to various forms of abuse. A nation could decide on certain rights that are deleterious to her citizens and threaten the well being of people of goodwill in other parts of the world. Benedict highlights in CIV the need for states to uphold laws promoting the integrity of the family (CIV, 45). Therein lies the need for a grounding of rights on a more secure foundation. As a moral code that expresses the natural law, the contract theory of right could be interpreted within the natural law tradition as an expression of an order which human reason can discover. Pope John XXIII teaches that the ultimate source of rights is not found in the mere will of human beings, in the reality of the state, or in public powers but in the human person and in God the Creator of the human person (John XXIII, *Pacem in Terris*, 55).

The second school of thought on the nature and foundations of human rights is the natural law theory. This is a school to which the Catholic tradition of rights belongs because its foundation for human rights is on human nature itself. This means that people have rights simply because they are people; human rights arise from a common humanity. I have rights which others must recognize, simply because I am a person. Further, my claim to rights on this basis necessarily requires my recognition of the rights of others. According to the document, *The Church and Human Rights, Justitia et Pax*, "The teaching of the magisterium on fundamental human rights is based in the first place or is suggested by the inherent requirements of human nature . . . within the sphere of natural law" (n.28). Not allying itself to any of the ideological positions of the liberals and the socialists, the Church's understanding of human rights is that it belongs to the order of creation and human nature, made known in natural law and discernable by reason. Pope Benedict in CIV reaffirms that natural law is the foundation not only of human rights but also for a just social order and economic system. He teaches thus; "In all cultures there are examples of ethical convergence, some isolated, some interrelated, as an expression of the one human nature, willed by the Creator; the tradition of ethical wisdom knows this as the natural law. This universal moral law provides a sound basis for all cultural, religious and political dialogue, and it ensures that the multi-faceted pluralism of cultural diversity does not detach itself from the common quest for truth, goodness and

God. Thus adherence to the law etched on human hearts is the pre-condition for all constructive social cooperation" (CIV, 59).

The Church's teaching on human rights has revolved constantly on two complementary lines. The first is the line of ascent, which is based on natural law, discoverable by reason, and confirmed and raised to a higher level by Divine Revelation.[50] This draws from Thomas Aquinas' notion of natural law, which we shall refer to later. It links natural law to eternal law. This is a link often ignored by the new natural law theorists like Finnis. This group fails to see the insufficiency of natural law to attain the final good of the human person. Hence natural law is subordinate to divine law and draws from it but does not exhaust it. This is why grace builds on nature, but stretching it to the transcendental end that is its goal. The other line from which the Church's human rights teaching is drawn is a line of descent.[51] In this sense, the coming among us of the Son of God and in sharing our human nature has ennobled our dignity and establishes once and for all the transcendent grounds for justice, rights, and charity. Human rights discourse in the Catholic Church is thus eminently both anthropological and Christological: Christ reveals man to man and makes his noble calling clear. Hollenbach argues that Catholic social teaching has always based human rights on human dignity. This dignity as we have shown is rooted in the image of God in us ennobled by the mystery of the Incarnation, "Human dignity is not an abstract or ethereal reality but is realized in concrete conditions of personal, social, economic and political life. The history of the papal teaching has been a process of discovering and identifying those conditions of human dignity. These conditions are called human rights."[52]

Jacques Maritain fully developed the Thomistic theory of natural law as the basis for the dignity and rights of the human person. The reliability of natural law as Heiko Oberman holds is a universality that goes beyond individual validity and offers a moral foundation that is in undisturbable harmony with eternal law.[53]

The term natural law has often been used in both ancient philosophy and in various religions. Antigone for instance defines it as

---

50. See International Theological Commission, "Dignity and Rights," 259.

51. Ibid.

52. Hollenbach, Claims, 68.

53. Oberman, Harvest, 108.

"the uncreated unwritten law"; for the Stoics, the existence of natural law, jus naturale was an emanation of "eternal law," that is the law of reason of the universe. They argued that the moral law is rooted in nature (*physis*) rather than only constructed by convention (*nomos*), and that moral virtues can be identified by reason reflecting on nature; "the existence of an inner reason in man linked everyone with the cosmic order."[54] Aristotle wrote of doing the right or the just act. He contrasted what is right by nature from what is right just by convention. In the Ancient Roman legal system, a distinction was made between laws that were specific to Romans (*ius civile*), and laws that are common to all nations (*ius gentium*). Time and space do not permit us to go into the full elaboration of natural law tradition in Greek philosophy, or in the writings of the patristic period. The articulation in a systematic way of the natural law within the Catholic tradition could be traced to Thomas Aquinas. St. Thomas defines natural law this way, "Thus implying that the light of natural reason, whereby we discern what is good and what is evil, which is the function of the natural law, is nothing else than an imprint on us of the divine light. It is therefore evident that the natural law is nothing else than the rational creatures participation of the eternal law."[55]

Natural law is thus an inclination towards the good which is discerned through reason and which conduces towards the common good. Maritain writes that this order which reason can discover and according to which the will must act in order to be attuned to itself is the necessary end of the human being.[56] How does one come to an awareness of the natural law? On the ontological level, Maritain writes that there is a "normality of functioning" in all existents, which is the proper way in which, by reason of its specific construction, it demands to be put into action. Indeed, all existing reality has a purpose, certain teleology, which according to Aristotle is good in itself. All beings move towards their ends according to their essences. Natural law with regard to the human person is ontological because the human essence is an ontological reality, which does not exist separately, but in every human being, so that by the same token natural law dwells as an ideal order in the very being of all existing things.

54. Encyclopedia Britannica, 716.
55. Aquinas, Theologia, 1/Q91/A1: ad 1.
56. Maritain, Rights and Law, 141.

On the gnoseological element, Maritain writes that natural law is unwritten law but known infallibly because it is self-evident: "Man's knowledge of it has increased little by little as man's moral conscience has developed."[57] This knowledge is not one acquired through ratiocination and conceptual judgments but knowledge through inclination (Aquinas), and this is a gradual growth process recognized by the human race in human history. The concept developed in the double protecting tissue of human inclinations and human society. Natural law is the basis for human rights according to Maritain because without it human rights will be meaningless and susceptible to varying interpretations and applications according to the whims and caprices of governments and individuals. Maritain argues;

> The same natural law which lays down our most fundamental duties, and by virtue of which every law is binding, is the very law which assigns to us our fundamental rights. It is because we are enmeshed in the universal order, in the laws and regulations of the cosmos and of the immense family of created natures (and finally in the order of creative wisdom), and it is because we have at the same time the privilege of sharing in spiritual nature that we possess rights vis-à-vis other men and all the assemblage of creature.[58]

Natural law is also the basis of the Church's teaching on Christian personalism and on human rights. We have rights because we are human beings created in the image and likeness of God. Through the revelation of Christ the basic human rights of humankind are made known in a fuller and more decisive manner. Human rights relate to the exercise of human freedom and hence enable human persons to freely undertake proper human acts that have moral components. The human person has rights because he or she has been created by God to freely respond to the call of love and through his or her acts ennoble creation and attain through moral acts to his or her ultimate human destiny. This is a much deeper foundation for rights than the rationalistic and individualistic foundation proposed by some schools of positivism and Marxist socialist school that subordinate the rights of the human person under the iron will of the state. It also protects the common good, while also safeguarding the full development of the

57. Ibid., Man and State, 88.
58. Ibid., 95–96.

human person towards his or her ordered end. *The Compendium of the Social Doctrine of the Church's* summarizes this teaching this way: "In fact, the roots of human rights are to be found in the dignity that belongs to each human being. This dignity, inherent in human life and equal in every person, is perceived and understood first by reason. The natural foundation of rights appears all the more solid when, in the light of the supernatural, it is considered that human dignity, after having been given by God and having been profoundly wounded by sin, was taken on and redeemed by Jesus Christ in his incarnation, death and resurrection" (n. 153).

Against the attacks of Bentham, Austin, Kelsen, Weber, Hart, and Raz (who repudiated the theory of natural law as a foundation of human rights), Finnis holds that the natural law provides the sure foundation for human rights and shows clearly the nature of the rights themselves because: (1) they assert the basic practical principles which indicate the basic forms of human flourishing as goods to be pursued and realized. (2) They offer a set of basic methodological requirements of practical reasonableness which distinguish sound from unsound practical thinking, right action from wrong actions, and just actions and unjust actions. (3) They provide the bases for general moral standards with regard to the common good, democracy, and the proper ordering of society. The social teaching of the Church with regard to human rights is not meant to externally impose a religious faith as such, but to assist in laying the foundations for a humane society. It provides a set of principles upon which a just and democratic society can be based. It supports freedom and values, which, though they may historically have been won largely in the teeth of religious opposition and political oppression, can never find an adequate foundation in purely materialistic philosophies or the iron will of state fiats.

Human Rights are universal, reciprocal, inalienable, and inseparable. They are universal because they are present in all human beings, without exception of time, place, or subject-no qualifications are needed. Also to be noted contrary to some thinking, is the truth that human rights are intrinsic to human history and connatural to all cultures and civilizations. However, not all cultures and civilizations have systematically articulated or fully embraced the heritage of human rights. This does not mean that the notion is absent in their history and social and community life. Thus I will disagree with views represented by Jack Donnelly that non-Western civilizations like African, Chinese, and Indian have a notion of human dignity but not that of human rights.[59] It may be right to argue that Western type liberal rights tradition are not shared by non-Western cultures who have often organized their societies within certain norms and communal ethos which respected individual rights without stifling the common good.

Rights are also said to be reciprocal meaning that my claims to rights must entail my recognition of the rights of others, and their recognition of mine. Further, it entails my obligation to respect and, if necessary, to defend the rights of others, especially the rights of those who cannot defend themselves. As Pope John Paul II said in his World Day of Peace Address (1999): "These rights apply to every stage of life and to every political, social, economic, and cultural situation. Together they form a single whole, directed unambiguously towards the promotion of every aspect of the good of both the person and society . . . The integral promotion of every category of human rights is the true guarantee of full respect for each individual right."[60]

The rights are inalienable in so far as no one can legitimately deprive another person of these rights, since this would do violence to nature. No state can deprive the rights of her citizens without just cause. Human rights are also inviolable and inseparable. No one can take them away from the human person since they are inherent in the human person and in human dignity. Because it would be futile to proclaim rights that would not be kept by governments and peoples everywhere in the world, these rights must therefore be protected. As a result, the history of the world and of nations has shown that various international laws and national constitutions have safeguards against the abuse of human rights. Within the legal system of nations, human rights are said to be actionable meaning that people can take legal action to safeguard their fundamental human rights.

David Hollenbach, Rodger Charles, and Donal Dorr have shown in their works how the doctrine of human rights developed in the Church and how from Pope Leo XIII to Pope John Paul II various aspects of these rights have been developed. Some of the significant magisterial works on human rights include *Rerum Novarum* (which

59. See his argument in Donnelly, "Human Rights and Human Dignity."
60. AAS, 91 (1999), 379.

defended the rights of the workers) *Mater et Magistra, Gaudium et Spes, Populorum Progressio, Centesimus Annus, Sollicitudo Rei Socialis* among others.

The Compendium outlines these rights and the duties which go with them and they are worth outlining in a very brief way: The most updated magisterial list of rights could be found in *Centesimus Annus* which includes; "the right to life, an integral part of which is the right of the child to develop in the mother's womb from the moment of conception; the right to live in a united family and in a moral environment conducive to the growth of the child's personality; the right to develop one's intelligence and freedom in seeking and knowing the truth; the right to share in the work which makes wise use of the earth's material resources, and to derive from that work the means to support oneself and ones dependents; and the right freely to establish a family, to have and to rear children through the responsible exercise of one's sexuality. In a certain sense, the source and synthesis of these rights is religious freedom, understood as the right to live in the truth of one's faith in conformity with one's transcendent dignity as a person" (*Centesimus Annus*, 47). We see in this enumeration that the first basic right is the right to life from conception to natural death because it is the basis for the exercise of other rights. Emphasis is also given to the right to work and the freedom of religion. There is also a high tenor placed on the right to decide one's own state of life, and the right to family life and education in a family. One can identify then five main divisions of rights within the Catholic tradition, namely:

- A human person is a living being. Hence, there is a life factor in each human person.
- Each human person is a psycho-somatic being. Each person is living body, hence there is a physical-psychological factor in a human person.
- Each person is a rational being with an embodied spirit. Hence, there is an intellectual-spiritual factor in a human person.
- Each person is a political being, hence there is an economic factor in a human person.
- Each person is a social being. Hence there is a social factor in a human person.[61]

---

61. Muyebe and Muyebe, Bishops on Rights, 14–15.

- Respect for these rights is an indicative sign of the authentic progress of any government, any society and any culture (Compendium, n. 155).

- Rights necessarily involve duties. Both rights and duties derive their origin, their sustenance, and their indestructibility from the natural law, which in conferring rights also imposes duties. Duties are linked to rights in the same person: the right to life is the counterpart of the duty to preserve it; the right to decent standard of living brings a duty to live in a civilized manner; the right to search for the truth involves the duty to do so. We are also obliged to respect each other's right (cf. *Pacem in Terris*, 28–33). Society must be orderly, useful and conform to human dignity in order to secure the rights of the human person. It must promote and protect the common good and establish just structures that advance social justice, distributive justice, and commutative justice. The teaching on rights and duties are clearly presented in the Compendium this way:

> The mutual complementarities between rights and duties-they are indissolubly linked-are recalled several times, above all in the human person who possesses them. This bond has a social dimension: "in human society to one man's right there corresponds a duty in all other persons: the duty, namely, of acknowledging and respecting the right in question." The Magisterium underlines the contradiction inherent in affirming rights without acknowledging corresponding responsibilities. "Those therefore who claim their own rights, yet altogether forget or neglect to carry out their respective duties, are people who build with one hand and destroy with the other" (n. 156).

This position is what *Caritas in Veritate* not only underlies clearly, but updates in its application to contemporary challenges facing today's world. It also goes further to teach that duties reinforce rights and call for their defense and promotion. Pope Benedict also teaches that arbitrary claims such as the inclusion of same-sex unions into the definition of marriage, cannot, through legislation or otherwise, properly be enshrined as rights, even as some countries are doing currently. The same principles apply to international organizations. Rights are not human inventions, but are drawn from natural law and the nature of things, especially human nature, and in new cosmologies from the revelation found in creation. Rights are intimately linked to duties, the right to family presupposes the duties of openness to life, procreation, and education of children as primary; the right to life applies to all. This is especially so to the vulnerable and the weak (as for example the unborn, the sick, the elderly, the handicapped among others). Environmental rights and claims are also specified by the duty of both the human subjects to respect and care for the environment as well as the duty to recognize the origin and destiny of all things in God.

The Dignity to Life

Human life is always a gift. All Christians are called to be pro-life. The question many people ask sometimes is: What is the relationship between being pro-life and development issues? In the first place, development is about people and creation. We cannot develop people or the environment by acts of violence and destruction. In the 1980's development proponents from the West heightened and in some cases exaggerated the claims of over-population especially in Africa and other Two-Third World countries. They argued that the world cannot be sustained by the over population in the world. There were covert and subtle attempts to impose population control measures, which included not only the evil of abortion but also contraception, and all forms of sterilization and anti-life policies. There also were, at least by some, intentions to apply such measures against specific (less desirable in some people's limited thinking) peoples through subtle forms of eugenics. Today, the agents of these false practices have become more silent as their failed theories continue to be subverted by the facts on the ground. Benedict XVI teaches that "due attention must obviously be given to responsible procreation, which among other things has a positive contribution to make to integral development" (CIV, 44). There is need for responsible parenting in many families, which requires that parents raise small or large families with due diligence and full consideration of the modern economic and social pressures and challenges to responsible parenting and family wellbeing. Pope Benedict is however, teaching that it is immoral to tie population control measures unacceptable to African culture, especially abortion, to development aid to Africa and other developing countries. In addition, there is urgent need to promote a healthy morality with regard to sexuality.

One will add that teaching young primary students and high school students how to use condom, as is done in many African schools, minimizes and distorts the moral demands and the choices to be made between the use of condom and life or death. This corrodes African and Christian morality. While there are many questions being considered in terms of the use of condoms for the prevention of HIV/ AIDS in conjugal acts between married couples, I believe that the question of prevention of pregnancy and the protection against contracting HIV goes beyond technical solutions. It is also paternalizing for people to condomize Africa without due regard to the cultural and social dynamics on the grounds. The use or lack thereof of condom in Africa needs a wider analysis beyond the ideologically driven debate today. It goes beyond a simplified appeal to the use of condom as the answer to the spread of HIV/AIDS in Africa. It involves the question of poverty and vulnerability, especially of young girls and women; the powerlessness of the very people who are being exposed to this disease through the use or failure to use condom. Also to be pointed out is the poor state of healthcare in Africa, the high level of ignorance and cultural traditions and practices with regard to sex, and corruption in the political and healthcare sectors in many African countries. It is important that the Church in Africa reads the signs of the times in our struggling continent with an eye on the principles set out in Catholic social ethics with regard to life and moral choices, and work towards better family life, strong sexual morality, poverty eradication, education, tolerance, and openness to discussion of matters of sexuality and relationship, and the protection of the vulnerable members of society, especially women and children.

Already one can see the danger of an anti-life ethics in many Western societies in the increasing number of abortions, high rate of pornography, the banalization of sex through a frightening rise in prostitution and teenage pregnancies. These anti-life forces manifest also in the deterioration of married life as demonstrated by examples of so many spouses stung by the rough edges of an unfulfilled love-life, in which they often feel used. There is also the danger of the myth of efficiency and physical productivity and effectiveness, wherein the elderly and the weak are often considered expendable and sometimes abandoned by society. The replacement value of the population continues to dwindle in many Western countries because of the low premium placed on child bearing. Indeed, in many instances, people celebrate the birth of a baby whale, or a cub of a polar bear more than they care about the millions of babies and unborn who are not allowed to live. Thus, when the Pope links development with both a life ethics and the principle of gratuitousness one can understand the link in a perfect way. There can be no authentic development without fidelity to the truth about the sacredness of human life. This truth and that of the sacredness of the created world should both be promoted, respected, and treated with love and care. I must add here as well the need for African countries to begin the process of abolishing the death penalty and impose stricter penalties for all criminal acts that threaten human well-being. One act of violence does not nullify a previous act of violence, and violence even if legislated by the state or religious institution as punitive or deterrent measures is a negation of good. Restorative justice, that seeks healing for both victims and perpetrators of crimes and evil, is more fitting for Christian humanism and the dignity of life than retributive justice of which death penalty is a sad example.

2

Catholic Theological Ethics Applied in Different Social Settings

SOCIAL ETHICS IN DIFFERENT SOCIAL CONTEXTS

IS THERE A VALID Christian answer to constant economic crises, environmental crisis, oil spillage, and natural disasters, all of which bring so much suffering on people? Catholic theological ethics deals with specific challenges facing the world today in the areas of social ethics that are highlighted, namely the relationship between business and ethics, international co-operation, science and technology, and ecological ethics. The first part of this chapter will deal with these important social-ethical considerations, we shall devote the final section of this chapter to a theological reflection on development. Some of these challenges we shall address in chapters 4 and 5 when we apply some of the principles developed in this encyclical and Catholic social teaching to Africa and the role of Christian charities, Christians, and churches in Africa in practicing charity in truth in Africa.

The Relationship between Business and Ethics

Pope Benedict writes in *CIV* 46 of the changing context of business and ethics. He calls for alternate entities that do not operate on the pure logic of profit. Some of these alternates will include micro-finance, co-operative unions, economy of communion, etc. Globally, one could see the reality of the Pope's proposal. There is an exponential growth in third sector organizations (especially not-for-profit groups) and social capitals who are working for a better possible world. These groups are grassroots movements. They also, each in their own way, manifest new approaches for living and co-operating and go beyond the profit and loss mentality. While these organizations (also called NGOs) in many countries have not been fully integrated into countries with juridical and legal frameworks, they are redefining the way businesses should be governed by ethics, especially applying the principles of charity in truth. As is the case with all reforms, there are imperfections. Pope Benedict challenges these organizations to be more transparent and accountable to their benefactors, who desire that their donations be appropriately, effectively, and especially ethically and charitably used for aid to the poor, as well as towards their empowerment. We shall return to this point later in chapter 3 as we wish to underscore the reasons why development aid and initiatives in Africa frequently fail. We have particular interest and responsibility when these failures occur in church based organizations, where the errors are often systematic and are uniformly painful.

It must also be added that business divorced from ethical principles is the root cause of the financial crisis and economic meltdown of 2008–2009 and possibly beyond. In an environment motivated by greed and selfishness, in societies driven by materialism and exaggerated utilitarian norms, people become mere objects to be used and exploited, while the uncontrolled passion to acquire more and more (so as to be "more"), within the limited space of time, becomes an idol. Such a vision of life is blind to the authentic goal of human life on earth, and is a destructive force that squanders the earth's resources without care about the common destiny of all things. Pope Benedict, therefore, appeals to each human being, and to each human group worldwide to strengthen businesses, especially those capable of viewing profit not as an end but as a means to make the market and all of society more humane, especially in poorer countries of the world who find themselves outside of the influential circles of the global market (*CIV*, 47).

This is also required in finance (*CIV*, 65), which should be directed towards improved wealth creation and development. The Pope teaches as follows: "Insofar as they are instruments, the entire econo and finance, not just certain sectors, must be used in an ethical way so as to create suitable conditions for human development of peoples. It is certainly useful, and in some circumstances imperative, to launch financial initiatives in which humanitarian dimension predominates" (*CIV*, 65). In this paragraph, Pope Benedict is arguing that the entire financial system should be governed by ethical principles in which the common good is promoted and protected, and where the poor are not mere instruments. The structural nature of the economic crisis is very much emphasized here. This basic systemic error is the result of socio-ethical failures at the personal level. It is in this regard that the Holy Father calls on all the stakeholders and men and women in the financial sector to rediscover the ethical foundation of their work.

Charity in truth is the foundation for co-operation among people, for just and equitable distribution of wealth within and among nations, and for protection of the vulnerable. In those cases where love and relationship are used as the bases for authentic inter-subjective interaction of economic, political, and social kinds, there are always peace and justice. But more importantly, these go beyond the requirements of demand and supply, and profit and loss to the condition of the human person who is the primary locus of development. This is why the Pope points to the new micro-credit unions and micro finances which have all become increasingly recommended in development discourse.[1] These are new ways in which society is attempting to spread wealth across the board. It is important, according to the Holy Father, that the weak members of society are not used as pawns, nor should loan become perpetual enslavement. Thus, financial systems should be so structured so that they become instruments for emancipating the poor, for creating jobs, and supporting equal access to opportunities for self-fulfillment. This way, everyone can be enabled to participate in building up the common wealth. The Pope also draws

---

1. One could draw attention to the impact which Muhammad Yunus made in Bangladesh with micro-credit unions through which he provided the poorest of the poor with small loans as small as $27 which helped to give them a head start in life. His principle was simple: loan poor people money on terms that are suitable to them, teach them a few sound financial principles, and they will help themselves. I think what the Pope is calling for here is that the poor are not content to be helped, but will like to take responsibility for their own lives if societies will build on the assets of the poor through better micro-credit support. See Yunus, *Banker to the Poor.*

creasing influence of consumer groups, and advices
sponsibility should be governed by moral principles
is on the common good. Thus, through the applica-
al principles, greater accent will be placed on ethical
out diminishing the intrinsic rationality and freedom of choice that are associated with the act of purchasing.

This is also important in the areas of export and import. The right
of the poor countries not to be dumping grounds for poor and inferior
products needs to be emphasized. Even though the encyclical does not
specifically mention Africa, the full consequences of consumer rights
in international market economy cannot be over-emphasized. How
much control do African nations have in determining the standard
and quality of the products coming into Africa? Is it not shocking that
in many cases machineries, automobiles, electronic products, cellular
phones, and in generic drugs which are no longer deemed safe outside
of Africa are sent or sold to Africans. The poor must not continue to
be the garbage dump for the rich; nor should Africans become the refuse place for dated textbooks, used cloths, disused weapons, decrepit
aircrafts, and other products which imperil human life and damage
environmental health. The poor quality of products being sent to
Africa from the industrialized nations has serious deleterious effects
on the building of economic prosperity and constitutional democracy
in Africa. In addition, they also have long term costs on human and
eco-system health, hence the need to adopt this principle of social responsibility to international export of products to Africa.

INTERNATIONAL CO-OPERATION AND AID

Pope Benedict states that the principle for international co-operation
should be based on truth and love. There is a divine plan about the
origin and destiny of all things. As a result, international co-operation
should aim at making human lives, political and economic systems,
and global history to conform to God's plan. God's plan is abundant
life for all of creation. In addition, God's plan passes through the human family beginning from each individual family, which takes its
name from God the father. Pope Benedict teaches that the development of peoples begins when humanity recognizes that we are one
family (*CIV*, 53). People must accept one another as brothers and sis-

ters and not simply tolerate each other. All tongues, races, peoples, nations, and religions make up the one family of God, and communion
among all peoples is proposed in *Charity in Truth* as the authentic
path towards international co-operation.

Pope Benedict returns constantly to his main argument that a
theological theistic anthropology is the only authentic way of understanding development. He continues the teaching of Paul VI that the
social question has become a radically anthropological question (*CIV*,
75). In this regard, all kinds of bioethics such as stem cell embryonic
research, eugenics, genetic mutation, cloning and other forms of human attempts to produce hybrid humans are considered destructive
of the very nature of the human person as gift. The inter-relationship
between the human family, and integral development can only be
properly understood when we appreciate the uniqueness and splendor of every human life, and the trinitarian origin and goal of human
life and the entire creation (cf. *CIV*, 77).

There are three implications of this papal teaching on development from a trinitarian perspective: (1) it makes manifest the intrinsic
unity among humanity rooted in the trinitarian origin of human life
and the social order. (2) The trinitarian origin of our human society
leads to the anthropological understanding of the human person as
created in the image and likeness of God, a truth that illumines our
understanding of human identity. (3) Human relationship is, therefore, to be based on this divine model of mutual relationship, intrinsic
openness to the other, communion and shared existence, solidarity,
different but related operations, and autonomy and divergence which
uphold each individual, while at the same time allowing their mutual
involvement in each other's lives. The *Compendium* summarizes this
perspective clearly when it teaches, "The commandment of mutual
love, which represents the law of life for God's people, must inspire,
purify, and elevate all human relationships in society and in politics.
'To be human means to be called to interpersonal communion,' because the image and likeness of the Trinitarian God are the basis of
the whole of 'human ethos,' which reaches its apex in the commandment to love." The modern cultural, social, economic and political
phenomenon of interdependence, which intensifies and makes particularly evident the bonds that unite the human family, accentuates
once more, in the light of Revelation, "a new model of the unity of

the human race, which must ultimately inspire our solidarity. This supreme model of unity, which is a reflection of the intimate life of God, one God in three persons is what we Christian mean by the word, 'communion'" (*Compendium*, 33).

Human relationships and co-operation from the lowest level of social organization to the highest levels of international co-operation are not accidental but are rooted in human nature. It is, therefore, open to a metaphysical interpretation of which appreciation of the truth about the human person and creation as such offers the necessary ground for promoting charity (*CIV*, 55). Charity draws from this theological anthropology of relatedness and commonality, and the ultimate destiny of all things. Our practical involvement in the shaping of history contributes to bringing this about. In this way of viewing co-operation among peoples and nations, God has a central place. The encyclical makes constant appeal to the divine wisdom and the recognition of God in the public square as primary for a proper moral and spiritual edge required for building a strong and enduring foundation for a better world. This is an important papal teaching because a purely secular notion of development that often relegates God to the private domain in many societies works against the very basis for development. Development without God will lead to inhuman development, and a warped sense of history, and a humanism without transcendental values. The vision of development that Pope Benedict proposes encourages dialogue between faith and reason, and between believers and non-believers. This way, humanity will mine the cultural and religious traditions of various civilizations and their interaction through healthy dialogues in working out sapiential models of development integrating the full truth about humanity and creation, and the destiny of all things in God (CIV 56–57).

In a situation where poverty and suffering significantly eats away a substantial portion of our humanity, then acts of solidarity should be manifested to changing such unacceptable situations in order to bring abundant life to God's people. This is why the Pope urges those involved in international co-operation to act according to sound moral principles relying on divine wisdom for the procurement of abundant life in which consists true development. He goes on to teach on how this should be done with regard to respecting and emancipating the poor; "From this standpoint, international organizations might question the actual effectiveness of their bureaucratic and administrative machinery, which is often excessively costly. At times it happens that those who receive aid become subordinate to the aid-givers, and the poor serve to perpetuate expensive bureaucracies that consume an excessively high percentage of funds intended for development (*CIV*, 47).

The Holy Father makes appeal to the principle of subsidiarity in international co-operation especially between believers and non-believers (*CIV*, 57). Here one must observe that the Pope proposes the possibility of a unified vision of development because the truth around which charity is built is metaphysical. Therefore, it is accessible to everyone irrespective of religious affinities through the application of their rational and moral faculties.

The Pope goes on to show the ways and means through which international co-operation and aid should be carried out to reflect the metaphysical principles he enunciates. The two principles he appeals to are subsidiarity and solidarity. These principles constitute the bases for the equal participation of every member of society in the promotion and protection of the common good. These also protect the poor from suppression under the weight of the powerful and mighty.

SUBSIDIARITY AND SOLIDARITY

These are two important principles in Catholic social teaching. Benedict builds on these principles and applies them to the social questions of the day. Subsidiarity is defined in *Quadragesimo Anno* this way: "Just as it is gravely wrong to take from individuals what they can accomplish by their own initiative and industry and give it to the community, so also it is an injustice and at the same time a grave evil and disturbance of right order to assign to a greater and higher association what lesser and subordinate organizations can do. For every social activity ought of its very nature to furnish help to the members of the body social, and never destroy and absorb them" (QA, 23). This principle is aimed at protecting the weak from the strong; while at the same time respecting and promoting the different forms of assistance for the human person through the autonomy of intermediate bodies (*CIV*, 57). On the basis of this principle, all societies of superior order must adopt attitudes of help (*subsidium*)—support, promotion, development—with respect to lower-order societies (*Compendium*, 186). We live in very complex and intimately intertwined societies. Some of the complexities of modern life have created anonymity, while in some cases social networks and new forms of human contacts have made human relationship more constant and diverse, albeit impersonal. As a social philosophy, subsidiarity is related to civil society in terms of how individual freedom could be better exercised within those primary units of interaction that help to firm up human relationship. This philosophy of subsidiarity has traditionally been evident in many African societies where there are small village groups, family units, co-operative groups, age-grades, ethnic and clan-based economic, political and social units who are promoting grassroots development and cultural life. In the large and mainly artificial boundaries created in many African states by colonial fiats, and political entities and organizations maintained by these boundaries, there has been a consistent suppression of these robust intermediate units, who could contribute to development at the most primary levels of societies. The development models which have often been foisted on many African societies have minimized and in some cases have totally taken away from them the things they could do for themselves. These have markedly suppressed their inherent traditional cultural and economic creativity.

This can also happen in international development aid wherein the development agents and governments in the West impose forms of development that destroy local initiatives and creativity. The goal of subsidiarity is to safeguard the creative subjectivity of citizens and small social units and to grant them the existential space to contribute in their own way to the growth of the community to the development of the wider and higher units of social organization. Put in other words, subsidiarity means that you cannot take away from someone what he or she can do for himself or herself; you should help or support individuals to help themselves. Thus, this principle is against all forms of excessive centralization of power or economic life on a large and overbearing state or institutional entity. It also rejects the bureaucratization of all economic, social, cultural, and political life in countries since these suppress human freedom and the free exercise of moral acts in participatory practices for promoting the common good. National governments must work out new constitutional structures in which subordinate units are allowed to carry out those duties that pertain to their spheres. Inappropriate centralization of many social, cultural and economic initiatives by governments has led to conflicts, injustice, and suppression of economic and ethnic dynamism in too many African countries.

Monopolies and protectionism in international relationship are thus rejected as principles for international co-operation. The same could also be said of the welfare state especially, for example in the excessive and unjustified presence of the state in every sphere of private mechanism. *The Compendium* states the basis for the practice of the principle of subsidiarity this way:

> respect and effective promotion of the human person and family; ever greater appreciation of associations and intermediate organisations in their fundamental choices and in those that cannot be delegated to or exercised by others; the encouragement of private initiative so that every social entity remains at the service of the common good, each with its own distinctive characteristics; the presence of pluralism in society and due representation of its vital components; safeguarding human rights and the rights of minorities; bringing about bureaucratic and administrative decentralisation; striking a balance between the public and the private spheres, with the resulting recognition of the social function of the private sphere; appropriate methods for making citizens more responsible in actively "being a part" of the political and social reality of their country (*Compendium*, 187).

Solidarity, on the other hand, highlights in a particular way the intrinsic social nature of the human person, the equality and rights and the common path of individuals and peoples towards an ever more committed unity (*Compendium* 192). Solidarity is an essential aspect of Christian gratuitousness incarnated in our human history by the total gift of our Lord Jesus Christ to the world. He came to help us when we were in need; he identified with our human condition in all its totality so as to save us. Through the life and deeds of Christ, we have hope that this world with all its troubles can become a center for the celebration of the civilization of love (Pope John Paul II), for friendship where the pain of the other draws the deepest acts of compassion from me, and challenges me to do something for the person, animated by the spirit of charity in truth. The life of Christ challenges us to reach out to everyone in love, especially those on the margins of society. It also calls on us to embrace new forms of sharing and communion, so that just as Christ gave us the inconceivable prospect of participating in the divine life, we too can give to our brothers and sisters the offer of sharing in what we have.

Solidarity is both a vocation and a mission. We are all called to mutual sharing in a world where many people are still on the margins of the good life, and where many are still starving of the basic necessities of life as well as thirsting for the good news. The Christian can be no closer to Christ than when he or she makes sacrifices and gives of what he or she has to others. Mutual participation between Christians and others will aid the reduction of poverty, suffering, pain, and isolation that is so often the case in our world. Solidarity is therefore, the call and the mission to willingly give of myself for the good of my neighbor, beyond any individual or particular interest (*Compendium*, 194). Solidarity is the only true path toward realizing the principle of participation wherein everyone shares in building up the common good and draws from it equally as well.

Solidarity is both a moral virtue and a social principle. It is a moral virtue because it seeks the restoration of the order of justice leading away from poverty, inequality, suffering, and pain. This demands consistent moral choices by people of good will to topple the structures of sin that often characterize the relationships among individuals in groups, and between nations. Solidarity draws from the moral virtue of doing justice in love, and practicing charity in truth. Thus, we cannot close our eyes to the truth that suffering in our society and in the world is the result of human greed and selfishness for which we all share a certain guilt. It also reflects the failings and limitations of human persons to build perfect and workable societies and just relationship when God is left out. Solidarity will, therefore, inspire Christians and men and women of goodwill to work towards a more just society where everyone can participate in the abundant life that God has provided in creation, and where sharing and co-operation becomes concrete. Solidarity is not simply a vain show of compassion. It is the concrete involvement in the eradication of human suffering caused by sin and the active effort to change the social, economic, juridical, and political structures which create conditions for suffering, inequality, and poverty.

As a social principle, solidarity is directed to the common good. The good of my neighbor is not removed from my own good; the good of the environment is not removed from the human good. Solidarity is a readiness to lose oneself for the other; it rejects all kinds of selfishness, exploitation of people and the environment, and it further rejects any international practices and structures which make it impossible for all to participate equally and freely in creating and enjoying the wealth of the earth. Pope Benedict shows how these two principles can help us meet the challenges of the day in many places in his encyclical:

Subsidiarity can help manage the rough edges of globalization by directing it towards a more humane and authentic development. The Pope proposes some form of authority to protect the global common good. This could, for example, be at the level of the state or through the reform of the United Nations (*CIV*, 67). This authority would promote world peace and security, food security, and manage the global economy through better international governance or what he calls "a true world political authority." This proposal of the Holy Father, which has come under severe criticism does not mean a unitary political or economic system, but a way of bringing some strong moral and political judgment and authority to control the tyrannical aspects of globalization and international relations. There are many common challenges that face the world today and many people the world over agree that today no single nation can alone meet the challenges it faces. There is so much interaction among peoples which calls for some strong international authority to hold everything in balance through moral and spiritual principles which will respect the autonomy of nations, and individual freedoms, while protecting the global economy, security, and disarmament to safeguard the world (*CIV*, 57).

International aid must respect both the principles of subsidiarity and solidarity to prevent what he calls social privatism and paternalistic social assistance which demeans the poor. Here the Pope is concerned about authentic development. A cycle of dependency has been created in international development today. It often locks the poor countries in Africa and many other developing countries within the trap of poverty. Like many other well meaning people Pope Benedict is obviously unsatisfied with the current state of development initiatives especially from North to South. Such aid fails in most cases because the development initiatives are driven by secondary objectives; they are not grassroots based and are often top-down. In many cases, they overlook the role of intermediate agencies and bodies who help to create robust civic culture and network for development. Pope Benedict, therefore, calls for a development model that is people-centered hence the need to push for development that helps to build on the human capital which should accumulate if development can be realized in many poor countries (*CIV*, 58).

Pope Benedict agrees with many people today who are calling for a new paradigm for human development in many African countries. Such a paradigm will promote human, spiritual, moral, and cultural development as the first and fundamental step. It will encourage the reform of institutions locally and internationally. In addition, it will create a new global market wherein poorer countries will be able to participate in free trade and it will allow greater involvement of the poor in trade, foreign investment and in development. In addition, there is need for more aid to be given by developed countries to poor countries to help stimulate their economies. Such aid should be given freely without stringent conditions that tie the poor to the apron strings of the rich in perpetuity (*CIV*, 60). This should be seen as a needed initial boost, rather than as a continuing handout. He also calls for fiscal subsidiarity in many countries wherein a system is worked out in which citizens would be able to determine how a potion of their taxes could be applied to supporting individual initiatives for development. This however, would work only in those countries where there are effective, efficient, and accountable systems of taxation. Taxation reform is a very urgent economic and political step that many African countries need to take if their common good is to be promoted, preserved, and protected for future generations.

International co-operation in development is not only economic but also is cultural. Technological and economic determinism have minimized the very important dimension of cultural life that is higher than economic considerations. There are other levels of human solidarity that reveal the deeper spiritual and transcendental dimensions of human interaction. In this regard, the pope teaches; "Technologically advanced societies must not confuse their own technological development with a presumed cultural superiority, but must rather rediscover within themselves the oft-forgotten virtues which made it possible for them to flourish throughout their history. Evolving societies must remain faithful to all that is truly human in their traditions, avoiding the temptation to overlay them automatically with the mechanisms of a globalized technological civilization" (*CIV*, 59). The Pope devotes chapter 6 to addressing the question of development of peoples and technology. The principle here is that "a person's development is compromised, if he claims to be solely responsible for producing what he becomes" (*CIV*, 68). Technology is not autonomous, it is always governed by moral laws based on the ultimate good of the human person who through his or her technological works expresses and confirms the hegemony of the spirit over matter. Authentic human freedom, according to the encyclical, is exercised when the human subject responds to the fascination of technology with decisions that are the fruits of moral responsibility. Technology, therefore, according to Pope Benedict, continuing the teaching of John Paul II, is the objective side of human action whose origin and *raison d'être* is found in the subjective element: the worker himself (*CIV*, 69). Technological development needs to rediscover its origin and destiny; humanity cannot on its own through technology create a new world.

As creatures, we exist because we have been made by God, and have received from God the human vocation to be stewards of creation and to fulfill ourselves through fidelity to the divine call to be. The intoxication of total autonomy could lead away from the proper moral and spiritual scale, towards the distortion of the meaning and destiny of human existence, and the destruction of human lives. What is possible is not always what is moral, nor is what is technically expedient, spiritually ennobling. The distortion of means and end which technological determinism has imposed with its attendant humanistic values poses a great moral challenge on contemporary society.

Herein lies the need for reconceptualization and reappropriation of what is the authentic use of human freedom for human fulfillment and for the attainment of ultimate human destiny. In this regard the Pope calls for both "professional competence and moral consistency" (*CIV*, 71), and the replacement of a "technical worldview" with a moral and spiritual worldview. This then requires understanding of the meaning of creation, what it means to be human, and the goal of creation as such. Some of the specific areas where the distortion of means and ends has taken place include but are not limited to the following:

(i) *Peace-Building*: The seeds of peace are sown through justice. A just order will promote respect, human dignity, and rights. This demands that everyone should be treated equally without regard to sex, creed, race, religion, or status. Technological supremacy or amassing weapons of mass destruction, cannot guarantee peace nor is the increasing marginalization of poor countries and socially disadvantaged people helping to bring world peace. The Pope's point here is that world peace can come about only when humanity places at the center of economic, political, cultural and social life those values which respect human life and the ultimate destiny of human beings. In this regard, co-operation between religions and civilizations is a vital step for development in which love, mutual understanding, mutual care for one another, and social ethics work together in upholding the fully human dimension of development and peace.

(ii) *Social communications*: the need for realizing the meaning and purpose of the media is also emphasized. This, Pope Benedict affirms is to be found in an anthropological perspective, the promotion of human good, and a vision of the person. Sometimes today's media have become ideological, often fronting partisan interests and in many cases anti-Christian values. These are particularly loud and aggressive in many Western media where there is, as it were, the clash of values, leading to a sub-cultural project, which is threatening to subvert traditional Christian values and mission. There is also especially with regard to Africa the feeding of the uncritical assumptions and stereotypes about Africa and Africans which have been championed by Western media. Many Africans are becoming very worried about the constant negative narrative about their continent in Western media as they constantly exaggerate the negative aspects of life in Africa, while minimizing the significant progress and exciting communal efforts being made at many levels in Africa to lay the foundation for sustainable development. The Holy Father brings out the foundation for authentic social communication, which is: "the voice of the peoples affected must be heard and their situation must be taken into consideration, if their expectations are to be correctly interpreted" (*CIV*, 72). The media should become the voice of the voiceless, and not the behemoth that silences the voiceless or imposes on them a voice without taking their conditions to heart. The need of the times demands a firm commitment to the truth, and a consistent appeal to charity and gratuitousness through solidarity and subsidiarity.

(iii) *Cultural exchanges*: There are other forms of cultural exchanges that could promote international co-operation and development. Pope Benedict, for example, calls for greater accessibility to integral education, which leads to the integral formation of the whole person. He calls for cultural exchanges through tourism, which should also be carried out in a moral and healthy manner to protect the vulnerable and to create more ethically conscious societies. When wrongly used tourism could lead to the dissemination of unwholesome values like sexual promiscuity, sex-trade and prostitution, human trafficking, drug trafficking, etc., in which the poor and vulnerable are exploited by the rich. This is also related to the problem of migration. While the Pope does not go into details about the causes of migration and the increasing number of people escaping from the less developed countries to the developed countries, migration which is a common human experience has become widespread today. Just as the geography of North America today was changed by migration, in the same way people's identity is being radically changed by the increase in migration in contemporary society. The increasing incidence of social dislocation, wars, famine, natural disaster, religious intolerance, poverty, religious fundamentalism, nationalistic, racial, and ethnic bigotry and the fight for cultural identity, and general random and widespread economic distress have all fuelled contemporary migratory practices and increased the number of refugees. The rights of migrants need to be emphasized, while the integration of migrants into their hosting communities should be gradual and sympathetic to the need to preserve the cultural and spiritual goods of migrant communities. Exploitation of migrants' labor is also condemned as morally wrong. Greater international co-operation in managing this human migration crisis and in diffusing wealth is shown to be the only proper way to achieve international development.

Pope Benedict further underlines the connection between unemployment and development. There can be no development in countries where there are no jobs. The link between work and unemployment cannot be over-emphasized. In many African countries, there are many young people who are roaming the streets of life without any prospect of work. These are people who become easy targets for people who will exploit them by leading them into crimes, violence, alcoholism, drugs and currency trafficking, religious fundamentalism, and sexual promiscuity. There is also the challenge of upholding just wages, a fair working environment, equality of access to jobs for both the rich and the poor, as well as women and men, and the rights of workers to organize themselves into trade unions to protect their rights and their dignity in the work places. There is also the need to remove all kinds of discrimination, and exploitation in the work places.

However, the Pope did not mention the fact that jobs cannot be created if the economy is not growing. Indeed, one of the first signs of recession in national and global economies is the lack of jobs. Job creation occurs when the economy is growing and when there is stable demand and supply, and the chain of goods and services is revolving to meet the needs of the community. The new context of work today has also seen the practice of outsourcing, where goods used in many Western countries are produced through cheap labor in many poor countries. There is also the increasing export and import among countries meaning that sometimes one may enjoy goods and services produced through unjust work environment and labor relations. There is also the scourge of inferior and substandard products that have made many African countries dumping grounds for fake and low quality products as we mentioned earlier.

In *Charity and Truth* (62–64) the Pope underlies the importance of work as both reflective of human dignity and intrinsically related to it. To work is to be human, and if being human is being a repository of dignity, we ennoble creation through our work, we ennoble God and ourselves through our work. The works of human hands bear the stamp of God who is the author and finisher of all things. Work is, therefore, not only the way of being human, but our way of being like God who created heaven and earth. We work not simply to make money, but to become instruments of God in the stewardship of the earth. Hence, all attempts must be made to provide people with dignifying labor and wages which will help them to take care of their families, especially their children, to take care of their health, and to retire with honor and with sufficient provision for the remainder of their lives.

Solidarity and subsidiarity play an important role here. In the first place, when labor unions are allowed to work for the interest of their members, they are also reminded that society is an inter-connected reality. They should also place the common good of the wider society into consideration. Life in the society is a chain of inter-connected relations. Efforts at protecting the interest of a particular professional group must be aimed not only at defending the socio-economic interest of that class, but the safeguarding of the common good of society at large following the principles of solidarity. In other words, society is a unit of integrated levels of work, and relations. Thus, the demands of workers in a particular trade for just wage are not inseparable from the desire of the entire society for a better living condition. Healthy societies are those in which all the vital cells, and levels of work operate in accordance with a just order. However, assessment of the just wage is the concrete way of verifying how the social economy works for the good of the workers, how it enhances their productivity and how it promotes integrated development. Wages cannot be fair and just in countries where the economy is not well managed or where the social and economic structures are broken. Since wages and fair working conditions remain the only practical and equitable means by which the vast majority of people can have access to goods and services intended for common use, governments and the private employers of labor are morally bound to manage the economy in such a way that workers receive enough wages to maintain a reasonable standard of living.

THE NEED FOR ECOLOGICAL ETHICS

In his 2008 message for World Day of Peace, titled, "The Human Family, a Community of Peace," Pope Benedict summarizes his vision for an ecological ethics when he calls the earth our home. He also demonstrates in his message the kind of anthropocentric view that he proposes should ground a new ecology of sustainability: "The family needs a home, a fit environment in which to develop its proper relationships. *For the human family, this home is the earth*, the environment that God the Creator has given us to inhabit with creativity and responsibility. We need to care for the environment: it has been entrusted to men and women to be protected and cultivated with responsible freedom, with the good of all as a constant guiding criterion. Human beings, obviously, are of supreme worth vis-à-vis creation as a whole. Respecting the environment does not mean considering material or animal nature more important than man. Rather, it means not selfishly considering nature to be at the complete disposal of our own interests, for future generations also have the right to reap its benefits and to exhibit towards nature the same responsible freedom that we claim for ourselves. Nor must we overlook the poor, who are excluded in many cases from the goods of creation destined for all. Humanity today is rightly concerned about the ecological balance of tomorrow."[2] We can better understand this concept by summarizing the important teaching of Pope John Paul II on ecological ethics, and thus appreciate the continuity of the teaching and the advancement and applications of this teaching in *Charity in Truth.*

On January 1, 1990, Pope John Paul II gave a message on the World Day of Peace titled. "The Ecological Crisis: A Common Responsibility Peace with God the Creator, Peace with all of Creation" which I believe is the best summary of the Church's teaching on ecological ethics. John Paul's address is divided into sixteen articles, each representing a claim that he makes or supporting or developing a preceding claim.[3] In the first article, the Pope sets the context of his discussion by stating that:

> World peace is threatened not only by the arms race, regional conflicts and continued injustices among peoples and nations, but also by a lack of due respect for nature, by the plundering of natural resources and by a progressive decline in the quality of life.[4]

Thus, world peace, in the thoughts of John Paul II cannot be divorced from an environmental consciousness. Humanity can no longer use the resources of the earth as she did in the past. There is, according to the Pope, an ecological awareness that is being studied by experts, political leaders, and policy makers, who are working out concrete programs and initiatives for a new ecological ethics. Some

2. Benedict XVI, "Human Family," 7.

3. References to this article will be based on the number of the articles. The copy of the address that I used is the one found under the title "Peace with all Creation," in *Origins* 19.28 (14 December 1989) 465–68.

4. John Paul II, "Peace," 1.

of these initiatives from other Christians have been pioneered by the World Council of Churches since the early 1970s.[5]

In article 2, the Pope argues that a "morally coherent worldview" is what is required to address the ecological crisis, because the development of a peaceful society or the articulation of a new ethics for ecology cannot come about unless there is a re-appraisal of the value system that brought the crisis in the first place. The answer to the ecological crisis, he notes, does not lie in the better and more rational management of the earth's resources, but in the development of an ecological ethics based on sound morality. In article 15, he argues decisively:

> When the ecological crisis is set within the broader context of the search for peace within society, we can understand better the importance of giving attention to what the earth and its atmosphere are telling us: namely, that there is an order in the universe which must be respected, and that the human person, endowed with the capability of choosing freely, has a grave responsibility to preserve this order for the well-being of future generations. I wish to repeat that the ecological crisis is a moral crisis.[6]

The bulk of the address is aimed at showing: (1) how to conceive the ecological crisis as a moral crisis. He does not, however, define this morally coherent worldview that he proposes, but indications of what he means can be found in this address. For instance, in article 2 he writes of "a worldview grounded in religious convictions drawn from Revelation."[7] He writes further: "when man turns his back on the Creator's plan, he provokes a disorder which has inevitable repercussions on the rest of the created order."[8] This teaching draws from Augustine's theology of sin as rebellion against God and turning towards creatures. John Paul II repeats in many other writings that sin is a rebellion, a disorder, which is opposed to the submission of Christ to God's will.[9] In this regard, we could understand that John Paul II

5. For a detailed account of some of these initiatives see Hallman, *Ecotheology*.

6. John Paul II, "Peace," 15.

7. Ibid., 2.

8. Ibid., 5.

9. For a detailed discussion of sin as the rebellion against the order in nature implanted by God see Congregation for the Doctrine of Faith, *Freedom and Liberation*, 31–43; for John Paul II's detailed Augustinian interpretation of sin as the disruption

perceives the ecological crisis as rooted in sin, the abuse of human freedom. This position reveals the whole range of the anthropocentric basis of the ecological crisis in the writings and teachings of the magisterium of the Catholic Church. One can, therefore, immediately identify some of the strengths and weakness of ascribing sole moral agency to the human person by examining the implications of an anthropocentric ecological ethics being proposed in this address. (2) The address argues that the moral agency of the human person, which has led to the ecological crisis, is only the reflection of a deeper moral malaise that has ramified to other aspects of human and societal life in general. In a sense, the argument is that the ecological crisis is only a symptom of a deeper moral crisis that has created a dysfunctional value syndrome in the human world.

In articles 3–5, John Paul II does a biblical analysis of the creation account in Genesis and brings in the theology of Paul on the restoration of creation in Christ and the rule of all things in Christ (*pantocrator*). In his interpretation of the Genesis creation account, he takes one stream—the anthropocentric stream, which is based on the first creation account. There are interesting lines of thought in this interpretation that show its anthropocentric reading; "God entrusted the whole of creation to the man and woman, and only then-as we read-could 'he rest from all his work' (Gen 2:3)."[10] He also writes that in God's creative plan a pride of place is given to the human persons because God gave them, more than to other creatures, those abilities and gifts that distinguish them from other creatures. Even though the human person has some fixed relationship with other creatures, the fact that he or she was created in the image and likeness of God is the greatest evidence that the human person is to exercise dominion over the earth with wisdom and love. By not pointing out the moral status of non-life forms, the autonomous existence of the other life forms in themselves in spite of the meaning that the human person confers on them, the traditional hermeneutics to which the Pope subscribes, places the whole creation story as the unveiling of the primacy of the

---

of the order in nature and the understanding of sin as related to rebellion against the ordered moral universe see his post-synodal exhortation, *Reconciliation and Penance*, 11–18; see also *The Catechism*, 1871; see also the discussion of the changing context of sin with regard to social sin and environmental sin in Ilo, *Face of Africa*, 186–87.

10. John Paul II, "Peace," 3.

human person. This revelation of the human primacy, which is presented in this address by the Pope, is shown to have been restored in Christ when he came to restore the human primacy that was destroyed by sin and rebellion that also affected the earth.

This hermeneutic has some advantages: it shows that the human person can still save the earth because in Christ all things have been restored to their original state of goodness and beauty. Hence, by submitting to the law of Christ, by respecting the moral universe that is implanted in creation, the human person can help to restore and maintain the harmony and beauty of the earth. However, this is a very pyramidal reading of revelation and creation, which creates a sense of human progress, and the primacy of human history and culture. In addition, there is a notion of a cyclic progress and decay, which unveils in salvation history as the whole creation moves towards the eschaton. This interpretation of the creation story could falsely create an inevitability to the whole destruction of the earth, which even makes some fundamentalist Christians to think of the ecological crisis as the inexorable movement of creation to the ultimate destruction or apocalypse, which will require the final consummation of all things in Christ.

Gary North has called for a new interpretation of the *imago dei* away from the substantial and functional anthropocentric motif that has predominated in the history of Christian theology. This static, hierarchical understanding of humanity's role in the cosmos that was systematized in Medieval Europe and found worthy proponents in the new dynamic and optimistic sense of human condition and progress in the Renaissance and Enlightenment period needs to be re-evaluated. I propose that Benedict XVI has begun a new recovery, a decentralization of the agency of the human person in creation as the Lord of the earth, by placing governance in God, and pointing to the principle of gratuitousness as the very character of human agency. The natural law theory could be summarized as both a creation-centered and God-centered reading of universal history, which subordinates human activity to divine governance relative to the eternal law. A reading of the creation story that is heteronymous and integrates a mutuality of functioning and relationality among all the members of the cosmic family (man, woman, plant, animals, water, elements,

stone, sky, earth, planets etc.) is immediately evident through a reading of Benedict's social encyclical.[11]

Even though through biblical theology Pope John Paul II ex-
pounds on the relationship between human activity and the whole
creation, he does not show how the anthropocentric reading of the
creation story establishes a relationship of co-dependence between
human beings and other life forms in the universe. There is a dualism
between humanity and the rest of creation in this interpretation of the
creation story. This may pose some challenges in the search for an integrated ecological vision, which places the whole creation in a mutual
implication of equality, inter-relationship, inter-connection, solidarity
and communion. William French articulates this very well when he
writes; "Where much of modern and post-modern thought has centered attention both on the inextricable historical character of human
experience and the diversity of cultural and religious histories that
shape the globe's multiple societies, the rise of the ecological sciences
has given us a critical reminder that equal emphasis must be placed on
humanity's unified bonds as a species, a biological community, bound
by common constraints and needs, and sustained by common ecological energies, food chains, and climate systems of a shared and pre-
cious planet."[12] Indeed, the blessings of the *deep ecology* (Arne Naess)
being advanced by a comprehensive ecological ethics is the admission
that the earth has a common story of which the human story is only a
layer. However, Catholic theology has always maintained the primacy
of the human person in terms of his or her transcendental and spiritual destination that is not reducible to intra-cosmic dynamics. This is
against some damaging trends that might reduce the human person's
origin and destiny to this-worldly ends.

The other danger is the Kantian turn to the subject which would
arrogate to the human person the master of creation defined and controlled by his or her freely chosen ends. Our eco-theology I propose
should admit that (1) the human person has a unique relationship
with God which no other life form has. The Holy writ does not say that
the sea for instance was created in the image and likeness of God. Any
attribution of God's image and likeness to other life forms will only

11. For a detailed Christian polyvalent reading and reconstruction of the Genesis
story see Bahnsen, *Theonomy*; North, *Dominion Covenant,* esp. 27–28.

12. French, "Ground and Skies," 373.

be an extended metaphor. (2) That the human person has a destiny with God which is unique because of his or her moral and spiritual life, which orients him or her to unity with God which is beyond what our cosmic calculation and consciousness could ever imagine or truly articulate. Newton's *Scholium Generale* makes an important contribution here in reminding us that the regularity of the planetary motion cannot be explained solely through mechanical causes. Human destiny cannot be fully understood through mechanical causes, or the forces of evolution.[13] It requires a metaphysical spiritual range that sees beyond the earthly horizon, the mysterious and transcendent destiny that lies hidden in the heart of God.

In articles 6–9, John Paul II gives four reasons based on some global phenomena as to why he thinks that the ecological crisis is a moral problem: (1) the indiscriminate application of advances in science and technology, whose negative consequences have revealed to humanity, that she cannot interfere in one area of the ecosystem without paying due attention both to the consequences of such interference in other areas, and to the well-being of future generations. Some of the harmful results of the failure to develop an ecological ethics are the gradual depletion of the ozone layer and the related greenhouse effects, industrial wastes, burning of fossil fuels, unrestricted deforestation, and use of certain types of herbicides, coolants and propellants all of which are dangerous to the environment and injurious to human health. (2) The lack of respect for human life, which reveals the moral implications underlying the ecological problem. He draws attention to poverty, the degrading treatment given to workers who are regarded as mere objects in the line of production instead of subjects of dignity, and the priority of economic interests over the goods of individuals and entire peoples. All these are seen as ecological in nature. (3) The delicate ecological balances that are being upset by uncontrolled destruction of animal and plant life or by a reckless exploitation of natural resources. These should be checked so that their ultimate threat to human and ecological good could be checkmated. (4) There is also the deep concern about the enormous possibilities of biological research that include the indiscriminate genetic manipulation and unscrupulous development of new forms of plant and animal experimentation. These forms of experimentation have also been

13. See Schonborn, "Fides, Ratio, Scientia," 87.

extended in many instances to the origins of human life. In all of these, John Paul II points out that there is a relevant moral principle, which is framed thus: "respect for life, and above all for the dignity of the human person, is the ultimate guiding norm for any sound economic, industrial or scientific progress."[14]

The complexity of the ecological question is evident to all, but the threats we face because of ecological degradation are often not taken seriously in our world. One will add with sadness as an example of the lack of seriousness and commitment in addressing the global ecological crisis, the failed 2008 Copenhagen conference on climate change. It is also important to avoid framing the global conversation on the future of our planet on apocalyptic terms, or precipitate and inconclusive scientific generalizations. Ecological consciousness has not become very global and hence the need to call attention to "a new ecological awareness *is beginning* to emerge which, rather than being down played, ought to be encouraged to develop into concrete programs and initiatives."[15] Why has humanity not taken bold steps towards resolving the ecological crisis if such an awareness is evident to all? The rest of the address is devoted to proposing the solutions to the ecological crisis based on the principle that no peaceful society "can afford to neglect either respect for life or the fact that there is integrity to creation."[16]

The solution to the ecological crisis is conceived as one that embodies three disciplines: theology, philosophy, and science. These all speak of a harmonious universe that has its own integrity, its own internal, dynamic balance that must be respected. This universe, he points out in article 8, is given to the human race to use while respecting its integrity. Theologically, John Paul II points out using a quotation from *Gaudium et Spes* (69) that God destined the earth with all it contains for the use of every individual and all people. Hence the ecological crisis should be jointly addressed from the realization that humanity and all creation has this earth as our common heritage, the fruits of which are for the benefit of all. He points out that the ecological crisis is teaching humanity that exploitation of the earth is

14. John Paul II, "Peace," 7.
15. Ibid., 1. Italics mine.
16. Ibid.

contrary to the order of creation, which is characterized by mutuality and interdependence.

The solution to the ecological crisis, according to Catholic social ethics will also involve the international community. Individual states must undertake "long-term and effective action," working out a "comprehensive plan" to stop the destruction of the biosphere and the atmosphere. There is also, he points out, a need for a careful monitoring program to check and control the dangerous effects of new technological and scientific advances. He suggests that the right to a safe environment should be included in an updated Charter of Human Rights. This call for an environmental rights regime is in my opinion, the most important, and radical and progressive point that this address makes. The 1948 Universal Declaration of Human Rights was framed to protect the dignity of the human person. The new environmental rights that the Catholic Church is calling for is one which should broaden the rights regime in such a way that it does not seek to protect the rights, dignity and well being of the human citizens of the earth alone, but also seeks to protect the rights, beauty and sacredness of the other citizens of the cosmos in their proper created order.

Environmental issues are discussed within the provenance of Catholic social teaching, which until the Second Vatican Council was a branch of ethics or moral theology. This is because the understanding of the moral demands is that of the attunement of the individual will to his or her ordered end, which is sanctification and eternal life. The world is, therefore, to be governed by the human person as a moral demand that requires that the right choices be made by the human person for his or her own temporal good and eternal salvation and for the salvation of the world. Thus, the whole proposal for solidarity should be diversified to reflect a new narrative of other life forms that share a common participation in the life of the universe, which is our home. This is a new form of solidarity that demands new analysis, and creative imagination and insights.

The call for a new solidarity is far-reaching with regard to human good. There is need for states to promote in complimentary ways the natural and social environment that is peaceful and healthy; there is the need for an end to reckless destruction of the environment; there is need for a proper ecological balance which addresses directly the structural forms of poverty that exist in the world. This is a link between poverty and the environmental crisis because for instance; "some heavily indebted countries are destroying their natural heritage, at the price of irreparable ecological imbalances, in order to develop new products for export."[17] This assertion is true of countries in Africa like Cameroon, Nigeria, Chad, Algeria and Ivory Coast to mention but a few. These countries are facing severe environmental crisis (oil spillage, desert encroachment etc.) as a result of the exploitation of the resources of oil, cocoa and coffee in these countries. John Paul II rightly points out that war is the leading cause of environmental crisis with the development of weapons of mass destruction and the use of very dangerous nuclear and atomic weapons that could lead to "incalculable ecological damage."[18]

John Paul points out that the ecological crisis is a common responsibility. Hence, he calls for an education in ecological responsibility (article 13), which would involve religious bodies, non-governmental and governmental organizations, and all members of society. Ecological crisis, he admits, is not one that could be responded to by religious men and women only, because men and women without any religion do have an acute sense of their responsibilities to the common good (article 15). Christians, he argues, are particularly challenged to respond to the ecological crisis because this is not only a moral issue but relates also to the call of faith. The environmental crisis is one that challenges Catholics, non-Catholic Christians, those adhering to other religions and even those without any faith at all.

John Paul II finally presents to all the example of St. Francis of Assisi whom he proclaimed as the patron of all those who promote the ecological concerns in 1979, citing St. Francis' example of genuine and deep respect for the integrity of creation. I think, his call for a return to the "aesthetic value of creation" is a fitting final claim to be observed in the address.[19] In this regard, he writes: "Our very contact with nature has a deep restorative power; contemplation of its magnificence imparts peace and serenity. The Bible speaks again and again of the goodness and beauty of creation, which is called to glorify God . . . Even cities can have a beauty of their own, one that ought to motivate people to care for the natural contours of the land as an indispensable

17. Ibid., 11.

18. Ibid., 12.

19. John Paul II, "Peace," 14.

prerequisite for ecologically sound development. The relationship between a good aesthetic education and the maintenance of a healthy environment cannot be overlooked."[20]

The address, however, shows the consistent anthropocentric foundation of Catholic ecological ethics. This position is reiterated in the *Compendium of the Social Doctrine of the Church* which argues among others: the biblical message and the Church's magisterium represent the essential reference points for evaluating the problems found in the relationship between man and the environment. The document, which quotes copiously from the papal message under consideration also states: "The Magisterium finds the motivation for its opposition to a concept of the environment based on ecocentrism and on biocentrism in the fact that 'it is being proposed that the ontological and axiological difference between men and other living beings be eliminated, since the biosphere is considered a biotic unity or undifferentiated value. Thus man's superior responsibility can be eliminated in favor of an egalitarian consideration of the dignity of all living things."[21]

This position is, however, refined by other voices in the Catholic tradition that demand a broader insight on the biblical theology being employed and the foundation of the teaching based on Tradition. I will only refer to three voices here for want of space. Barely one year after the release of the papal message under consideration, the United States Conference of Catholic Bishops (USCCB) in its message "Renewing the Earth" points out that arrogance and acquisitiveness led time and again to our growing alienation from nature and that safeguarding creation requires human beings to live responsibly within creation rather than manage creation as though the human person is outside of creation.[22] This position re-echoes the wise insight of Irenaeus of Lyons who wrote that it is not the human person who confers beauty and meaning on creation but God because all created beings have an intrinsic value independent of any human agency.[23] According to Irenaeus: "It is safer and more accurate to confess the truth: the creator

---

20. Ibid.

21. Pontifical Council for Justice and Peace, *Compendium*, 463.

22. See United States Conference of Catholic Bishops, "Renewing," 426–27.

23. On the argument on the intrinsic value of created forms see Kavanaugh, "Value, Persons, Stewardship," 72–75.

who formed the world is the only God and there is none besides him who received from himself the model and figure of things which have been made. Weary with impious and circuitous description, we are compelled at some point or other to fix our minds on some one and to confess that from him came the configuration of created things. From himself God found the model and form (*exemplum et figurationem*) of created things."[24]

According to Osborn, Irenaeus saw the world as a harmony, just as the lyre has many and opposite notes but one unbroken melody arises from the intervals and differences between notes, we do not divide the world but, we prove the judgment, goodness, and skill shown in the whole world. We listen to the melody, praise the artist, admire the tension of some notes, attend to the softness of others and discern sounds between these extremes, the special character and purpose of each, and the cause of their variety, while at the same time holding the rule that there is one rule, one artist and one God who is within and beyond creation. [25]

This view of beauty and mutual implication and submission to God of all creations including the human person is what a polyvalent reading of the creation narrative could help us to achieve. Arguments being advanced in the Catholic tradition that an unfortunate aspect of the new ecological awareness is that Christianity has been accused by some as partly responsible for the environmental crisis has not been able to vitiate the danger of an undue anthropocentric eco-theology. It is necessary to broaden the scope of the conversation to include the new voices of the new cosmologies.[26] The biblical account especially the second creation account offers us some grounds to shift from an anthropocentric approach to an approach of mutual functionality and communion of all created things. Sean McDonagh points out that the second creation account sets out to situate the history of God's saving act on behalf of Israel within the broader parameters of human and cosmic history; it shows that the human person is earthy and not supra-earth and could even be a basis for re-reading the Genesis story

24. Quoted in Osborn, *Irenaeus*, 60.

25. Ibid.

26. For a Catholic defense of the anthropocentric based approach to ecological ethics see International Theological Commission, "Communion and Stewardship," esp. 72–80. Elizabeth A. Johnson shows the weaknesses of the anthropocentric response and the evolution of this worldview in "Losing and Finding Creation," 3–23.

in evolutionary terms with the emergence of the human from the earth as being part of the earth and not over the earth.[27]

In the same way, we can use the natural law tradition to advance a new eco-theology in the Catholic tradition. We can advance a view of eco-theology that is both anthropocentric on one hand, and cosmic on the other based on natural law. Moving from below through nature and the reality of the universe, and coming down from above by admitting that the laws of nature are not autonomous but arise from eternal law which point towards the destiny and design of all things by God. Thus, the origins of all created things including the human person, their survival, and their destiny could be interpreted as a related narrative. Jacques Maritain, Germain Grisez, John Finnis among others who use natural law as the foundation of human rights, did not attempt to conceive an ecological ethics or an environmental rights regimen from natural law. The possibilities for such articulation, I argue, already exist in Aquinas and Augustine.

Augustine did not develop any systematic treatment of law (temporal, natural or eternal) in his rich corpus. Augustine particularly had argued that temporal law can only be accepted if it is based on justice. However, temporal law can be changed, but the eternal law which he calls 'highest reason' (*summa ratio*), through which the evil suffer and the good prosper must always be obeyed.[28] Every law, therefore, relates to justice because the eternal law that orders all things is the standard with which the temporal law is formed. The eternal law is the law of justice. Natural law in many of Augustine's writings has the following meaning: divine providence, physical laws of nature. It is written in the hearts of the godly, it is the will of the Creator, it is the *ratio* of the order in nature, or the law by which God rules creation, it is rational and knowable through human reason, is implanted in the conscience, and is a principle of order. It also governs all things including human, plants, animals (*Doctrina Christiana*, 1, 26, 27) as well as physical bodies, and determines the path of all things.[29] Natural law is the principle of right order, which it governs and is not subordinated to the human regulation of the earth. Indeed, the only higher reality

27. McDonagh, *Greening*, 123.

28. Augustine, *Libero Arbitrio*, 1/6:14–15. I have based this analysis from Dougherty, "Natural Law," 583–84.

29. See Dougherty, "Natural Law," 583.

to which natural law is subordinated in Augustine is the eternal law. We can also extend this reasoning to mean that natural law as the law of justice and rightness of action, could open a possibility based on reason and rightness of action to ethically evaluate human actions as just or unjust with regard to how we relate to the earth and the environment. Furthermore, the inner law of nature governs all life forms according to the eternal law of God which constitutes their end. Thus, human agency is seen in the light of Augustine as solely ordered to maintaining justice in creation, which simply means respecting the "sphere" proper to all creation, through good stewardship.

According to Jacques Maritain's interpretation of Aquinas' natural law theory, natural law is an inclination towards the good which is discerned through reason and which conduces towards the common good. This order, which reason can discover, and according to which the will must act in order to be attuned to itself is the necessary end of the human being. How does one come to an awareness of the natural law? Natural law is unwritten law but known infallibly because it is self-evident. This knowledge is not one acquired through ratiocination and conceptual judgments but knowledge through inclination (Aquinas), and this is a gradual growth process recognized by the human race in human history. This concept developed in the double protecting tissue of human inclinations and human society. Maritain argues that the same natural law which lays down our most fundamental duties, and by virtue of which every law is binding, is the very law which assigns to us our fundamental rights. It is because *we are enmeshed in the universal order*, in *the laws and regulations of the cosmos and of the immense family of created natures* (and finally in the order of creative wisdom), and it is because we have at the same time the privilege of sharing in spiritual nature that *we possess rights vis-à-vis other men and women, and all the assemblage of creatures*.[30] I think the insight here on natural law that we are enmeshed in the universal order, and in the laws and regulations of the cosmos, of the immense family of created natures, opens a new perspective on natural law and the moral order within Thomistic thinking on natural law for an ecological ethics that is not overly anthropocentric.

One significant point to note is that even within the Thomistic tradition—represented by Jacques Maritain and to a less degree

30. Maritain, *Man and State*, 95–96.

theologians and philosophers like John Finnis, Bernard Lonergan, Henri de Lubac, Yves Congar among others—there is no consensus on the meaning and full moral implications of the natural law theory for ecological justice. It is within the moral and dogmatic domains, and to a less extent the sacramental systems that Catholic theology has always understood natural law. Since the publication of the encyclical *Pacem in Terris*, (1963) there have been attempts in the Catholic doctrinal system to use the natural law as the foundation for grounding her social teaching with regard to Christian personalism, human rights, democracy and the rights of workers. This emerged with the separation of social teachings and social ethics from moral theology as a separate area of theology. The understanding and application of natural law specifically to morality (in the *Catechism of the Catholic Church* just to give one example), Christian personalism, and anthropology which privileges certain restricted interpretation of law and the good has been accepted in Catholic social thought.

Africans, for instance, do not justify moral agency and moral autonomy through natural law. On the contrary, moral discourse and the ordering of society in Africa draws from an anthropocentric worldview in which natural law has a place. Africans, however, accept a cosmology that is based on order and laws in nature, based on the vital force which fills all creatures and mutually enriches all creatures as they remain attentive to the presence of the sacred and life in all things. All created things, in African cosmology, have life because they give vital force. Being is co-extensive with vital force. Most African theologians and philosophers, who question the use of natural law as the ultimate foundation for moral norm, limit their critique to the ethical template, which applies to moral theology and the sacramental economy. They argue that moral norms are justified in Africa not by an *a priori* deductive process, but by a discursive ethics that places the individual and the community, the living and the dead, the human and the natural in a symbiotic relation and dialogue. Nature also speaks because it has its own unwritten laws, which humans must obey just as the natural world of animals and plants, rivers and seas keep the laws of nature in order to sustain life for the human. The "reason" of nature will more appropriately be understood in African theology not as "rational" but "vital" the discovery of which is based on how one is attuned to the wisdom of and in relationship with the community and the eco-system as such.

James Nash argues for a new reading of natural law foundation to include an ecological ethics in which cosmic harmony is to be found and not determined by anthropocentrism or physicalism.[31] His argument is capable of enriching the natural law foundation of eco-theology. His interpretation chimes with African cosmology, where values are not given to "other life forms" but rather are discovered through "listening" to them and respecting their autonomy. Moral autonomy is not only an anthropological construct; it is also a construct of nature understood in its totality and in its individualities (including the human person, animals, plants, water, sky, and the cosmos in general). The over-emphasis on the "order of nature" as discoverable by the human person through the rational-experiential method establishes an anthropological primacy in nature, which denies moral norms to other life forms. This anthropological primacy, which is culturally conditioned, has made it possible for the abuse of both nature and the human through the unfettered application of human will and freedom to nature.

The presupposition of a non-changing moral regime, which an unchanging reason could discover, should be modified, to include the new life forms and a new sense of history which shows that revelation is ongoing. Rationality here, whose ultimate movement is the embrace of truth in its fullness, could be widely interpreted to embrace new forms of rationality that lie beyond the limited reason of the human person. This is because the understanding of eternal laws as the source of the order of nature and as the defining norms for understanding the good, the beautiful, and the true, is not exhausted through human reasoning or a narrow anthropocentric ethics. The cosmology that gave birth to the natural law wherein the heavens were as unchanging as the eternal laws of God, has given way to a new cosmology that shows that change is the logic of life, that there are things that remain, but the tension between what changes and what remains cannot be resolved by an anthropologically defined moral universe. On the contrary, the way forward is to recognize natural law not as past, but rather to begin to articulate an ecosystematic compatibility discoverable in nature, the recognition of God as creator of all things, and the formation of

31. See Nash, "Seeking," 227–50.

the values and virtues of this new ecosystem where every being finds a home. This, I propose, is a viable path to be followed because the human and the non-human are tied in the garment of a common destiny which can no longer be determined by a natural law that places the heavy burden of lordship over all creation solely on the human person or human reasoning and willing. As one Hindu saying goes; "Dharma requires that one consider the entire universe an extended family, with all living beings in this universe members of the same household."[32]

There is the need to constantly re-evaluate the foundations of our eco-theological ethics in order to broaden its scope and adapt it to changing situations and other cultural rationalities on eco-spirituality outside the West and the new cosmologies. This obviously calls for a new theological hermeneutical approach that calls humanity away from anthropocentric arrogance to an ethics of the stewardship of humility, care and concern for the planet's general good; and an appreciation that we are part of nature and not above it: "If we read the various creation texts together with Genesis 1, an underlying picture emerges of a stable, structured, habitable world constituted in response to God's royal decrees. The world is both a kingdom over which God rules and a cosmic building where a variety of creatures may live fruitfully together and flourish."[33]

This should be the goal of an ecological ethics informed by a Christian vision. This will no doubt help bring peace on earth, restore the harmony in creation the absence of which is causing climate change, global warming, industrial pollution, toxic waste dumping in many poor countries, ocean salination, etc.

Pope Benedict's teaching on the environment follows and builds on the teaching of previous popes especially John Paul II's. Benedict however, takes the teaching forward in many ways. In the first place, he acknowledges the centrality of the human person as the primary subject of development. He begins to show a broader understanding of an anthropocentric worldview in which the human good is tied to cosmic good and the good of the eco-system, and in which the human family has an intimate bond with creation as a whole and the cosmos. The earth is called our home by Pope Benedict. The human person and the rest of creation are not two binaries in contention, but two

32. Quoted in French, "Ground and Skies," 384.
33. Middleton, *Liberating Image*, 81.

sides of the same coin. All kinds of reductionism or evolutionary determinism characteristic of New Age thinking is therefore, overcome by seeing creation in the Thomistic framework of *exitus-reditus*—the emergence of rational creatures and all things from God and their return back to God. Benedict sees the right order between the human person and the rest of creation in terms of a relationship that should be governed by charity in truth. However, it is the human person who has stewardship of creation because he or she is the rational member of the cosmic family whose moral choices are decisive for the survival of creation for both present and future generations. Authentic human development requires that we do not subordinate the human person to nature. This, according to Pope Benedict, could lead to attitudes of neo-paganism or a new pantheism because human salvation cannot come from nature alone understood in a purely naturalistic sense (*CIV*, 48). Nature should always be seen as a gift from God which points to its source and leads back to God.

In the second place, Benedict's teaching also adds the element of "grammar" to the Church's teaching with regard to the environment-that is, the intrinsic rationality of creation is prior to human rationality and therefore sets forth the ends and the criteria for the wise and respectful use and stewardship of creation (*CIV*, 48). He also adds that nature is not simply pure matter; it is also spirit and is thus endowed with transcendent meaning and aspirations that are also normative for cultural self-understanding. Human beings can thus relate to the environment in a meaningful way; they can interpret the grammar of the environment in the creation of culture, infrastructure, and superstructure. This can proceed morally through the responsible use of human freedom in accordance with the dictates of moral law. He reiterates the dimension of solidarity in ecological ethics that is the inter-generational justice in different contexts: ecological, juridical, economic, political, and economic.

From this ethical and theological framework, Pope Benedict goes on to address specific questions linked to the care of the earth. He demonstrates a firm grasp of the contemporary ecological concerns in articles 49–52 where he addresses the hoarding of non-renewable energy by developed countries, and the unethical exploitation of the earth's resources. He employs the principle of solidarity to address this concern and the stewardship of the earth. It is important to note that solidarity is not advanced solely as a social principle in inter-personal relations, and in communities and the globe like John Paul II did in his New Year message. Instead, Pope Benedict advances solidarity further, and applies it to the way we treat the earth and its resources. The kind of ecological ethics we need for sustainable development is "a responsible stewardship over nature" so that all members of the eco-system will be accommodated. In his words; "On this earth there is room for everyone: here the entire human family must find the resources to live with dignity, through the help of nature itself—God's gift to his children—and through hard work and creativity"(*CIV*, 50). Sustainable development which guarantees the health of the earth and everything in it today and protects and preserves creation for the future can come about by ethical, personal and collective choices aimed at strengthening that covenant between human beings and the environment, which will mirror the love of God and our co-operating with God in bringing all things under his governance.

In addition, protecting the environment demands a moral evaluation of lifestyles, because the senseless exploitation of the earth arises from wrong moral choices, unrestricted consumerism and materialism. Cutting down consumption of domestic energy, countering all kinds of hedonism and lessening attachment to material things, cleaning up industrial pollution, and helping to reduce the high ecological footprints especially in the industrialized world demands significant personal and collective changes in life style. Thus, the answer to the ecological crisis, according to the Pope is a change in the moral tenor (*CIV*, 51) and the moral senses with which people see reality. Here again an appeal is made to the truth of things. We receive this earth and our lives as a gift from God. Development is not solely a human project. Human genius should and does produce abundant life and the shape and texture of the quality of life desired by all. However, the teaching of the Pope here is that in the attempt to construct the kind of world modern men and women crave for, we have lost something fundamental: the quality of existence as gift and the mystery about life, and the ultimate destiny of all things. Drunk by the sweet nectars of human progress, human ecology has become threatened and humanity appears to have forgotten that she does not and cannot fully explain existence outside of the divine compass. However, existence as such is an integrated reality, if human ecology is debased, environmental ecology will also be threatened. When human life, family life, social relations, and international relations are driven by a lack of charity, selfishness, and greed, the same kind of mentality will also be applied to the way we treat nature and the earth. We cannot hope for a better future when we fail to understand the integration of all things: the human person, the environment, sexuality, peace, international co-operation etc. In a sense development should integrate two related combinations: (1) God and the triple bottom line: God, people, planet and prosperity (G+3BL). (2) Faith, compassion, care, courage, and community (F+4C). We can then say that F+4C is the Christian ethical framework required for the emergence of a cosmic regime in which there is God at the center of the triple bottom three (G+3BL).

Integral development should begin with setting the right order of things, and in applying the right moral principles to our relationship with one another. Once these are established, extending the same kind of relationship to the earth will become a necessary consequence. It is a relationship of respect, love, and mutuality; a relationship in which our solidarity for the earth demands that we make the right choices to protect the earth and care for it as God would. The book of nature is one indivisible unit (*CIV*, 51) of which the human person is intimately linked to the rest of the members of the eco-system. Thus, while Pope Benedict continues the theological anthropology that places the human person above creation, there is a shift to understanding the relationship from sole dominion to that of love, care, and mutuality. This is because he understands that the ecological crisis today is a moral problem caused by an exaggerated application of an anthropocentric view of the earth. So with Pope Benedict we can say that the earth is our friend, the earth is our family, the earth is our home, and the earth is a gift. Since we have received the earth as such, loving the earth is not only commanded of us, it attunes us to the truth of who we are: dust you are and unto dust you will return.

SOME FUNDAMENTAL SOCIO-THEOLOGICAL CONSIDERATIONS ON DEVELOPMENT

It is now possible for me to apply some important principles from Benedict XVI's social encyclical and the Christian social gospel in proposing a theology of development. Development has become a key word globally and locally especially since the launching of the Millennium Development Goals. But not everyone agrees on the meaning of development. I will define development in this work as *the fulfilment and enrichment of the human person, the human race, human culture, nature, and the cosmic world in a wholesome manner.* Development means to unlock the hidden potentials of a person, and to make manifest what is present or latent, hidden or unrecognized in a person. Development takes place when both humans and nature and the cosmos are healthy, flourishing, and actualizing themselves in the continuing quest for abundant life for all members of the planet. A developed person is one who has actualized his or her potentials. It is only developed people who build up developed cultures and societies. Development is an inward unravelling rather than an externally predetermined emergence. The external forms and structures of development arise mainly from the inner emergence of the good held within the human person, culture, nature, and the created world.

An evolutionary understanding of development sees it as the progressive emergence of the cosmos and everything in it in a wholesome manner. However, it does not give an account of the inner principle that governs this emergence. Is creation automated to move in the direction of its completion and fulfillment? Is God the hidden hand that controls the forces of nature and the human in the journey towards the ultimate good? However one answers this questions, it is obvious that human, cultural, and cosmic development is not without purpose or direction; nor is it an autonomous emergence or merely dependent on accident or chance. I must note that the cosmos is not always evolving to higher degrees of complexity nor does the human race always develop to higher levels of existence. There are times when we see all around us signs of growth, and stagnation, and simultaneously at other times, we see some signs of decline and decay. One can conclude that development is not a constant upswing or growth. Sometimes cultures, persons, civilizations, nature, etc. simply remain as they are or experience decline and fall into the law of stasis or inertia. Authentic development as a result has to be seen as both an inward growth and an external manifestation.

This understanding of development overcomes the often-anthropocentric understanding of development as the realization of the human potentials and the cultural and economic advancement of a people. In this anthropocentric understanding, the human good is pursued as an isolated end without due consideration to the inter connection between humans, the ecosystem as well as the whole world of nature. It helps to make human beings humble before the majesty of the created universe that is held in care by God, who has given us a share in his ordering of the universe.

Today there is an increasing conviction that to enjoy and promote the mutual flourishing of human life in mutual relationship to the flourishing of all life on earth is the ultimate meaning of human history and integrated and sustainable development. This is because many of the crises that afflict humanity are environmental in nature: for example climatic change, pollution, water shortage, defaunation, decline in arable land, depletion of marine fisheries, tightening of petroleum sources, persistent pockets of severe poverty, the threat of pandemics, and a dangerous disparity of resource appropriation within and between nations are related to the environment.[34] According to Jeffery Sachs, we share a common fate in a common planet, and an activist philosophy that is based on an ethics of global and cosmic solidarity should draw humanity away from a univocal understanding of development. This narrow understanding is based on the false conviction on the self-organizing forces of the market economy. In its place, humanity should adopt the overarching principles of social justice, environmental stewardship, deep spirituality and morality, and an attitude of care and compassion for all the equal players on the cosmic field.[35]

The contemporary understanding of development is very alienating. It excerpts humans, nations, and cultures and civilizations from each other, and from the whole of creation. It also glorifies an economically driven moral template that relativizes the questions about authentic morality and spirituality in creating both a healthy human vision for survival and authentic existence. In addition, it ignores the fundamental questions about the meaning and value of life in general and community in particular. Furthermore, it marginalizes the decisive import of human ecology and moral development for an integral understanding of development. The model and metaphor for a new

34. Sachs, *Common Wealth*, xii.

35. Ibid., 4

world ethics is one that should be rooted on the intricate and intimate mutuality of cultures and civilizations, the inner spiritual ecology between the human species and other members of the ecosystem, nature, animals, the air, rivers, trees, and a moral tenor which embraces transcendental values and virtues.

Indeed human ecology should not be seen as an exclusive anthropocentric ethics of development, rather it is very inclusive and comprehensive. The word, ecology, is a Greek term that deals with the logic and organization of a household. Defending human life is intrinsic to safeguarding the good of the earth that is our home. Protecting the animals and preserving the forests are matters connected to the health of the eco-system of which the human person is a member. Thus, human ecology as distinctively pro-life is also by the same token pro-earth. The *Earth Covenant* adopted in 2001 is one that sees the relationship between ecology and development, between an earth-affirming and human-affirming sensibility, and one that sees integral development as linked inextricably with sustainable development.

A new global ethics that recognizes development in terms of cosmic unity is what a theology of development advances. This should move us as humans to act in such a way that we meet conditions for the progressive creation of mutual relations within and between humanity and the rest of life. This understanding will lead us to see as unhealthy and mutually destructive a situation where some members of the human family are wrenching in poverty or where some members of the ecosystem are suffering. Development thus conceived will involve pro-active concerns on how to sustain everyone here in the cosmos, and make the earth healthier for successive generations.

A theology of development seeks the foundations from revelation, history and faith for a *regenerative ethics of communion, solidarity, friendship, mutuality, and care.* It is a theology of hope that recognizes that the earth is a gift which we have received from God, and that our ultimate human destiny is tied to the moral and spiritual choices we make today. In this regard, morality and spirituality have an important place in determining those choices and human responsibilities and commitments that are right and those which are wrong. Charity becomes decisive in drawing people to gratuitous acts rooted in self-sacrifice, while faith shows the way in leading people to a deeper appreciation of the beauty of the earth, and the source and destiny of all things: God. Hope gives the impetus to embrace values that are spiritual and moral as a way of securing our future by making the planet conform to God's plan which is the fulfillment of every member of the cosmos in a wholesome manner, or their possession of abundant life. Regenerative ethics of communion and friendship will lead to empathy for any one who suffers, and a consciousness to the fact that my choices, my lifestyles, indeed all my actions have a consequence for others, the living and the not-yet-born, and also for my ultimate destiny as well. I am the fruit of other people's choices before me, and I am accountable to God for how my actions have healed the world, and helped to begin here on earth the coming forth of the signs of God's kingdom. A regenerative ethics will be pro-life, for it seeks the good of life, and all life, and seeks to give birth to love, and newness through communion, mutual exchanges, solidarity, compassion, and friendship.

This notion of development will also lead to some moral tenor for doing what the German philosopher, Martin Heidegger, calls "the enframing of technology." This is a situation where humans use science and technology to serve the human and cosmic good and not to build weapons of mass destruction, new and horrific ways of killing and terrorism, biogenic distortion of the mystery of human life or to sustain a structure of injustice and exploitation. Making available to developing nations of Africa and the Third World the fruits of science and technology will no doubt help to spread prosperity through the stimulation of dormant human, natural and material resources of poor nations. Development is about how our common patrimony is serving all of us in a progressive and organic manner in this earth which Pope Benedict calls our home. It is about attuning ourselves to the grammar of the earth and the hymn of the universe so that we can be held in care by the loving hand of God, and build for ourselves a better world through submission to the laws of God which he has hidden in the laws of nature. Development is, therefore, the positive emergence or unfolding of the human person within cosmic forces and nature in a holistic manner, and their movement towards their fulfillment in Christ.

Peace is another name for development. Peace is development because it is the presence of harmony in creation and between creatures and nature. Harmony, on the other hand, is right order, which many people see as the meaning of justice. Injustice is the principle of disorder in our world today, wherever there is injustice there will be found violence, anger, bitterness, ungodliness, selfishness, and greed. That means that unjust international structures, unfair trade relations, protectionist tendencies, exploitation of the weak by the strong whether in international relations or within nations bring about disorder in creation, threaten global peace and security, and lead to under-development.

This harmony as the fruit of development and peace is the result of fulfillment that comes from the actualization of that which is good and noble in us. It is, in addition, the full flowering of nature that gives the rhythm and rhyme for creation. When poverty, wars, conflicts, and ecological disasters rob people of the freedom to pursue their ordered end, something fundamental is lost. It causes disharmony, suffering, and pain. It also significantly reduces the fulfillment of creation. There is an inner harmony that creation longs for, which can rightly be called "the hymn of the universe" (a title of the book of respected Christian palaeontologist, Teilhard de Chardin). This comes about when people are at home with themselves and their world, because they live fully and in the direction of God. They can go to bed without thinking of where to get the next meal or being afraid for their safety. It is the harmony that exists when men and women even from different cultures and civilizations, love and respect each other as friends and not as rivals and enemies to be defeated and humiliated. It is a harmony that comes from the deepest human springs which arise spontaneously from a good heart which is moved by human suffering, and set aflame by human excellence. It is the harmony that exists when nature is at one with humans because humans respect and love nature, so that nature will preserve and protect humans. This harmony is what development is all about; the inner peace of creation in its condition of organic growth. This mutuality, communion, and friendship will draw all men and women to defend the rights of every person to live, and every member of the ecosystem to survive and flourish and fulfill their God-given purpose. It will respect the interior sacredness of creation as permeated with beauty and relationality, etc., etc.

The two dimensions of development as inner and external have to be held together. We must, therefore, avoid the danger of a one-dimensional understanding of development to a more inclusive and extensive understanding. This also brings into sharper focus the often forgotten moral and spiritual dimension of development. Can we build structures for development without strong ethical and spiritual foundation? Can nations of the world flourish without seeking ways and means of polishing through moral and spiritual forces the inner soul of their citizens? Within Africa, for instance, no understanding of development of Africa can be meaningful without taking into consideration the full range of the African condition with all its ambiguities, beauties, and tensions. The *total picture approach model* comes in here because an African unified vision of life will demand a more unified and organic notion of development that will include both the spiritual, economic, ecological, moral, and communal elements.

Philosophical anthropology has often defined development in terms of human actualization. This is based on what we consider as essential components of the human person. Thus, the more developed person or the more developed culture in comparative terms will be the person or cultures that more fully realize what they have potentially. Thus, we can actually speak philosophically of under-developed person or cultures in terms of the quality of life, and the level of the human fulfillment index. This is an area that will take us far afield because people are not agreed upon the nature of the human person's inner hunger that needs to be fulfilled: material, intellectual, emotive, affectionate, spiritual, psychic, conational as well as environmental.

However, there seems to be a consensus that authentic human development must respond to four levels of human consciousness: Mind, body, spirit, and environment. Hence, development in the way I conceive it here is about creating a healthy environment in which the human hunger at the levels of mind, spirit, and body is fulfilled in each person. Each culture and each civilization defines itself by the values that it espouses, and the ends it pursues or projects as ideals for members of society. I do not wish to go into cultural criticism to question whether economic development—which is often at issue in a world that is governed by quality of life as constitutive of human fulfillment in terms of economics—is a good index for proceeding, but I will highlight what I understand as development from the perspective of African rationality. There are important aspects of development that I think we can draw from African philosophy and traditional rationality that summarize our discussion in this section. They are also in need of further elaboration, but there are no practical approaches to development and aid by the Church or other institutions and agencies in Africa that should not begin with a consideration of the following essential elements:

- Development is about *people* and is *located in the collectivity or community.*

- Development is about *culture and tradition* = cultural growth and handing over of knowledge and wealth. Development happens from inside-out.

- Development is *integral* including the whole of creation.

- Development brings *fulfillment today* and secures *fulfillment for tomorrow.*

- Development is *cosmic*; it is total and involves every member of the universe. It is regenerative growth for every citizen of the earth; it is opposed to decline.

- Development is about spiritual *ecology*, human ecology, and harmony. Socio-economic progress must go in tandem with spiritual progress, moral transcendence, and community.

- Development is about freedom to be, to act, to relate, and to flourish.

There is no development without freedom: if people cannot apply themselves to their world in a meaningful way, then they cannot develop. Indeed, the greatest tragedy in contemporary Africa is the stifling condition of existence (poverty, instability, diseases, and joblessness for example) that makes it impossible for many people to use their freedom in a creative and meaningful way to build up wealth, and thus actualize and secure their cultural and human capital.

This is well captured in Amartya Sen's book, *Development as Freedom* when he writes in what appears to me a perfect conceptualization of African development thinking: "What people can positively achieve is influenced by economic opportunities, political liberties, social powers, and the enabling conditions of good health, basic education, and the encouragement and cultivation of initiatives. The institutional arrangements for these opportunities are also influenced by the exercise of people's freedoms, through the liberty to participate in social choice in the making of public decisions that impel the progress of these opportunities".[36] In the next chapter, I shall examine through economic and social data, the changing faces of Africa, and the effects of development aid and charity in Africa.

SOME THEOLOGICAL PRINCIPLES ON DEVELOPMENT AND AID IN AFRICA

How can we conceive sustainable development in the world today through an African Christian reflection governed by the principle set out in *Charity in Truth*? What is the kind of development that the Church in Africa should work towards? There are five fundamental aspects of development that the encyclical recommends, namely:

(1) *Development is not a merely human achievement.* The perfection of creation can never be pursued as an end but as a means towards an end. Thus, even though human beings through their right moral choices can bring about authentic, integral and sustainable development, the possibility was first and must continue as a divine initiative. God has already offered such a prospect through the gift of creation and through human capacity to reason, believe and will that which is right, just, beautiful, and true.

(2) The *application of human reason to development will flounder without the fundamental sapiential edge driven by faith,* which orders all things to God as their source and destiny. Thus, development must include not just material growth but spiritual growth. There cannot be holistic development and universal common good unless people's spiritual and moral welfare is taken into account. Material understanding of development is very narrow and limiting.

(3) *Development in today's world is to be carried out through application of charity in truth.* In *CIV* 78, Benedict teaches that the greatest service to development, then, is a Christian humanism that enkindles charity and takes its leads from truth, accepting both as a lasting gift from God. It is also to be driven by a Christian realism that places worldly concerns relative to and a means towards ultimate human destiny. Openness to God makes us open to our brothers and sisters and towards an understanding of life as a joyful task to be accomplished in a spirit of solidarity.

36. Sen, *Development*, 5.

(4) *Development requires a theological anthropology* which is capable of showing the dignity and nobility of the human person, and animating the interior life of the human person, and illuminating this inner life through the experience of God's love, mercy, and forgiveness. This gives the courage and trust to face the future without fear and shows the bond we share as a common human family through the adoption we have in Christ. The sense of common humanity, and a common human family through fellowship with Christ give humanity the grace to overcome the sins of greed, selfishness, and pride, and to make sacrificial acts of love, self-denial, acceptance of others, and acts of solidarity to heal the wounds of brokenness in our world through justice, peace, and active involvement in reaching out to everyone.

(5) *Development is about the whole creation, and cannot be completed here on earth.* It is the beginning of the full revelation of the whole creation in Christ. It demands a constant appeal to Gospel principles, and natural law principles, and a judgment of global trends and life styles whether economic, political, or social in the light of these gospel principles. Development is a cultural event for the human person. In the sight of God, creation is developing when it is emerging from the bondage of sin, poverty, injustice, inequality, discrimination, violence and evil to its fullness, and the realization of the purpose of creation. Thus, the eschatological nature of human history has to be kept in focus by all Christians. Hence development is open to Christian evaluation and demands the involvement of the Church and Christians, but it also calls for dialogue and mutual relations with non-Christians, in the search for solving the constantly evolving social and economic challenges of the times. The principles provided by Christianity can be applicable universally because they are drawn from natural law, and thereby revealed by God, and are rooted in human nature in its essence.

A deeper reading of African history today challenges us to a more radical and broader reading of development beyond prosperity, often narrowly measured in economic terms as the level of the gross domestic product (GDP), per capita income, and life expectancy, among other indices. Economic prosperity in Africa need not be identical to economic prosperity in the West. Africans need to pattern and shape their economic development, and it might not come about through the kind of clinical economics that Jeffery Sachs and many other well-meaning economic activists are projecting. A critical study of African cultural life in the brave new world, immediately reveals that African development at all levels of life may need a different approach.

Many years ago, the foremost African social scientist, the late Claude Ake wrote an influential book, *Democracy and Development in Africa*, which in my opinion contains perhaps the most profound insight into the reason for Africa's development problem as rooted in improbable options. He argues that development as such has not started in Africa because the necessary ingredients for development are not in place yet in the continent. His judgment may have been grim since he was inspired to write that book after the collapse of the economies of African nations. This was due to the failed economic and development policies presaged by the Structural Adjustment Policy of the 80s imposed on Africa by the World Bank and IMF. Today, however, I do not see any reason to dispute the conclusions of Ake in 1990 that development has not started in Africa despite the enthusiasm about the Millennium Development Goals (MDGs) that will hopefully be realized in 2015. There may be random successes here and there in Africa in terms of constitutional democracy, and perhaps in marginal economic growth, but there are no strong and sustainable structures nor have the human and cultural components that are decisive for development been truly enriched.

Although Africa has the potential to be the richest continent on earth, its present and future, like her past remain the objects of arguments, propositions, manipulation, exploitation and ridicule.[37] Since the late 1960s there have been about twenty-three different resolutions and benchmarks for development for Africa reached either at the level of the UN or the OAU. That these have not translated into sustainable development is a concern that should be placed in context. It all boils down to whether the cultural world of the Africans has been understood by Africans themselves and also by the non-Africans who are aggressively pursuing a path towards spreading Western development models. There are obviously some new initiatives coming up both from Africans and from Westerners that are beginning to evolve into some participatory practices in small communities. These initiatives place emphasis primarily on building on the assets of the

37. Africa Institute of South Africa, *Africa's Development*, 17.

local communities, while also addressing the obstacles (the needs) to development within those communities.

One must admit with Pope Benedict that development is about people and creation, and that only the people themselves can be the agents of their own development. Europe and North America on their own cannot develop Africa, but through solidarity they can support Africans to develop Africa. Thus the answer to Africa's development rests squarely on Africans. This is because, as Pope Benedict shows, development is about the agency of people in creating prosperity, and abundant life for the people in their world and on the whole planet. This was also the considered judgment of President Obama in his first visit to Africa as the first black president of the US when he said in a speech to the Ghana Parliament that *Africans* hold the key to African development.

One thing should be obvious to every one: There is nothing fundamentally wrong with African cultures or African societies; there is nothing intrinsically wrong with African clime and peoples. Rather, something is fundamentally flawed with the political institutions and structures of many African states. Something is wrong with governments who embezzle international aid for treating AIDS and malaria patients and use them instead to buy palatial mansions in Europe and North America. Something is wrong with NGOs, and church development agencies that use social advocacy and charitable causes as means for personal enrichment, and social connection. Something is obviously wrong with presidents who are consumed with a false sense of self-importance and messianism and who will trigger off national crises and watch thousands of African children die of hunger and starvation, while the common folks are weather-beaten by poverty and suffering because these political leaders wish to perpetuate themselves in power. Something is tragically wrong when African political and religious elites exploit the fragile ethnic and religious sentiments of the common and poor Africans for their selfish economic and political goals. This is the thudding blow that continues to destroy national integration, the protection and promotion of the common good, and human rights in many African countries.

The unacceptable ethics of the African public square have debauched the salient communitarian social ethos of African traditional political ecology. This has provided the fodder for power adventurers and predatory sit-tight leaders, whose tensile praetorian paternalism have brought many African states to their knees. The rationality of Obama's prognosis draws not only from the empirical reality of progress seen in many well governed African states like Ghana, Botswana and Tanzania to mention but a few, but from the fact that Obama speaks from the point of view of an insider who has Africa in his blood. If his speech was made by a white president, many Africans would have interpreted it as a continuing tradition of Western paternalism perpetuating accustomed and unwelcomed post-colonial profiling. However, Obama's call is for a new narrative for reading Africa and a new charter for a better future for a continent long adrift from the global radar of economic development, political stability and relative prosperity.

There are two narratives about African under-development each of which has struggled for space in intellectual and political discourse about the fate and future of Africa. First, is the position held by many Africans that Africa is victim to external forces that hold her land and peoples in chains. This has been loud in much post-colonial discourse about Africa. This position blames Africa's present predicament on slavery, colonialism, racism, and the forces of neo-liberal globalization. For many Africans, the line is simple and clear: Western prosperity has been bought at the expense of African impoverishment. Africa is claimed to be the victim of Western exploitation as shown in the fact that Africa's natural resources are being controlled by Western conglomerates who do not care about the ecological disasters of their exploitation of Africa's wealth, and who prey upon the unjust and undemocratic political climate in their hosting countries. This narrative is very popular and somewhat comforting. This is because it spews all kinds of conspiracy theories and plays the blame game about how Western governments are propping African dictators. It also argues that Western businesses are supporting the weaponization of Africa through many rebel groups whose asymmetrical warfare continues to hunt many African states. For Africans, as for many individuals, this habit of blaming others for our problems, rather than facing them ourselves, is an attractive but deadly trap.

For many Westerners who buy into this logic, Africa is seen as a helpless land of desolation, crimes, wars, and suffering which demands a crisis interventionist approach at all times. Africans, the reasoning goes, cannot help themselves as they are victims to certain ineluctable global cultural and economic forces which have left them with broken polities and unworkable political and economic structures. This explains why Western charitable initiatives dealing primarily with Africa's needs continue to grow exponentially with no significant contribution to Africa's long-term development. In my work with Canadian Samaritans for Africa, and Engineers Without Borders-USA, I notice that it is often harder to raise funds in Canada and the USA in support of building schools, skills centers, granting scholarships to African kids, etc. However, many other charities that deal with feeding the hungry, rehabilitating AIDS orphans, and refugees get quick and immediate funds. The difference must lie in part with the perceived immediate need for a band-aid solution as against the more fundamental need for development such that the band-aid is no longer required. Many Africans living abroad and Western activists for Africa, spend so much time and many resources showing how and why these kinds of immediate charitable needs define Africa. They give the impression that Africa is a land of constant emergencies; that people are dying unless something is done urgently. While one may admit that the latter have more obvious urgency because (in many cases it is a matter of life and death), it is clear that it also builds into a certain narrative about Africa as a lost, hopeless and hapless continent. It must be stated in a most obvious way that attending to the growing needs of Africa is not development, even though it may help to remove the obstacles to development. Thus, the image of a dying African child will attract more sympathy than the image of a healthy African child who is studying with a kerosene lamp. These represent two ways of seeing Africa, one as a continent of needy people, and the other as a continent with people who have assets waiting to be discovered.

The second narrative that Obama alludes to is the one that accentuates the agency of Africans in African development. It argues that Africans have the answer to Africa's problems. Valorizing the agency of Africans to reconstruct the contoured face of Africa will demand mining the interior cultural forces within the African continent and the stimulation of human and cultural development. This narrative does not minimize the historical forces that have stunted Africa's growth, but it argues that these forces should not be seen as absolutes and deterministic for the future of Africa. This position places the responsibility for Africa's development on the shoulders of Africa's governments and peoples. It seeks a more introspective approach to problematizing the African condition that looks at the interior circumstances and cultural factors that have stymied growth and political integration in Africa. It also seeks to locate the problem of the failure to establish constitutional democracies in Africa, and build inclusive national structures squarely on the shoulders of African peoples. Canalizing the divergent ethnic and religious polarities which have divided African countries into one common national channel for economic and cultural development is a task which Africans must take up for themselves. No foreign country will wield a magic wand that will make African peoples to live together in peace and work together across ethnic and religious lines for the common good.

This conclusion is not simply a patronizing assertion. It draws from concrete reality. If we Africans continue to play the victim, our so-called victimizers will not stop victimizing us. We have to pull ourselves up by our bootstrap and begin to imagine, work towards, and collaboratively seek in small and modest ways, the path towards integral development in Africa. I am, therefore, not in agreement with many African scholars who blame all but themselves for Africa's woes. An African proverb says that he or she who points one finger at others should know that the other four fingers are pointing at him or her. We should look more at the inner dynamics in Africa, and the internal factors that have made Africa and Africans vulnerable to foreign exploitation, and incapable of building sustainable development structures, along with stable and workable constitutional democracies. As we shall see, there are some obvious international hypocritical actions, and there is a woeful lack of commitment in some quarters to African development. "Helping Africa" has become an easy way to become a celebrity for some in the West or to seek international attention and leverage. Third Sector approaches and individual-led approaches for partnership or intervention in Africa are helpful and valid in seeking some strong grounds for stabilizing Africa for needed structural changes in African society.

What I am arguing for, however, is for *more comprehensive and coordinated approaches to African development* with regard to Western involvement, and the decisive aspect of African agency in viable participatory practices in the development efforts in the continent. This is what the Catholic socio-ethical principle of subsidiarity and solidarity is all about. The approach being advocated here should be multi-pronged, based on assets and not merely on needs, and directed towards capacity-building not towards interventionist approaches. It should also be driven by Africans and not by foreigners and Western conglomerates with their neo-liberal, clinical capitalism. However, I still emphasize that Africans, especially political and religious leaders in post-colonial Africa must take responsibility for the progressive exploitation of the people and the destruction of the beautiful continent. What this means in a more concrete sense is that we *cannot push away Africans or African cultural realities, or African worldviews, or African agency in African development.* Unfortunately, as long as development initiatives between the North and Africa are seen as patron-client relationship, or teacher-student relation, or father-child relation, Africa will continue to suffer a crippling handicap in development partnership. There will persist a pre-existing expectations level among Africans with regard to Westerners who come to Africa to work, which will only perpetuate a dependency syndrome, wherein Africans fail to take responsibility for their future. This is true not only for non-religious charitable organizations but also for Church-based NGOs as well.

3

Changing the Face of Africa through Aid and Development Initiatives

THE CATHOLIC SOCIAL ETHICAL framework for doing charity in truth is an invitation for humanity to embrace the whole picture of reality. It means at a practical level that one has to understand and embrace the reality of the people whom one wishes to serve. I wish to highlight some significant aspects of Africa's social context today and why and how development aid could help or hurt Africa. I will concentrate in this chapter on general principles that I am proposing for humanitarian and development aid initiatives in general. In the next chapter, I will apply these principles with specific reference to the Church and Christian-led charitable activities in Africa. I have used the image of the face to show the dreams and despair of Africa, and the hopes and expectations of the continent. It also helps one to understand better the search in Africa for abundant life, the homelessness of Africans, the challenges of poverty, racism, diseases and illiteracy in Africa. Because Pope Benedict interprets the grammar of contemporary society as one defined by globalization, I shall devote a significant part of this chapter to discussing the implications of globalization for Africa's social context.

THE DREAMS AND DESPAIR OF AFRICA

If a stranger came down to Earth from Mars to visit Africa what will the person see? The person will be amazed at the enthusiasm and vibrancy of African peoples. He or she will immediately experience the happiness of the people even in the face of some real challenges and suffering. If the stranger is spiritually sensitive, he or she will observe the lively liturgy, the energy and Spirit-filled atmosphere in the Churches. He or she will also notice that there are many churches in Africa, and that the traditional churches like Roman Catholic, Anglican, Methodist, Presbyterian, etc., are now facing serious competitions for membership and loyalty with a resurgent Pentecostal and Charismatic brand of Christianity, as well as from African Initiated Churches. The visitor will also notice the strong religious sentiments of the people, in various cultural symbols, behaviors, attitudes that are all colored by religious candor. The spiritually attuned visitor will also notice that the Islamic religion has also found a place in many African countries and is growing among the young people. The visitor will be refreshed by the warm hospitality of Africans and their interest in knowing about others and receptivity to strangers. The stranger from Mars will no doubt be shocked that there is a great disparity between rural communities in Africa and the urban cities. He or she will also observe that even in large cities, there are many slums and poor neighborhoods that show the injustice in the land and the plight of the poor and ordinary people. If the visitor visited some families in the cities, he or she will notice that every household of means has domestic servants who do not eat at the same table with the family of their masters and mistresses, and who look different in dressing and general appearance because they are poor. The visitor will wonder why there is so much wealth in the hands of a few people of means in Africa, while the majority of the people suffer, but he or she will notice that the people generally look happy and content. He or she will see many beggars, hawkers, jobless young people on major streets and highways. He or she will see also many sick people who are being treated at home because they could not afford to pay for hospital treatment. If he visited the hospitals he will really be shocked at the poor quality of the health care system. But he or she will be lifted by the vegetation of the land, the natural beauty of the environment, and eco-system's health, that is if he or she did not visit the African Sahel, the drought-stricken Horn of Africa or portions of the Rift Valley, and parts of Kenya, and Tanzania. The visitor will not be interested in going to places like Darfur, North-Eastern Congo, Northern Uganda, Saharawi Arab territory of North Africa, parts of Nigeria's Niger Delta, and some other hot spots in the continent where life and community living is very precarious.

Our visitor will also be impressed with the industry of Africans especially African women as they work hard in their farms, in their trades, in the market, and in offices, and in various skilled and semi-skilled professions. The visitor will be convinced that there is a dream that is strong in the hearts of Africans but he or she will admit that there are many obstacles. However, the people are strong enough to face the pain and work hard for a better and prosperous tomorrow that lies within their reach. This judgment is similar to that made by the Secretary-General of the UN, Ban Ki-Moon in 2008 at the midpoint in the global efforts to achieve the MDGs for Africa by the year 2015. He wrote of the potentials of Africa this way: "Africa is endowed with human and natural resources, environmental diversity, and cultural and archaeological richness. The region is a youthful continent with over 920 million people, of whom 60 per cent are under 25 years of age. The last decade witnessed the end of several long-running wars and the consolidation of democratic rule in a majority of states. The resumption of growth in many African economies since the mid-1990s has been similarly noteworthy. In 2007, Africa's real growth averaged 5.8 per cent, a rate comparable to and even higher than those of many other developing regions."[1]

Is this vision of a renascent Africa shared by many Africans today? Is this the face of Africa which Africans and non-Africans see? What is the dream of a typical young African growing up in the continent today? What are the despairs that have flooded the hearts of many Africans? In my book, *The Face of Africa: Looking Beyond the Shadows,* I argued for a comprehensive approach to reading African history that integrates the full story of the continent. Africa does not have a single story but many stories and histories. I believe along with many Africans that the dream of Africa will one day come true, and the promise of God on this continent is not far from being realized. However, hope is not achievement; we need to tell ourselves the truth

1. UN General Assembly, "New Partnership," A/63/130:4.

and paint the correct picture of the continent in its beauty, possibility, ambiguity, and complexity. This is how we can be faithful to the message of Pope Benedict that charity should begin with truth, seeing things the way they are, and thus envisioning in the light of the Christian faith, how they should be.

When most African countries gained their independence in the early 1960s there was some strong belief that the day was dawning for the continent. Even those countries like Namibia, Zimbabwe, and South Africa that gained their independence later had some genuine sentiments of joy and hope. For instance, when Zimbabwe got its independence from Britain in 1980, the former Tanzanian president Julius Nyerere was said to have told the then Prime Minister, Robert Mugabe that he had inherited a diamond and should keep it the same. Most African nationalists fought for the end of colonialism because they believed that Africans were better placed to manage their countries. They also were convinced that Africans can and should be allowed their self-determination to secure the future of their countries for generations yet unborn. The nationalists in Africa, who took over the reins of their respective African countries, gloried in the establishment of independent political entities, but failed to see the shifting sands on which their respective countries were built. As a result, they failed to set Africans to task in working concretely and realistically for a new Africa and laying the building blocks for a truly liberated and prosperous Africa. Within a decade of gaining independence, most African countries rumbled through nights of violence because of a statism that centralized and personalized every economic activity around the state's several "African big men." Thus, arose political instability, civil unrest as a result of rising poverty and suffering, and civil wars. The center, according to the famous expression of Africa's foremost novelist, Chinua Achebe, could no longer hold and things fell apart in Africa.

Today, the living condition of Africans is worse than it was when most of their countries gained independence in the early 1960s. The former Special Envoy to the United Nations Secretary General on HIV/AIDS in Africa, Stephen Lewis agrees with this position when he writes, "It must be understood, without any hint of heady romanticism, that Africa in the 1950s and 1960s . . . was a continent of vitality, growth, and boundless expectation . . . There was something about the environment of such hope, anticipation, affection, energy, indomitability. The Africa I knew was poor, but it wasn't staggering under the weight of oppression, disease, and despair; it was absolutely certain that it could triumph over every exigency. There were countless health emergencies—polio, measles, malaria, malnutrition—but it never felt like Armageddon. In fact, life expectancy began to rise in the late 1960s, until the reversal induced by the Structural Adjustment Programs on the one hand, and AIDS on the other."[2] There is the need to understand the reality about Africa, and the nature and extent of the present African condition so that we can fully explore some proposals on the role of the Church and Christians in changing Africa's social context.

HOMELESSNESS AND AFRICA'S SOCIAL CONTEXT

There are two faces of Africa's social context, one of hope and another of despair. The despair of the African continent is what I have described in many writings as homelessness. The African condition is one that can only be correctly interpreted through a historical and cultural analysis. The question of African identity is rooted in these two factors: the historical factors which have created the political structures of African nations, and continue to influence African economy, social integration or social dislocation in most of these countries. The cultural crisis which touches on identity, worldview, status, equality, gender issues, family life and traditions, the social capital, the common good, and the bases for living and working together among various ethnic nationalities and diverse cultural and religious communities in Africa. Both the cultural and historical factors raise similar but related perplexities: What does it mean to be an African today? What are the rights and obligations of a citizen in each African country? How do Africans see themselves in the complex and troubling social, economic, and political contexts of their respective countries? What are the values around which Africans build their lives? What roles will religious profession and conviction especially the phenomenal growth in Christianity play in the identity formation, and the regenerative ethics of communion and friendship needed for the reconstruction of the

2. Lewis, *Race*, 44–45.

soul of Africa? It is immediately obvious to everyone who looks at the face of Africa that there are deep cultural and historical crises in the continent that have spread misery and ethical confusion in the land of Africa and inaugurated a season of anomie among the young and the elderly. This crisis can be fully explained as homelessness, which is a general human condition, but has a specific ramification according to historical contexts.

Homelessness is the restlessness of the human heart in our search for foundations, transcendence, union with God, human fulfillment, and meaning. Homelessness goes beyond the pain of the present moment or the anxiety about tomorrow; it is an existential condition constitutive of human temporality, finitude, and orientation towards the future. In this sense, every human being experiences homelessness more or less depending on how one has reconciled one's self to the full picture of life, faith, culture, human destiny, disappointments, joy, sorrow, etc.

Christianity teaches that one's homelessness can be resolved when one makes a constant and ongoing response to the offer of love that has been made on the cross for human salvation by our Lord Jesus Christ. Jesus Christ has already made an offer to all humanity of a home here on earth and beyond the shadows of present life into the fullness of glory in heaven. Jesus Christ is our home (2 Cor 5:6–9; John 14:2–10; John 15:5–7; Matt 7:24–27). In him is the eschatological fulfillment of human temporality as both *presentia Christi* as well as *adventus Christi*. He is the genuine newness that fulfills all our human expectation. He alone offers us the definitive answer to the questions and uncertainties of the human heart, and the worries and anxieties about tomorrow. He is the concrete norm of human existence for he shows us the path to life, and the model for authentic human living. This new way of living transforms human action beyond the imprisonment of selfishness and pride to the wider horizon of service and humility. This new way of living in Christ inspires us to stoop to wash the feet of the other, and to love the other without any precondition or attachment other than our common identity in the light of Christ.

In Christ alone are our wandering hearts at rest, because he frees us from the fear of the other or the fear of tomorrow; he assures us that God's grace and blessing are enough and that the other person, the other ethnic group, race, or nationality do not impoverish me or threaten my own fulfillment but they widen my humanity and possibility in a rich and infinite manner. The present angst about the scarcity of means whether of food or natural wealth, or the loss of status or privilege, which so often draws us in Africa to exclude the other, could be overcome in the light of the promise of the Lord that he will grant us abundant life (John 10:10).

Human homelessness is heightened when one lives a life without God. Such a life is led without any anchor, without any clear purpose, deprived of any eschatological thrust, and without any firm and consistent ethics of love that moves human action beyond the merely self-satisfying goal of immediacy for one's self or group referent. We are homeless when we deliberately try to exclude others because we unconsciously choose to live an exilic life, or to shut ourselves from those who are not "like us." This condition can afflict Christians when we fail to manifest in our lives what we profess; or when we use religious practices and authority as cover for our own personal agenda or to advance our own limited vision of God's kingdom that has no resemblance or relationship with the present and coming reign of God which Christ built on submission to divine will and faithful commitment to following all that he has commanded.

Homelessness viewed in this light reveals the absence of reconciliation with one's self or group identity or with one's personal and group history. Homelessness breeds violence and intolerance; it nurtures anger and despair. It is not the absence of God in one's life or one's culture, but rather the failure to recognize the presence of God that leads to panic existence and the flight of hope. Homelessness is the clearest sign of cultural and religious crises because it topples the values of authentic cultural and religious practices and breeds false hope and expectation. Homelessness leads to a culture of blame and failure to take responsibility. When a person blames everyone else but himself or herself for a personal tragedy, there is no basis to hope that the person can overcome the personal tragedy.

Homelessness also manifests in the cultural and historical process for groups, and nations, and the wider global community. Many Africans will immediately point to slavery, colonialism, apartheid, racism, and globalization as the causes of the unacceptable condition in Africa today. They will blame the ethnocentric intolerance in most African countries or random racially charged tension in countries like

South Africa and Zimbabwe as well choreographed schemes by imperialistic forces. Within the Church, many African Christians will lay blame on the missionaries and on a centralizing tendency of the institutional Church for the lack of creativity and dynamism in the Church in Africa that has made the churches in some African countries marginal players in the present task of addressing the social challenges of Africa. There are many who will also blame foreign forces for the failure of the Church in Africa to build strong ecclesial structures and communities that will move the peoples towards greater integration and reconciliation. We have already broached in the previous chapter the answers to these questions, but raising such questions are signs of the homelessness which we are describing here: the question of the true identity and destiny of African peoples especially as seen in our analysis from a Christian reading of the social context.

Homelessness as a condition is a call to step out of the imprisonment of self-alienation that sin, human temporality, fear of the other, and our false securities impose on us. It is a call to become more human, to move out of our comfort zone, to transcend our limitations and the specious and shaky walls that we have built that excludes the other and deprive us of seeing the whole picture, and the richness and beauty of diversity. Viewed in this sense, the recognition of my homelessness invites me to take some steps towards embracing the whole truth about myself, the other, the world of nature, and above all submitting the specific and varied terms of my homelessness to the saving grace of the Lord. Two biblical figures exemplify for us how the recognition of one's homelessness gives one a new identity and changes one's vision and mission: Moses, and the Prodigal Son. I will give brief anecdotal pointers about these two figures in the light of our discourse on homelessness, because of the limitations of space.

Moses stands tall among Old Testament figures, as the giver of the Torah, the one who saw God face to face, the one who led Israel out of slavery in Egypt to the Promised Land, and one who presided over the Sinai covenant constituting Israel as God's people. The biblical portraits of Moses vary based on the different OT traditions (Yahwist-Elohist, Deuteronomic, and Priestly traditions) with their specific confessional themes about God, which colors their interpretation of Israel's history and the place and unique presence, action, and direction of God in this history. Delving into these traditions is not our concern here, since we are interested in a theological reading of the text. The Yahwist-Elohist account in Exod 3:1–12 relates the actual call and commissioning of Moses to the theophany of the Burning Bush. This call begins as a dialogue between Moses and God, who had seen the plight and suffering of the people of Israel and wishes to set them free. Obviously, like many great religious figures in the life of God's people, Moses was prepared for his mission: the nature of his birth, the miraculous find and rescue by Pharaoh's daughter, his protection in the royal palace, and eventual flight into the land of Midian. However, even though Moses was protected from the suffering and pain of his people in (1) Pharaoh's royal court in his later life (Exod 2), and (2) in the secure environment provided for him by the his father-in-law in the land of the Midians, Moses was not internally reconciled with his identity and the identity of his people.

The reason he gave to his father-in-law, Jethro, for wanting to leave to return to Egypt is a key to understanding the homelessness of Moses. Moses said; "Give me leave to go back to my relatives in Egypt and see if they are still alive" (Exod 4:18). Moses wanted to return to his people because he was not at home in the land of the Midian. He was inwardly not reconciled with his own condition and that of his people. Moses' experience was that of homelessness. Moses, as depicted in the first four chapters of Exodus, was a man in search of his vocation and deeply troubled about the condition of his people. At times he was a wanderer, searching for a home; at other times he was fighting for his people, believing perhaps that the victory over slavery in Egypt will be won by force of arms; at other times he did not believe in his abilities and the possibility of liberation for his people through the conquest of Pharaoh. He thus showed that authentic exercise of freedom, the experience of liberty from stifling conditions, enables one to become really and truly oneself and to take one's place in God's plan. Homelessness takes us away from our divine destiny, and is thus essentially a limiting condition, and in most cases an evil situation. His experience of the divine was, however, the beginning of his conquest of homelessness. He will constantly make appeals to that experience in his leadership of Israel. At the end, God not only brought Israel to himself, but also brought Moses to understand the direction of his personal history and that of Israel. Moses saw that the reconciliation of his personal destiny and that of his people were ineluctably tied to the covenant with God.

The homelessness of Moses was existential; it was not brought upon Moses because of his wrong choices, it was a historical condition he found himself in because he belonged to the house of Israel. The condition of Moses could be compared to that of many young Africans who were born into poverty, conflicts, and wars. These young Africans came into the world carrying the deadly HIV/AIDS virus, and some of them find themselves in failed states where they have no immediate prospects of the good life. They are innocent victims to the historical process, and have limited abilities to change their fortune. Their homelessness is simply existential, historical, and accidental. However, we observe from the condition of Moses that the reconciliation of the homelessness of Israel was only when Israel found her destiny in the Covenant with Yahweh. In the same way the reconciliation of the homelessness of Africa will come about when Africans find their true destiny with God and begin to live God's dream for Africa through embracing the virtue of charity in truth with the regenerative ethics of communion, friendship, and mutuality. Here, the liberation of the house of Israel was not simply the freedom from slavery from the land of Egypt but the acceptance of a new identity that was tied to the covenant with God. Being free from slavery was not enough; their liberation from exile and slavery in the land of Egypt was simply the beginning of their search for their identity that they received on Mount Sinai. The leader in this journey was Moses who received a new identity as he and the house of Israel accepted their real destiny as not simply being a liberated people but God's people whose destiny was now determined by God's offer of a covenant in perpetuity.

Homelessness often inspires one to search for one's destiny and in Moses we see that the resolution is found in one receiving a vocation or purpose for existing from God. However, even though Moses' destiny and vocation were tied to the destiny and vocation of Israel, we learn from reading these events in the light of Christ that Moses and Israel prepared the ground for a more universal mission that Christ brought through a new covenant in his blood. However, we also learn that reconciling the complexities of Israel's religious or political destiny was far from being completed by an act of deliverance from slavery; it was a continuous reception and response to God, and ongoing reconciliation and being at one with Israel's destiny.

In the parable of the prodigal son in Luke chapter 15, we find another example of homelessness that relates more to wrong choices. The analogy of this parable in the papal document, *Reconciliation and Penance*, brings out very clearly this aspect of homelessness as an existential condition that comes from the rejection of God. "There was a man who had two sons; the younger of them said to his father, 'father, give me the share of property that falls to me.'" The condition of the homelessness of the prodigal son who leaves the father is reflected in the adventurous but futile departure from his father's house, the squandering of all his property and inheritance in loose and empty living; the dark nights of exile, emptiness, and hunger; the lost dignity, humiliation, shame, and nostalgia for his home; the courage to go back to his father, and the conviction that his father will receive him back. We can apply that to Africa in terms of the squandering of the wealth of the land, on one hand, by African leaders and elites, and the exploitation, extortion, and abuse of Africa's wealth by the industrialized countries on the other. We can see also in Africa the rejection of communion and community when ethnic groups fail to live together in one country, when religious groups and Christian denominations reject each other's rights and freedoms, and when we fail to live together as one family in spite of our differences. Is it not homelessness when, like the prodigal son, African ethnic groups wish to break apart from one another? When ethnic groups marginalize people from outside their group? When rebels and political oppositions fail to work together as one and thus create divisions and rifts? In a sense, the homelessness of Africans in the continent especially is best explained in terms of the narrative of prodigality, rejection, alienation, waste, isolation, breakdown of community and communion, greed, and selfishness among others.

Here again, we find exile and homecoming at play in the search for ultimate human fulfillment and our ultimate destiny. The possibility of homecoming or reconciliation when we have gone away from the path of authentic human existence or when we lose our Christian calling is rooted in the love, grace, and power of God to bring us back. Homelessness at this level is a rupture in human authenticity, human freedom, and human relationship. It is also the result of a failure to understand the communal and universal nature of our Christian calling and ultimate destiny.

Can we not see then in the light of the many sad events in some parts of Africa, that this is not the kind of destiny that God willed for Africa? How do we as Africans reconcile within our personal and group history the evils of genocide, ethnocentric killings, millions of Africans who have died and will die from HIV/AIDS, or the increasing incidents of violent crimes, assassinations and murders, and other evils which take place in our continent since the end of colonial rule and apartheid? Do these acts that we find in our society not show a clear sign of homelessness as loss of human authenticity at this level?

Putting these two biblical analogies together, we can conclude, that (1) homelessness is an existential condition, which can also arise spontaneously from the fact of our being human, or from our group history and culture; (2) homelessness can also be the direct consequence of human choices and actions especially when these actions draw people away from God and from others, and the world of nature; (3) homelessness can be overcome through the path of reconciliation of individuals and groups to their true human destiny which is to be found in God. An African theology of reconciliation will show us as a people of God on a journey to our Father's house how God in Christ can reconcile the homelessness of our African condition through the call to conversion and to practice charity in truth.

In analyzing the implication of homelessness for Africans, one needs a deeper religio-anthropological reflection, framed within a wider political and economic discourse on poverty, cultural alienation, unjust structures, racism and lack of an educational framework, which passes knowledge with regard to skills, ethos, and technology from one generation to the next, supplemented by the educational heritage from outside Africa. The homelessness of Africans does not merely refer to the fact that there are millions of Africans who are far from their physical home nor does it mean the pervasive effects of the brain drain on African economy and social life. The homelessness of Africans refers to the abandonment of the African continent by Africans physically, but more fundamentally, an emotional and cultural abandonment of Africa by Africans. It means the alienation of Africans from their cultural and spiritual roots, which affects their sense of identity and negatively hampers the evolution of their societies whether in the African continent or outside it. It is the existential exile into which the historical conditioning and socio-cultural dislocation of Africans have placed them, making it impossible for the full blossoming of the African personality and the emergence of truly liberated, self-regenerating and organic African societies and ethnic nationalities in various African countries. It is also the root cause of the seeming failure of Africans to work together locally and internationally to evolve robust frameworks for a new era in which the light of African existence extinguished in the night of historical injustice can be relit through a cultural rebirth. Homelessness leads to a lack of faith in the future of the continent, an unstable and unacceptable social condition, and the failure of Africans to tap into the positive energy of the continent to re-invent its soul. I am referring above all to the failure of African countries to take a critical look at their social condition and find from within the heart of Mother Africa the road they should take. The homelessness of Africans also refers to the loss of identity of millions of Africans and the unending search by Africans for who they are and their place in today's world. This homelessness is what defines Africa's present social context.

THE DREAMS AND HOPE OF AFRICANS

One of my earliest and saddest childhood recollections was when I was eight years old: the sad discovery of a mass grave when some workers were digging a toilet for our school. My father was the headmaster of the school and, with a child's eye, I saw my father cry for the first time. I later learnt from my mother that my father was crying because those fresh bones could have been those of some Igbo soldiers who were killed during the civil War in Nigeria from 1967–70. My father's stepfather was killed in the war along with some other family members because he refused to leave his ancestral home when the federal forces were approaching. The sight of those bones and skeletons brought to my father's memory the unknown graves of his stepfather and other family members who were cut down by the advancing federal forces in 1969. My question that night was: Why do people kill each other? Why should people suffer this way? Why can't we live together in peace and prosper as one? It was in that night of childish anguish and pain that I began to dream of a better society, a new world freed from hatred, poverty, suffering, injustice, and pain; a better Africa, and a prosperous world in which Africa will have a share. Thus, in spite of homelessness of Africans, I do have a deep conviction that African countries can still become a promised land; a land of hope; a land of beauty, and a land where men and women, young and old can find fulfillment and pursue their ordered end in peace and love. I have never ceased to dream about better days that shall come to Africans and many long suffering regions of the world, minorities, and poor and suffering people in any part of the world. It started as a childish dream, but even as an adult, I have not stopped dreaming and hoping for a better future for everyone especially those on the margins of global prosperity.

The frustrating and unacceptable situation in Africa appears to be giving birth to a new spring of hope welling up in the hearts of many young Africans, like myself, who were born more than one decade after the decolonization process in Africa. Most Africans born since the decolonization of Africa have never known the good old days in Africa. The imposing mountains of economic and social ruin, the rising moans and groans of numberless Africans can sometimes conceal the inner energy and ardent hopes of millions of Africans. These Africans are struggling against the untested assumption that the inhibiting conditions and the suffocating strain of the cracking social, political, and economic foundations of present day Africa, are incapable of supporting the structures of a new Africa. Africans are not searching for univocal paradigms for a better future constructed along different ethnic axes. Nor is Africa in need of patronizing generalizations about the continent or paternalistic recommendations and unrealistic mercenary total development packages from Western ideologues, politicians, and philanthropists, forced down the throats of Africans as pre-condition for aid and technical support and assistance. Just as there is no single answer to the African condition, so also is there no single answer to the question many children in Africa are asking: "Why do many of us go to bed hungry? Why is the world so silent about our fate? What is God's plan for us?"

I am convinced that the present African condition is not part of God's plan for Africa. God's dream for Africa is the dream he has for the world and for every child that is born to earth. His dream is that the world should be a peaceful and safe place for everyone; that no human person on planet earth should go to bed hungry and unsure of tomorrow; that people should have a place they can call home and have access to the basic necessities of life and mutually benefit from the fruits of human civilizations; and that all should be happy and healthy and sing their own special song to the world. God dreams of a world which mirrors the fruits of his kingdom, and which prepares men and women to enter that kingdom. It is only when people shine through with human fulfillment and human security that they can give glory to God, because God is glorified in a person fully alive (Irenaeus). Unfortunately, we men and women are individually and collectively destroying the world through greed, selfishness, unbridled passion for power and domination, unrestrained exploitation of the earth, unjust and unfair acts, and wars. This explains the African condition. The problem of Africa like all global problems is, as Pope Benedict points out in *CIV*, a question of moral choices which cause human suffering and injustice. Africans can only find a home in the world when we lay solid foundation for the building of God's kingdom in Africa. *What will the kingdom of God in Africa look like? What is a vision that can capture the essence and beauty of the reign of God in our land?*

The kingdom of God is the situation that emerges where no man or woman cries because of the wickedness, injustice, or weakness of the other; a world where peace would be maintained not by force of arm, but by the force of universal love. It is the situation where children grow up in peace and the elders live with dignity and respect; and it is the presence of charity in truth as the dynamic that governs human relationship. The kingdom of God is the emerging new situation that renews the human spirit and brings about positive energies in the hearts of men and women. This kingdom will come about through conscious and consistent positive moral choices and great strides in the positive direction by good men and women who I see everyday as I pass through the path of life. These are men and women who are rejecting the structures of sin in religious, political, international, and financial institutions that have sustained injustice, poverty, global financial crisis, and terrorism in the world. They are discovering convergences, not so much in institutions, but in real human needs that must be met and evil forces that have to be defeated. This world is not an accident; otherwise our collective mistakes would have destroyed it permanently. There is someone who has placed us here to do some good; to make a difference and to be a light; no matter our station in life or our condition, there is someone out there who would and can intervene in our long nights and dark days. This person is God working in and through us. He calls us always to account in the direction of love and in the values of his ever-present and coming kingdom.

An Afro-Christian vision of hope is built on this dream of God. It is the certain and concrete belief based on African Christian thinking, that there is a possibility of liberation in all aspects of life in Africa and the world from all negative factors which make it impossible for peoples and cultures to blossom with fullness of life. It is also anchored on the certainty of salvation in every aspect of life by the power and presence of Christ working in the lives of men and women, freeing them from selfishness and evil, so that in their lives and actions they rise above the imprisonment of immediacy and self-gratification and see the good of all. It is a vision that draws people together as they work as one family through a regenerative ethics of communion, love, friendship, solidarity, and mutuality. They are thus impelled to look beyond the shadows of today to the bright promise of tomorrow, which is possible through the mutual effort of all and the practice of charity in truth. This way, the life and well being of all is enhanced and every man or woman in society is thus given the offer of realizing their ordered end, living the promise of God and fulfilling their own dreams. It is possible to imagine a new world in Africa by embracing the gospel truths clearly articulated in Benedict's *Charity in Truth*. The dream of God for Africa is the same dream for the whole world, it is a dream which is wrapped in the abundant life which Jesus Christ brought to the world so that the world can be freed from sin and its attendant evils, to enjoy the refreshing newness of living together in charity, mutual respect, and reverence as friends of God and friends of one another. It is a vision that demands the fulfillment of the promise hidden in every human heart, of the young African child in her beauty and innocence, and the full consequence of our being created in the image and likeness of God.

DEVELOPMENT AID AND DONOR INITIATIVES IN AFRICA: SUCCESS OR FAILURE?

Pope Benedict teaches in *Charity and Truth* that aid and development programs should not be driven by secondary goals. This, one observes, is the main reason for failed development aid and donor initiatives in Africa. Some of the secondary goals that could be identified in aid and charitable initiatives in Africa include non-economic objectives on the part of the donor countries, military and strategically driven aid. Others include aid that is meant to create markets for goods from the donor countries (many aid come in terms of goods, and finished products). Other reasons include ideologically motivated aid to promote an African government that supports certain policies of the donor country, as well as charities aimed at advancing the particular evangelical goals of religious groups and bodies. These aid initiatives—whether they are for economic development, social and ecological support, promotion of human rights, education, and democratization, or military support or humanitarian objectives—require a proper understanding of the context, clarity about the aid being administered, and sincerity and commitment to the goal of each aid. The *primary goal* of aid and donor initiatives should be *the common good of Africans, which is to be built up, protected, promoted, and preserved primarily by Africans.* What is needed is solidarity in supporting Africans to pursue their own ordered end. Thus, a distinction should be made between humanitarian relief and support which address human needs with a view to removing obstacles to development; and capacity building aid and grants which build on the assets of Africans. Thus, improving the human, cultural and social capital of the continent should be the primary goal of all aid to Africa. This will not only lay solid foundation for African development but will also contribute to global development, security, and peace.

Unfortunately, aid and development initiatives have most of the time not supported the improvement of the human and cultural capital of Africa, and in some cases have promoted a culture of dependence, and encouraged corruption, waste, mismanagement, and cronyism, on the part of both donor organizations, and recipients of aid. Indeed, today's international aid and grants have become a business of its own and taken a life of its own which raises fundamental question as to whether they are meant to be a permanent aspect of global life or an intermediary stop-gap which will be phased out as the developing countries stand on their feet. There is the need for a new thinking on how to move Africa away from the poverty trap and the ever-revolving cycle of random aid, constant distress, emergencies, natural disasters etc. There is need to seek the paths towards doing charity in truth in Africa which will demand the abandonment of Western philanthropic plan and grand economic recovery narrative which supposedly will socially re-engineer Africa within some specific time line. In its place, a more sober, gradual, and modest approach should be embraced which builds from the cultural knowledge, arts, artifacts of Africans with supplementary additions in an incremental manner from outside Africa. However, it demands understanding African history and culture, and x-raying the secondary objectives of most donor initiatives and development programs which lead to their failure in Africa.

Time has come for Africans and non-Africans, who have been involved with Africa within the last four decades, to admit the simple truth that most development programs and donor initiatives in the continent since independence have largely been unsuccessful in bettering the condition of life of Africans. Many people will agree that past and present development paradigms in Africa have not helped in laying the foundation for sustainable development. On the contrary, they have sustained a structure that has spread poverty with greater intensity among Africans. This is not to say that the people, especially from the West, who have given a lot to Africa and who continue to sacrifice for the continent have not been well-meaning. The reasons for failed development initiatives are many and well documented. Two of the most comprehensive are the seminal work by Ostrom and Gibson et al. and the 2009 edited work, *Smart Aid for African Development*. Both of these works discuss the challenges of international development aid and donor initiatives within the last four decades and identified more than a hundred reasons for failed development aid.[3] While I do not wish to go into details on this topic as there are many books and articles that an interested reader could consult, I wish to develop three reasons which I have identified for failed development initiatives in Africa.

The first reason is *internal factors*. There are those who blame internal factors in Africa for failed development programs in the

---

3. See Ostrom et al., *Aid Incentives*; and Joseph and Gillies, *Smart Aid*.

continent. The argument is usually made by Westerners who have worked in Africa mainly as journalists or administrators of aid, grants, and loans for Western governments and agencies, or the IMF or World Bank. These people usually work with government officials and base their analysis on unworkable and complicated institutional state apparatus. Some of the analysts in this camp do not in most cases work with Africans at the grassroots level: age-grade, women's groups, village social networks, village elders, and co-operatives, etc. The most recent argument in this regard is Robert Calderisi who devotes a subsection of his book to "The Trouble with Foreign Aid." Calderisi worked for the World Bank in Africa. His argument is clearly stated this way:

> Most people reading Western newspapers or watching TV will not be aware that Africa has steadily lost markets by its own mismanagement; that most countries—including supposedly "capitalist" ones like Ivory Coast—have been anti-business; that African family loyalty and fatalism have been more de-structive than tribalism; that African leaders and intellectuals play intentionally on Western guilt; that even Africa's "new" leaders are indifferent to public opinion and key issues like AIDS; and that, in recent decades, Africans have probably been more cruel to each other than anyone else has been. Nor is it generally known that, far from ignoring Africa, the world has made special efforts to help the continent, including writing off its debt continuously over thirty years.[4]

He makes the argument that around the world, successful countries are those that have chosen the right policies for their own reasons and seen foreign aid as a complement to their own efforts rather than as a bribe for undertaking difficult reforms. Aid, he opines, works better where governments are already on the right track, establishing priorities, implementing policies, and developing key institutions for their own reasons rather than trying to impress people in foreign capitals.[5] He also argues that people-to-people aid and humanitarian assistance are much more effective in communicating values and shoring up African morale than official assistance. However, such aid does not reach the local population. There have been some successful aid programs, he points out, like the successful fight against river blindness

4. Calderisi, Trouble with Africa, 7.
5. Ibid., 160.

in West Africa which took more than twenty-five years; cultural exchanges between Africa and the West, small and targeted grants for intellectuals and professionals among others. However, his verdict is that aid has not worked in Africa and success has been small, ephemeral, or too expensive to reduce poverty or reproduce any sustainable development on a large or small scale. He argues that Africa does not need a Marshall Plan but some space to internally address the numerous factors hampering foreign aid. Calderisi's ten points on improving aid in Africa, however, reveal the fundamental flaw of his analysis. He accepts as given the present structure of African states and builds his development strategies around strengthening the states' capacity to set priorities and meet basic needs. He largely ignores the impact of private, church and faith-based charitable organizations (FBOs) in Africa which have impacted the lives of ordinary Africans in many ways. He forgets also the strong impact of organizations like WHO in the eradication of small pox, the five deadly childhood diseases, and the improvement of vaccines which have reduced the risk of yellow fever, cholera, and diphtheria in Africa. Even though he identifies the internal factors militating against African development, he ends up offering patronizing dosages on how African development should be supervised by the international community, how African elections are to be monitored by international organizations, etc.

One of the strongest arguments against this kind of reasoning is that of Thomas Pogge, one of the leading thinkers on a more integrated analysis of poverty, development aid, and social justice within the whole compass of human rights discourse. Caderisi's view is a restatement of the argument of the political philosopher John Rawls, that when societies fail to thrive, "the problem is commonly the nature of the public political culture and the religious and philosophical traditions that underlie its institutions. The great social evils in poorer societies are likely to be oppressive government and corrupt elites."[6] Rawls holds that charities to poor nations will only be a duty of assistance because the political culture of "burdened society" is the most decisive factor in development along with the population policy. However, we must note that political culture is historical, and not ontological, being the function of the interaction of several factors like political socialization, external influences, cultural elements, etc. In the words of

---

6. Quoted in Pogge, "Severe Poverty," 31.

Pogge, "Existing peoples have arrived at their present levels of social, economic, and cultural development through a historical process that was pervaded by enslavement, colonialism, even genocide. Though these monumental crimes are now past, their legacy of great inequalities would be unacceptable even if peoples were now masters of their own development."[7] Referring specifically to Africa, he points out that colonialism is not too long ago to explain African poverty: there was a 30:1 gap in per capita income in 1960 when Europe released Africa from the colonial yoke. Even if Africa had consistently enjoyed growth in per capita income one full percentage point above Europe's, this gap of ratio would still be 19:1 today and Africa will only catch up with Europe in 2302. Domestic policies are not the sole reasons for the lack of divergence and growth in the economic trajectories of poor countries in Africa. Even though they are contributory factors, the *global economic structure* plays a more decisive factor. Thus transformative strategies required for a more effective service of charity in truth will demand a more comprehensive analysis of the international and local structures of sins and injustices which have stymied development and aid initiatives. Thus, the failure of aid in Africa is also because of the international economic structure that makes local processes unworkable because they are made to fit into certain given "plans" which were formulated outside the frame of reference of the local structure.

The point here is that if African development and aid from the West is to work, it must be anchored on the agency of the people; that is, the human, natural, social, and material capital has to be improved through clearly defined paths. It will demand a restructuring of many African states, because statism (which emphasizes state control of economic activities, and de-emphasizes the dynamic creativity of local processes, and regulated market forces) is the primary cause of aid failure and stunted development at the institutional levels (and Church charities and Islamic charities, which parallel the state structure) in Africa. However, as constituted today, African states do not offer an enabling environment for sustainable development. What is prevalent today is the absence of what John Mukum Mbaku calls components of laws and institutions for sustainable development which will: (1) guarantee economic freedoms; (2) minimize corruption, rent seeking, rent extraction, and other forms of political opportunism; (3)

7. Ibid.

enhance indigenous entrepreneurship and hence wealth creation; and (4) provide structures for peaceful co-existence of population groups (that is ethnic and other social cleavages).[8]

The argument that failed aid and development initiatives in Africa is the results of internal factors has some merits because it shows that Africans cannot claim perpetual victimhood when it comes to matters of how they use aid, and how they set economic and social policies and implement them. There is much to be said about the failed development aid in Africa which shows that African governments failed African peoples and sometimes that non-governmental organizations and even Church-run charities in Africa parallel the state structures and reproduce the same reality: so much promise but little results.

The second factor is *external*. There are many Africans and non-Africans who believe that development models and donor initiatives are pursued with secondary goals and are ideologically driven and hence end up not achieving any minimal benefit for Africans. They also argue that donors set out their objectives and goals without taking into consideration the input of Africans. In these kinds of donor initiative and development programs, Africans are merely passive objects of patterns and models of development, which were tried elsewhere or conceived elsewhere and are imposed on Africa. This is a kind of development imperialism that seeks to reproduce development models in Africa that in most cases do not relate to the African social context.

One of the best presentations of this position is William Easterly, who argues that, "The West spent $2.3 trillion on foreign aid over the last five decades and still had not managed to get twelve-cent medicines to children to prevent half of all malaria deaths. The West spent $2.3 trillion and still had not managed to get four-dollar bed nets to poor families. The West spends $2.3 trillion and still had not managed to get three dollars to each new mother to prevent five million child deaths. The West spent $2.3 trillion, and Amaretch is still carrying firewood and not going to school. It's a tragedy that so much well-meaning compassion did not bring these results for needy people."[9] Easterly's thesis is that the failure of Western aid in Africa is due to the West's application of simplistic answers to complex internal prob-

---

8. Mbaku, "Ideologies," 393.
9. Easterly, *White Man's Burden*, 4.

lems in Africa.[10] He makes a distinction between planners (those who sit down in Washington, Vatican, London, Ottawa and make plans for aid and development in Africa *without the input of Africans*) and searchers (who adopt a vulnerable approach, seeking from within the people what works for them and enabling the maximization of the people's abilities and the removal of obstacles to their being realized). The failure of development aid is not so much the failure of African institutions but rather the externally imposed frameworks: Big plans, bogus targets, and unrealistic benchmarks. "The prevalence of ineffective plans is the result of Western assistance happening out of view of the Western public. Fewer ineffective approaches would survive if results were most visible. The Big Plans are attractive to politicians, celebrities, and activists who want to make a big splash, without the Western public realizing that those plans at the top are not connected to the reality at the bottom."[11]

In the first place, we must admit that African development is unpredictable. The predictability of social progress and development can only happen in those societies where there are basic social, political, and economic structures that are resistant enough to other unforeseen variables that impinge on the socio-economic process. The foundations for national development in Africa are very superficial and largely fragile, because of the political and economic structure of African nations that make them susceptible to unstable governments, corruption, ecological disasters, and ethnic and religious conflicts. These make long-term goals and planning largely unrealistic. Thus, setting benchmarks and timeline for development is often counterproductive because they ignore the fundamental elements of development, which should be put in place in the first place in most African countries: human and cultural development, constitutional and participatory democracies, robust and accountable local economic processes anchored on the industry and ingenuity of women, age-grade, local churches and religious groups among others. Long-term development goals in Africa are often hampered by the failure to address the immediate short-term concerns that relate to the human capital and the shape and structure of political, economic, and social institutions that determine the direction of African societies.

10. Ibid., 10
11. Ibid., 17.

The MDGs, for instance, were imposed on African countries without sensitivity to the peculiar problems and challenges facing individual African countries. Africa is a continent of fifty-three countries; each country has its own peculiar history and challenges. How can the MDGs be realized, for instance, in Zimbabwe, which is suffocating under the iron hand of the worst dictatorship that has gripped an African country in the last thirty years? How can the MDGs be a reality in Darfur and other parts of Sudan, where the basic question is about identity, nationality, and survival? Are the challenges of national reconciliation facing countries like Rwanda, Congo-Kinshasa, Sierra Leone, Cote d'Ivoire, and Liberia the same as that of South Africa, Nigeria, or Kenya, where the concern is how to evolve a constitutional democracy which will help actualize the hidden human and natural resources of these countries?

One would think that a more country-specific approach to aid should have been adopted in pursuing clearly defined and context specific challenges that meet local needs and goals. More sadly, is the fact that some of the parties that are in the African steering committee for the realization of the MDGs like the World Bank and the International Monetary Fund were the same banks that created the debt burden in Africa. Their exogenous, neo-liberal capitalism and worn-out death-dealing economic orthodoxies stifled the African economies through the much-hated Structural Adjustment Program. The stringent conditions tied to loans and economic assistance to African countries by these two organizations are part of the reason why African countries cannot make any economic progress. Development in Africa can never be based on mercenary solutions championed by the World Bank, the IMF, and the World Trade Organization. Their past failed policies in Africa, which are now being keyed into the steps for realizing the MDGs in Africa through NEPAD, will harm the weak and struggling economies of most African countries.

In recent times, Western governments, IMF, World Bank, and donor agencies, as well as international development and aid agencies have imposed strict benchmarks for African countries seeking aid. Development aid and grant seeking in Africa have taken on a life of their own. They have become a burgeoning business with their own peculiar logic, profit rationality, and unchecked accounting processes. They have become, in many cases, bureaucratic because governments, agencies, and NGOs in Africa struggle to produce evidence in order to meet externally imposed conditions and benchmarks for aid. In many cases, the evidences are phantom. Thus, the structural basis and projects for which aid are sought for, received, and accounted for are often false and empty.

In the final analysis, African countries must take control of their destiny. The repeated failure of the promises made to African countries by the international community should challenge *African countries to seek African solutions to African problems.* A holistic approach to socio-economic change demands the understanding that human development does not subsist only on economic variable. Change should be situated within the social, political, cultural, religious, and economic values and institutions of Africa The most solid foundation for sustainable development in Africa is the infrastructure of human capital, especially anchored on emerging skills midwifed by locally based science and technology, supplemented with skills and technology from other civilizations and cultures outside Africa. This cannot come about unless African countries evolve a stable and enabling environment for human development. This obviously is not a task that any country outside Africa can do for Africans.

The thirty-member Organization for Economic Cooperation and Development (OECD) of industrialized, market-economy countries can only support Africans when the suitable environment has been created. Development, partnership, and co-operation should be in the area of trade, education, women development, skills and technical transfer and exchanges, and support for building the foundations of a stable society, and the building and development of educational and political structures. Realizing the millennium goals in Africa through aid and donor initiatives will demand a new set of targets, a new country-based approach, a new direction that addresses African development through grass roots actions and direct initiative.

There are many economists and development experts on Africa who think that both the internal and external factors conspire to work against aid in Africa. As a result, they are calling for the abolition of aid in Africa. Some Africans in this abolitionist camp include Andrew Mwenda, James Shikwati, Herman Chinnery-Hesse, George Ayittey, and Moeletsi Mbeki.[12] The most radical is the 2009 book by the

12. I am indebted to the work of Maarten de Zeeuw and Mwangala Mubita for

Zambian economist, Dambisa Moyo appropriately titled, "Dead Aid." She argues for the abolition of aid to Africa within the next five years. She notes that aid initiative in Africa has led to a vicious cycle of aid, more under-development, corruption, dictatorship, and other negative consequences. In her words; "With aid's help, corruption fosters corruption, nations quickly descend into a vicious cycle of aid. Foreign aid props up corrupt governments—providing them with freely usable cash. These corrupt governments interfere with the rule of law, the establishment of transparent civil institutions and the protection of civil liberties, making both domestic and foreign investment in poor countries unattractive."[13] This camp argues that aid has not improved the quality of life of any single African country nor has it led to an increase in the GDP of any country. They point to the good intentions of the donors but show that these do not translate to any economic growth for Africa, nor has it reduced poverty or stimulated prosperity that could have reduced the need for more aid. This group also rejects the aid mentality, that is, that those who are rich should give aid to the poor. This, they further point out, has created a culture of aid instead of a culture of responsibility. Aid has hampered the capacity of the private sector to pursue wealth creation, and has not provided any catalyst for development in the most basic component of society at the grassroots. The abolitionists therefore, see both the internal and external factors as hampering the self-reliance of African societies.

However, there is a strong case made for successful aid regimen in the global scene today. The aid and grants given to African communities that achieve some reasonable success are those that are targeted, manageable, measurable, and procure direct and immediate results. In addition, its operation is less bureaucratic. In many cases, the grassroots structure is strong and stable; a situation which cannot be said of most African states. So the third perspective on whether aid should continue in Africa and the reasons for failed aid initiatives in Africa will demand for greater clarification of who is receiving the aid? Who is asking for aid and support? Is the aid interventionist (humanitarian) or pro-active (stimulating development and economic growth)? These questions are important in determining the success or failure of

---

their seminal article, "Dr Moyo's Proposal," 26–29

13. Moyo, *Dead Aid*, 49.

such initiatives. This is the middle of the road position which says that aid works in some cases, and does not work in others.

This position will argue that there are specific factors which can work against aid in a particular case, but which will be a saving grace in another case. Therein lies the need to avoid generalizations, and to examine both public and religious charities (the origin of aid and the destiny of aid) in terms of their goals, their operation, their implementation, etc. Roger C. Riddell argues in *Does Foreign Aid Really Work* that aid works; and that development initiatives are producing results in many communities and countries in Africa. However, he points out that the aid initiatives that are succeeding in recent times are the ones that are driven not by ODA (official development aid, mainly by Western governments) but by NGOs, which represent 30 percent of aid globally. He focuses his book on the NGOs and their impacts. He argues that the reason aid is working in many instances is because aid-giving is now done within the framework of human rights wherein the needs, capabilities, and rights of the recipients are taken as starting point for determining how much is given and the ways in which it is given. Thus, it is no longer up to the donor to determine when to give, how much to give, and conditions for giving, and how long the giving will last. Today, he observes, aid is seen as inter-connected to global human rights promotion, greater respect for indigenous knowledge and culture, and promoting solidarity and mutuality through aid. He argues that a rights-based approach to aid yields more result than a needs-based approach because it places the claims of the poor to a decent living on the same level as enhancing their power to take control over their lives through involvement in aid initiatives and shaping their likely outcome. In addition to the people being part of setting the goal and determining where they need help, rights—based approach does not create a culture of dependence on the part of the people who are receiving aid but rather seeks to strengthen their independence and freedom. The rights-based approach makes the donor agencies accountable to the poor and not only to sources of their donations.[14]

Riddell argues that aid does not work in many cases because of wider systemic and institutional factors both within the organization itself, with the local communities or groups to which they are providing

---

14. There is so much information contained in this magisterial work which I recommend to aid agencies especially in the third sectors. Riddell, *Foreign Aid*, 158–60.

aid, and country specific challenges in both the donor agency or the recipient of aid. Peter Singer shows that aid indeed works but that it is important for people in the West to hold the donor agencies and governments accountable for the millions they spend in places like Africa without any visible results. He shows that GiveWell (2007), a non-profit organization dedicated to improving the transparency and effectiveness of charities, and Charity Navigator (2001) are some of the organizations in the US, for instance, now showing the mismanagement of aid, on one hand, and the charities who are touching lives and producing positive and sustainable results for the poor in Africa and elsewhere. For instance, of the fifty-nine organizations that applied for GiveWell grants in 2007, only fifteen produced adequate information about their activities. The remainder described their activities by offering stories or newspaper articles about particular projects, but no detailed evidence showing the number of people who benefited, and how they benefited, from the organization's activities, and what those activities cost.[15] This is just one example out of many to illustrate that there are also internal incoherence, lack of accountability in many Western charities all of which contribute to the failure of their donor and aid activities in Africa.

In conclusion, the following could be summarized as the reasons for the failure of aid, which I think apply to Africa in a very specific sense: "Many problems with aid arise because of poor decision-making. Some problems with aid are specific to particular projects and programs, and arise from wrong decisions made by individuals and agencies as to the type of aid that should be provided to particular recipients, often as a result of insufficient understanding of what is needed, and how aid may help. Some problems with aid arise because of individuals and agencies making over-optimistic assumptions about the capacity of the organizations receiving aid to use it effectively. Other problems arise because donors or recipients either fail to undertake risk assessments or make assumptions about the external environment which turn out to be wrong, and the unexpected effects of these errors undermine or eclipse the expected beneficial outcomes."[16] These factors apply more to non-governmental organizations especially to private and religious groups involved in charitable works in

---

15. Singer, *Life You Can Save*, 87–88.
16. Ibid., 357.

Africa. Most of these groups unlike official development agencies do not usually work with the state or the state parallel organizations, but with small groups and agencies in African countries.

Aid will work better in Africa if both Africans and non-Africans interested in doing charity in Africa took time to understand that Africa has great diversity in form, culture, structure, and traditional economic engineering. These diversities are also decisive in terms of the burgeoning social capitals that are decisive in any economic development program. They should also understand the peculiar history of the country or ethnic group in which they are working and the particular cultural traditions in each case. I will elaborate more on this in chapter 4, where I will discuss how Church charities should operate in Africa. Unfortunately, the social context of Africa continues to be interpreted through many stereotypes.

Despite many philosophical, cultural, and historical studies of Africa, it is strange that the richness, diversity, and complexity of Africa have not been appreciated by Africans, let alone by non-Africans. Many people still see Africa as one unit or even one country. V. Y. Mudimbe,[17] Kwame Anthony Appiah[18], and George B. N. Ayittey[19] have all been very rich in their insight on the true face of Africa, which is different from the invented Africa made manifest in generalizations about the continent without recourse to data or specificities. I have also undertaken a similar task in my work, *The Face of Africa: Looking Beyond the Shadows*.[20] I think that this lack of clarity and understanding is what makes aid in Africa very problematic. For instance, the water needs of Ethiopia are not the same as the water needs in Ghana, so the cost of digging a well in Ethiopia will not be the same as digging a well in Ghana. In East Africa, for instance, most elementary and high school students live in boarding houses, which will entail more investment in education, and reduced contributions of the children in economic activities at home, while in West Africa such practices have long been abandoned as there are more students going to elementary and high schools from home. Thus, a charitable organization working on education in Uganda and Nigeria will have to adopt different

17. Mudimbe, *Invention of Africa*.
18. Appiah, *Father's House*.
19. Ayittey, *African Unchained*.
20. Ilo, *Face of Africa*.

approaches for each group. Even in one country, a strategy might work better in one province than in another. However, no matter how effective these aid initiatives become, the truth is that the reconstruction of Africa cannot come about through aid alone. However, if aid will make any meaningful contribution to Africa through the practice of charity in truth especially with private and religious charities, there is a need to understand Africa and treat the continent as a subject of solidarity and not objects of charity, sympathy, and relief.

Unfortunately, Africa has always been very marginal in world history and has often been misunderstood. George Hegel had no place for Africa in his cartography of world's history and civilization. The journey of the human spirit at the level of consciousness, in his interpretation of history does not pass through Africa because Africans' consciousness has not attained to the level of any substantial objective existence. According to Hegel, "Africa is the land of gold, closed upon itself, the land of children, it is the gold-land confused within itself—the land of childhood, which lying beyond the day of self-conscious history, is enveloped in the dark mantle of night."[21] This is the kind of mentality that regards Africa as a land of darkness and death or as one early explorer described it "a universal den of desolation, misery, and crime." Olufemi Taiwo has demonstrated in a well-researched paper that at the ideological level, this perception of Africa can be traced to G. W. F. Hegel.[22] According to Taiwo, for Hegel, Africa proper is shut up from the rest of the world by its geography as well as by the strange character of her peoples. Africans lack the category of universality. "This arises from the fact that they are one with their existence; they are arrested in immediacy. This means that they have not separated themselves from nature. 'The Negroes,' wrote Hegel, 'exhibits the natural man in his completely wild and untamed state.' As such, the African is shorn of the idea of the self that is separate from his needs and, simultaneously, has no knowledge of 'an absolute Being,' an Other and a Higher than his individual selfs."[23] Hegel, who wrote that Africa is "enveloped in the dark mantle of the night" disparages Africa this way: "At this point we leave Africa, not to mention it again. For it is no historical part of the world; it has no movement or development to

---

21. Hegel, *The Philosophy of History*, 91.
22. Taiwo, "Hegel's Ghost."
23. Ibid.

exhibit. Historical movements in it—that is its northern part—belong to the Asiatic or European world. Carthage displayed there an important transitionary phase of civilization; but, as a Phoenician colony, it belongs to Asia. Egypt will be considered in reference to the passage from the human mind from its Eastern to its Western phase, but it does not belong to the African Spirit. *What we properly understand by Africa, is the Unhistorical, Undeveloped Spirit, still involved in the conditions of mere nature,* and which had to be presented here only as on the threshold of the World's History."[24]

There are many non-Africans today who still think like Hegel. This kind of thinking is based on a lack of adequate information about the African continent. It is also based on prejudice and untested assumptions and stereotypes of Africa and Africans built and sustained by Western media and partisan Western commentators which go back to the end of slavery in the later part of the nineteenth century and in missionary work in Africa. Easterly documents a few of such notions of non-Western societies, which often contribute to failed aid based on wrong motives and condescending treatment of the Rest: "Must we not then . . . endeavour to raise these wretched beings out of their present miserable conditions?"—William Wilberforce, anti-slavery campaigner. "These vast lands—need only assistance from us to become civilized"—The Marquis de Condorcet.[25]

Helping Africa, civilizing Africa, humanizing Africa, wiping away Africa's tears, supervising Africa's growth and development, etc., all grew out of the wrong notion of Africa. Indeed, terms like "uncivilized," "under-developed," "savage peoples," "backward people," "barbaric culture" all evolved to "Third World," which today has been refined as "Two Third World." However, they all reveal distorted images of Africa and the rest of the world through the lenses of the West. Development aid as a Western policy is attributed to the American President Harry Truman who on January 20, 1949, said, "We must embark on a bold new program for . . . the improvement and growth of underdeveloped areas. More than half of the people of the world are living in conditions approaching misery . . . For the first time in history, humanity possesses the knowledge and the skill to relieve the

---

24. Quoted in ibid. Italics mine.
25. Easterly, *White Man's Burden,* 23–24.

suffering of these people."[26] After more than sixty years, what Truman said is still true. However, what is no longer true is the notion of suffering as the face of non-Westerners especially in Africa. There is an obvious paternalistic mindset among non-Africans with regard to Africa. Africa is not all about naked children rummaging for food in refuse dumps or dying men and women with wasted flesh hanging on mere skeletons; Africa is not a land of violence and turmoil. There is *much more* to Africa than what is presented in the Western media; there is another face of Africa which is not easily seen in Western media. These negative images of Africa, even though sometimes stemming from pure motives, rob Africans of their dignity and give false impressions on the possibility of a better future for Africa.

For instance, let us examine one recurrent theme in Western post-colonial discourse that Africa is held back today by corruption and that corruption is the major internal factor for the failure of aid in Africa. According to the United Nations Millennium Project Report, *Investing in Development*, corruption and bad government are not the main causes of poverty and underdevelopment in Africa. The report calls for a deeper and broader understanding of the African situation so as to appreciate the failed development initiatives in the continent. According to the report,[27] while there is a highly visible sign of poor governance in places like Zimbabwe, widespread war and violence in Angola, Democratic Republic of Congo, Liberia, Sierra Leone and Sudan, there are many well governed countries like Ghana, Malawi, Mali and Senegal who are caught up in the same grinding poverty like the badly governed African countries. Using formal statistics from organizations like Transparency International (corruption perception index) and Freedom House ranking (democracy ranking), Jeffery D. Sachs argues that relatively well-governed and less corrupt African countries failed to prosper, while extensively corrupt countries in Asia like India, Indonesia and Pakistan enjoyed rapid economic growth.[28]

According to World Bank indicators, Africa's governments are not worse, on average, than other governments elsewhere in the world. In addition, Africa's corruption is not worse than what is found in many parts of the Western and Asian countries. What Bernard Madoff,

26. Quoted in ibid., 24.

27. See UN Development Group, *Investing in Development*, 147–57.

28. Sachs, *End of Poverty*, 191.

through a ponzi scheme, fraudulently amassed was more than the corruption in the whole of Africa for the last decade. However, while corruption in many industrialized countries can be discovered and prosecuted, in Africa it is disruptive and destructive of the economy, and is often not investigated nor are the perpetrators held account-able. There is, therefore, the need to take a more comprehensive look at the African situation and the unexamined assumption that Africa is a land of corruption and misrule. It should not be assumed that all the fifty-four countries in Africa are corrupt and that all of them are reeling under the iron fist of bad leaders. Unfortunately, corruption negatively affects Africa and because of unstable structures it per-petuates Africa's poverty and weakens and even destroys the fledgling structures being laid for sustainable development.

The point that we wish to emphasize here in understanding the African situation with regard to failed aid initiatives is that one can-not lay the cause of the present failed development models in Africa on corruption alone. Corruption and misrule in some parts of Africa should be seen as symptoms of a deeper problem. This is well presented in the *Millennium Report* when its authors argue, "Our explanation is that tropical Africa, even in well governed parts, is stuck in a poverty trap—too poor to achieve robust and high levels of economic growth, and in many places simply too poor to grow at all. More policy or governance reform, by itself, is not sufficient to break out of this trap. Africa's extreme poverty leads to low national saving rates, which in turn lead to low or negative economic growth rates. Low domestic saving is not offset by high inflows of private foreign capital, such as foreign direct investment, since Africa's poor infrastructure and weak human capital discourage private capital inflows. With very low do-mestic saving and low rates of market based foreign capital inflows, there is little in Africa's current dynamics that promotes an escape from poverty."[29]

However, the pervasive effects of corruption and conflicts in African cannot be over-emphasized; they threaten any sustainable development initiatives in Africa. The material resources in the continent have become sources for conflicts and bitterness. For in-stance, the presence of diamonds in West and Central Africa has become a source of illegitimate business with arms dealers from

29. UN Development Group, *Investing in Development*, 147–48.

Europe and the Middle East who sell arms to African rebel groups in exchange for illegal trade in diamonds. According to Douglas Farah, author of *Blood from Stones: The Secret Financial Network of Terror,* "One of the most alarming and shocking things in my dealing with the diamond trade in West and Central Africa was the willingness of Israelis and Arabs, who want to kill each other in their homelands, to do business with each other on the ground in Africa. I met Hezbollah diamond dealers who were selling to Israelis and Israelis who were selling to Hezbollah, knowing that Hezbollah was trying to kill Israelis in the Middle East, and Hezbollah knowing, that the Israelis wanted to kill their family members back there. I think it is one of the truly extraordinary demonstrations of the depth to which people will sink in their greed for diamonds."[30]

This could be said of the oil wealth of countries like Nigeria, Gabon, Equatorial Guinea, Libya, Chad, and Algeria. According to the 2004 corruption index of Transparency International, oil wealth is the breeding ground for corruption. In some of the oil-rich countries of Africa, public contracting, in the oil sector, is plagued by revenues vanishing into the pockets of Western oil executives, middlemen, and local officials. Communities in the oil-producing countries of Africa continue to suffer from environmental destruction and ecological disasters from oil exploitation. Many Nigerians in the Niger Delta oil-producing area cannot forget easily, the full-scale destruction of Odi, a town of over 50,000 people, between November 20–24, 1999, because the residents resisted the Western oil companies who were extracting oil in the area, without any regard to the environmental degradation that it brought to the people.

This raises the questions: Why can't Africans manage their own resources? Why are African governments failing to prioritize educational goals to respond to the technical lack that is hampering industrialization and making their respective countries susceptible to Western exploitation? Why are the natural resources in Africa becoming sources of conflict and war (as we see in Nigeria, Congo-Kinshasa, Sudan, Cote d'Ivoire, Liberia and Sierra Leone) instead of means for improving the quality of life of the people? African leaders must take some part of the blame for their failure to take control of their natural resources and their usurpation of the oil wealth of their land for

30. Quoted in Ilo, *Face of Africa,* 360.

their selfish end. Referring to how national governments waste the oil wealth of their respective countries, Friedman writes, "As long as the monarchs and dictators who run these oil states can get rich by drilling their natural resource—as opposed to drilling the natural talents and energy of their people—they can stay in office forever. They can use oil money to monopolize all the instruments of power—army, police, and intelligence—and never have to introduce real transparency through power sharing. All they have to do is capture and hold the oil tap."[31]

The same could be said of cocoa, cereals, and cotton that are produced in many sub-Saharan African countries. In late 2004, the British High Commissioner in Kenya, Edward Clay, accused the Kenyan government of massive corruption, noting that the money lost through corruption is able to build half the number of schools needed in Kenya. Between 2002 and 2004, Kenya, a leading country in tourism and coffee trade, lost over $188 million through corruption. Kenya lost over $4 billion to corruption during the long regime of Daniel arap Moi. Despite the promise of the Kibaki regime to stamp out corruption in Kenya, there are still many mountains to climb. In the 2005–2006 Kenyan federal budget, the government is reported by the *National Post of Canada* to have earmarked the sum of $6.5 million to buy a fleet of new vehicles for the Office of the President; a further $6.3 million has been set aside for the maintenance of his existing car-pool.

The roll call of African leaders with unenviable records of corruption is long and shameful: General Sani Abacha impoverished Nigeria of over $6 billion during the five years of his evil regime in that country. His predecessor, "the smiling dictator," General Babangida also left a shameful record in public accountability. All Nigeria's extra earnings from oil during the first Gulf War (totaling about $12.4 billion) were stolen during the regrettable regime of Babangida, who shamelessly calls himself "the evil genius." William Keeling, of the *Financial Times*, who wanted to investigate how such a large amount disappeared from Nigeria's national vault, was forcibly deported from the country on June 30, 1991. That money alone could have given water and electricity to every Nigerian village (over 65 percent of Nigerians do not have access to water and power supply). The Economic and Financial Crimes Commission of Nigeria, estimates that over $500 billion of

31. Friedman, *World is Flat*, 460.

Nigeria's oil wealth has been embezzled by Nigerian dictators since the sad invasion of the military into Nigeria's politics in 1966. This amount represents approximately all Western aid to Africa in the last four decades!

In spite of the prevalence of corruption in Africa, we cannot justifiably say that corruption *alone* accounts for failed development programs or aid initiatives in Africa. Nevertheless, corruption does contribute to the growing level of poverty in Africa and eradicating poverty in Africa will require eliminating corruption in public and private life. However, the practice of charity in truth in Africa demands knowing the complexities and challenges in the African social context. It demand also removing the obstacles which poverty places on the path of African development, as Okot p'Bitek put it so wonderfully in *The Song of an African Woman*: "I have only one request/I do not ask for money/ Although I have need of it/ I do not ask for meat . . . / I have only one request/All I ask is/That you remove/the roadblock/from my path."[32]

POVERTY IN AFRICA

What do we mean by poverty and how does it apply to Africa? My definition of poverty is the absence of adequate means to meet immediate needs; this could be less or more according to the extent of the needs relative to the absence of means. Poverty designates in the first place, material poverty, that is, the lack of economic goods necessary for a human life worthy of the dignity of the human person. In this sense, poverty is rejected by contemporary society and considered as evil and an abuse of the human rights of people. However, Christians have often distinguished between material and spiritual poverty. The first referring to the absence of means, while the second relates to the poverty of spirit which demands detachment from material wealth. When Pope John XXIII said in a radio message on September 11, 1962,[33] that the Church is a church of the poor, he was only trying to underlie the fact that the Church is a church that should identify totally with the cause of the poor. In other words, material poverty is

32. Quoted in Novogratz, *Blue Sweater*, 79.
33. See Pope John XXIII, *Pope Speaks*.

an evil that the Church should confront because her members and societies to which she ministers are made up of poor people. Removing poverty in the face of the earth will entail making an option for the poor and the weak.

The preferential option for the poor, as it has often been interpreted in Catholic theology, means a constant and consistent action to defend the cause of the poor and the weak and removing the factors that give rise to poverty from the root. This demands restoring the dignity of the human person who is suffering; fighting against injustice, reigniting in the hearts of all Christians, and all men and women of goodwill, a collapsing platform of compassion in contemporary society and the often alienating self-imprisonment that has made our society selfish, egocentric, self-serving and profit-driven etc. In summary, the Church neither supports capitalism—which has made competition and survival of the fittest a new creed—nor does the Church support communism or the welfare state where the individual is swallowed up in the anonymity of the collective, or where his or her right to actualize himself or herself and benefit from the fruits of his or her labor are denied.

In other words, doing charity is not enough; there is also the need to fight against injustice so as to eradicate the root cause of poverty. This means in concrete sense the removal of selfishness and greed whether at the individual or group or national levels. *Doing charity in truth will demand an uncompromising commitment to love. The measure of the true value of the Christian religion is to the extent to which it promotes the peace and happiness of humankind and projects the ideal of love. The Christian religion we need in the world of today is not the one that tends to totalize and swallow everyone in the blaze of dogmatism, but one that creates conditions for love and peace and readily concretizes in the hearts of adherents genuine concern for others, especially the weaker members of society. It is this kind of Christian faith that will inspire change in societies, challenge settled prejudices, and create the suitable ground for a new society where no one goes to bed hungry and angry because of injustice and the wickedness of the other. Such Christianity should conquer hatred through saving love and overcome despair via the incarnation of hope as concrete transformation of individuals and cultures in the historical process. Any religion that preaches ultimate peace with God but promotes war, terrorism and division; any religion that preaches love but does nothing to reduce the suffering, powerlessness and rejection of the poor and the weak, is one that has lost its soul. Every true Christian religion, must make people to be at home with who they are and to see themselves in a spiritual and temporal chain that connects one to all. This kind of attitude can help conquer poverty in our world.*

In the Scripture, poverty is presented as a scandalous condition inimical to human dignity and therefore contrary to the will of God. The poor person is presented as *ebyon*, which translates into a "beggar," a "destitute person." It appears seventeen times in prophetic oracles and twenty-three times in the Psalms. Let us mention some instances in the Old Testament of the condition it describes: in Isa 14:30, "the poor are dying of hunger and the beggars are searching for food in the fields." In Amos 8:14 it refers to those who are thirsty and hungry, those who are treated unjustly. This word, *ebyon*, is also used in the prophecy of Amos to refer to those who are exploited and who do not receive fair wages and those whom social structures have put down in a poverty trap. The term *ebyon* translates then properly as someone who is needy and implies an expectation that this need will be met either by God or the community. In many cases *ebyon* appears with the word *tzaddik* (righteous person). Rabbi Jacobs explains this connection in two ways: In the first place, the *ebyon* is assumed to be someone suffering economic want because of his or her refusal to pursue money-making at all cost. He or she is dependent on God, and thus enjoys God's special favor. God is presented in the Bible as being on the side of the poor over the powerful and the wealthy. Secondly, the *ebyon* suffers poverty because of injustice. This is the import of Amos' prophetic oracle. Poverty increases in society when injustice is on the rise. When many people pursue wealth with so much passion at the expense of meeting human needs, the *ebyon* and the *tzaddik* suffer, and the *tzaddik* could actually become *ebyon*. "When those in power fail to prevent the exploitation of others, and when it becomes impossible for those who act fairly to become wealthy, there is a greater likelihood that the righteous will become poor, and that the wealthy will lose any commitments to righteousness."[34]

Another Hebrew word for "poor" is *dal* referring to the weak ones, frail ones who cannot work—those who are unusable, who in modern society could be expendable, or those who lack skills. Another

---

34. Jacobs, *No Needy*, 50.

Hebrew word is *ani*, meaning one who is bent over with suffering or who works so hard but cannot get enough to sustain life. He or she labors night and day without rest; one who is humiliated and one whose labor does not gain him or her enough sustenance. The idea of the poor in the Old Testament is that of a person who by virtue of bad luck or circumstances has landed upon hard times.[35]

Another word for poor is the one often used in the New Testament, *ptokos*; that is, the one who does not have enough to sustain life; one who is lacking in the basic necessities of life and so cannot subsist on his or her own. Poverty is presented in the Christian Scripture as a great scandal; an evil of injustice which demands immediate action to put an end to its dehumanization of God's people. The scandalous condition of the poor anywhere is condemned in the Christian Scripture, which presents God as one who is on the side of the poor. God makes a preferential option for the poor to lift them up to enjoy the dignity and fullness of life worthy of the human person, made in his image and likeness.[36] Jesus came to bring the good news to the poor (Luke 4:18–19) so that all God's children will have abundance of life. This is the message of salvation. Jesus himself went about in the course of his ministry reaching out to the poor and the marginalized. He gave food to the hungry, he gave water to the thirsty; he reached out to the sick and the abandoned; he served the needs of the widows and the orphans. He was always found among the poor, the *anawim Yhwh*, that is, those who are poor materially as well as those who are poor in spirit because they recognize their need of God and abandon themselves into his hand. Pope Benedict reiterates the message of the Church on the conditions of the poor when he writes in his New Year message for 2009, "Our world shows increasing evidence of another grave threat to peace: many individuals and indeed whole peoples who are living today in conditions of extreme poverty. The gap between rich and poor has become more marked, even in the most economically developed nations. This is a problem which the conscience of humanity cannot ignore, since the conditions in which a great number of people are living are an insult to their innate dignity

---

35. Ibid., 51.
36. Gutierrez, *Theology of Hope*, 291–92.

and as a result are a threat to the authentic and harmonious progress of the world community."[37]

The international community has set a benchmark for establishing the meaning of poverty. At the Global Summit to set the Millennium Development Goals in 1999, the United Nations declared 2005–15 as the decade for the eradication of poverty in the world, which is to halve the number of people who are poor and to eradicate extreme poverty in world by 2025. Today, the Make Poverty History Campaign continues to grow in numbers as millions of people around the world are coming together to say "No" to poverty on earth. Whether they will be able to create an awareness of the structural basis of poverty in terms of global injustice, failed national policies and the danger of neo-liberal capitalism is yet to be determined. However, it is a positive step and points to the fact that poverty is increasingly been seen as a man-made evil, which could be eradicated through joint efforts by all right-thinking men and women the world over.

For technical and statistical purposes, poverty is usually measured by establishing a poverty line, set at some multiple of income necessary to purchase a basic food basket that provides sufficient nutrition for an active, productive life. People whose income is below the level necessary to purchase even that basic food basket are called absolutely poor, or in deprivation."[38] National governments set the benchmark of what constitutes the basic financial equivalence to the food basket. Jeffery Sachs observes that one sixth of humanity is caught in a poverty trap, which makes it impossible for them to escape from extreme material deprivation; they are trapped by disease, physical isolation, climate stress, environmental degradation, and by extreme poverty.[39] Sachs distinguishes between three degrees of poverty: extreme or absolute poverty, moderate poverty, and relative poverty. *Extreme poverty* exists when households cannot meet basic needs for survival and are chronically hungry, unable to access healthcare, lack the amenities of safe drinking water and sanitation, cannot afford education for some or all of their children, and lack rudimentary shelter,

---

37. Benedict XVI, "Fighting Poverty," 1.

38. Youn et al., "Dying for Growth," 207.

39. My exposition on the meaning of poverty will be based on that given by Jeffery Sachs in his influential work, *The End of Poverty*, 17–25.

clothing, shoes, etc. Extreme poverty unlike moderate and relative poverty occurs only in developing countries.

Moderate poverty occurs when basic needs are barely met, while relative poverty is generally construed as a household income level below a given proportion of average national income. The relatively poor in high-income countries, according to Sachs, lack access to cultural goods, entertainment, recreation, and to quality healthcare, education and other perquisites for upward social mobility. The World Bank uses the income of $1 per day per person, measured at purchasing power parity to determine the number of people in extreme poverty, while income between $1 per day and $2 per day can be used to measure moderate poverty. Sachs argues that based on this grading, half of Africa's population is deemed to live in extreme poverty and it continues to rise in absolute numbers. The statistics bear this out.

According to an assessment report, *Investing in Development*, by the UN Development Group on how the different regions of the world are working towards reaching the Millennium Development Goals, in sharp contrast to Asia's progress, most of Sub-Saharan Africa faces significant challenges in meeting the Millennium Development Goals on almost every aspect of poverty. Many African countries are falling behind all other regions. The World Bank reported that in 1990 there were roughly 375 million people in China living in extreme poverty, on less than $1 a day. By 2001, there were 212 million Chinese living in extreme poverty, and by 2015, if current trend hold, there will be only sixteen million living on less than $1 a day. In South Asia primarily India, Pakistan, and Bangladesh the numbers went down from 462 million in 1990 living on less than $1 a day to 431 million in 2001, and is projected to go down to 216 million in 2015. In Sub-Saharan Africa unfortunately, there were 227 million people living on less than $1 a day in 1990, 313 in 2001, and an expected 340 million in 2015.[40] In other words, half of Africa's 880 million people live on less than $1 a day. The precipitous decline in Africa's per capita income is such that some countries of Africa enjoyed a higher standard of living in 1960 than they enjoy today. Indeed, according to Martin Meredith, the entire economic output of Africa is no more than $420 billion, just 1.3 percent of the world's GDP. Its share of world trade has declined to half of what it was in 1980, amounting only to about 1.6 percent,

40. Friedman, *World is Flat*, 315.

while its share of global investment is less than 1 percent. Africa is the only region where per capita investment and saving has declined since 1970.[41] Robert O'Brien and Marc Williams draw attention to this limited way of judging poverty in terms of development as misleading as it does not factor in cultural and sociological aspects of development, and the internal variables that reveal the dimensions of redistribution, which is not easily seen in the undue attention to aggregate growth.[42] However, our concern here is more on material poverty in Africa.

The African continent has a more than fair share of the poor of the earth. In the 2004 *Human Development Report* published by the United Nations Development Program, African countries are, by *all* indices, in the lower rungs of development. The report looks at such issues as life expectancy, educational attainment, adjusted real income, access to water, food, and social amenities and the all round choices open to people the world over in terms of the quality of life. The Index shows that of the twenty countries that suffered reversals since 1990, thirteen are in Sub-Saharan Africa. While life expectancy in Norway is seventy-nine years, that of countries like Angola, Central African Republic, Lesotho, Mozambique, Sierra Leone, Swaziland, Zambia, and Zimbabwe has fallen to forty years or less.[43] While Norway has a per capita Gross Domestic Product of US$36,600 (adjusted by purchasing power parity), Mali has a GDP of US $753.

Of the thirty-two poorest countries in the world in the *2009 Human Development Index*, thirty are in Sub-Saharan Africa and the five countries with the lowest levels of human development (except Afghanistan) in the 2009 rankings are all in Africa: Niger, Central African Republic, Mali, Burkina Faso, and Sierra Leone. Twenty out of fifty-three countries in Africa have been witnessing a frightening and heart-wrenching decline in the standard of living of their citizens since the 1990s. The average people in these countries are poorer now than they were in the last decade. In eleven African countries, more people go hungry than they did a decade ago. It is a tragedy that many people live in Africa without access to the basic necessities of life like water, electricity, education, healthcare services and food; it is a tragedy that the margins of the life of comfort in the Western world

---

41. Meredith, *Fate of Africa*, 682. See also Sachs, *Investing in Development*, 15.

42 O'Brien and Williams, *Global Political Economy*, 255.

43. See "Human Development Report."

merely intersect in a parallel way with the squalor that is witnessed in many African societies. Some of the most important issues which have caused poverty in Africa in the last two decades are: the impact of HIV/AIDS, tuberculosis, and malaria, the debt crisis, foreign aid, international trade, rapid population, ecological crisis and climate changes which has led to drought, and low rainfall in many regions, food insecurity and scarcity, urbanization and unemployment, defor-estation and environmental degradation, marginalization of women in development process, domestic and international conflicts, global economic crisis and unstable world economy, structural adjustment program and the role of the World Bank, the IMF, the UN, the African Union, and internal problems of poor management and inefficiency among other factors in specific African countries, poor agricultural techniques, and the absence of science and technology, food crisis, soaring energy prices, and the use of modern means of communica-tion among others.[44] We cannot address all these causes of poverty in Africa, but it is important to point at the danger of the HIV/AIDS pandemic, malaria, illiteracy and racism and the effects of economic globalization which all have impacts on Africa poverty.

HIV/AIDS AND MALARIA

HIV/AIDS continues to undermine all development initiatives in Africa. From the available statistics, Africa is at the epicenter of this global pandemic. Africa makes up about 12 percent of world popu-lation, but it accounts for the highest global proportion of AIDS-infected population.[45] According to the *2008 Report on the Global Aids Epidemic,* the global target of 2015 as the year of moving close as possible towards universal access to HIV prevention, treatment, care, and support may not be attained in Africa if serious efforts are not made by Africans and the international community to aggressively wage war against this pandemic.[46] The overall number of people living with HIV has increased as a result of ongoing number of new infec-tions each year and the beneficial effects of more widely available anti-

44. DeLancey, "Economies of Africa," 124–25.
45. See April Gordon, "Population, Urbanisation," 223–30.
46. UNAIDS, *2008 Report.*

retroviral therapy. Sub-Saharan Africa is the most heavily affected by HIV accounting for 67 percent of all people living with HIV and for 72 percent of AIDS deaths in 2007. The report also observed the stabilization of infectious rates in Africa for the first time since 2007, but in some other African countries the infection has jumped up for example in Kenya where it increased from 6.7 percent in 2003 to between 7.1 percent and 8.5 percent in 2007. In the worst hit African country of Swaziland, life expectancy has plummeted from sixty years in 1990 to thirty years in 2009.[47] Of the estimated 2.0 million children under fifteen living with AIDS globally 90 percent live in Sub-Saharan Africa. The report also notes that women are most at risk in Africa because of cultural, economic, health, and social reasons that make women dependent on men. Improving the capacity of African women to become part of the economic process through empowerment will help reduce the economic pressures that make women vulnerable.

According to UNAIDS, almost thirteen million people are at risk of starvation in six Southern African countries—Lesotho, Malawi, Mozambique, Swaziland, Zambia, and Zimbabwe. A combination of factors is at play here ranging from drought, floods, and a lack of adequate manpower; there is also the lack of consumer protection, the selling of food reserves, misguided governance and political instability among others. With the alarming rate of HIV in these countries where human resources are critical in reenergizing and stimulating the agricultural sector, the fact that HIV/AIDS strips bare the farmer, the farm-worker households as well as the agricultural extension workers and the state personnel unfolds a scene of hunger, starvation and hopelessness.

In the hardest-hit countries, the epidemic has wiped out decades of progress made in health, education, and social development. If the rate of spread continues in Africa, a majority of today's fifteen-year-olds will not reach their sixtieth birthday. In the six hardest-hit countries in Southern Africa, the life expectancy has plummeted radically to forty-nine years (thirteen years lower than it was before the outbreak of this horrible epidemic). The epidemic affects all sectors of life in Africa, including the business sector, which suffers from absenteeism in the number of people who are sick, organizational disruption, loss

47. See IRN Plus News: Global HIV/AIDS News and Analysis: www.plusnews .org/ReportID=86161.

of skills, and the increasing cost of funerals. In Kenya, for instance, 400 people die everyday from AIDS. "With education and prevention program starved for funds, access to medications is limited to the very rich or the very fortunate, victimization of the infected all too common, Africa and the international community failed to halt the spread of this disease, or ease the suffering and economic and social devastation it has wrought."[48] Of the estimated thirty-four million orphans living in Africa, more than eleven million under the age of fifteen living in sub-Saharan Africa have been robbed of one or both parents by HIV/AIDS. This represents 12 percent of the population of children in Africa. Seven years from now, according to UNICEF's estimates, their number will grow to twenty million, meaning that at that time on average about 20 percent of all children living in Africa would be orphans. "Orphaned children are disadvantaged in numerous and often devastating ways. In addition to the trauma of witnessing the sickness and death of one or both parents, they are likely to be poorer and less healthy than non-orphans are. They are more likely to suffer damage to their cognitive and emotional development, less likely to go to school, and more likely to be subjected to the worst forms of child labor. Survival strategies such as eating less and selling assets intensify the vulnerability of both adults and children."[49]

Some skeptics ask whether the figures of African mortality and infection were deliberately inflated to breed negative views of the continent. Perhaps thousands of Africans are dying from the same diseases that killed their parents and grandparents. This line of thought, however, flies in the face of the reality. This was the kind of argument brought forward by former South African President, Thabo Mbeki, that HIV was not the virus that causes AIDS. This porous argument misled many of his countrymen and women who could have been saved from the deadly disease. There are also many untested myths about this disease, and some empty religious claims that spiritual forces and charms could protect one from contracting the disease, and could also cure one who contracts it. It is ridiculous in this day and age and a scandal that many religious leaders in Christianity use the supposed cure of AIDS as a testimony to their supernatural power and healing gifts. While, we cannot under-estimate what the Good Lord

48. See UNICEF, *Orphaned Generations*, 1.
49. Ibid.

can do, it is important that we do not tempt God or mislead our young people in Africa with false promises of quick cures and protection.

The truth must be told that Africa is in the midst of a continental calamity of apocalyptical consequences, if it is not controlled. HIV/AIDS is killing more Africans than the many wars fought in the continent within the last four decades put together. "The disease fractures and impoverishes families, weakens work forces, turns millions into orphans and threatens social and economic fabric of communities and the political stability of nations."[50] No meaningful and sustainable development can occur if the AIDS epidemic is allowed to drain the human resources of Africa. According to UNAIDS, if allowed to go unchecked, HIV/AIDS weakens the capacity of households, communities, institutions and nations to cope with the social and economic effects of the epidemic. Productive capacities—including the informal sector are eroded as workers and managers fall prey to the disease. Flagging consumption, along with the loss of skills and capacities in turn drains public revenue and undermines the state's ability to serve the common interest of development and human well-being.

This cycle is both dynamic and vicious. It is the poor who are edged further towards the margins and exclusion as the worsening social indicators in countries with serious AIDS epidemic reveal. Unfortunately, the endless civil strife in many African countries is worsened by the economic and social crises precipitated by this epidemic. HIV/AIDS thrives amid social displacement and disintegration. The food emergency sweeping through Southern Africa highlights how vulnerable countries are to shocks that disrupt food production.

The global economic crisis has also seriously impacted on the prevention, care, and support of people living with AIDS and those who are HIV positive. According to the report, *The Global Economic Crisis and HIV Prevention and Treatment Programs: Vulnerabilities and Impact*,[51] there are shortages to antiretroviral drugs and other disruptions to AIDS treatment in those countries that are home to more than 60 percent of people worldwide receiving AIDS treatment. In thirty-four countries with 75 percent of the people living with HIV there is already significant impact on HIV prevention programs. The global

50. Skard, *Continent*, 31.
51. UNAIDS, *Global Economic*.

economic crisis all which made a new social encyclical necessary has severe and negative impacts on Africa with food shortages, the drop in aid and donor assistance, and the weakening of community support networks for people suffering from AIDS. It also threatens the availability of antiretroviral drugs due to falling revenues and budget cuts. There is the need to sustain the prevention and treatment regimen that have stabilized this pandemic in most countries in Africa through a greater commitment to the 2001 Declaration of Commitment. Africa is also the continent where the political Declaration on HIV of 2006 is not being applied. The protocol is aimed at removing the stigma, shame, and pain of those who have HIV and to help to encourage voluntary screening so that everyone will know their HIV status and still be treated with dignity and respect. This disease should not be treated as death sentence for those who are found to be positive. Some of the rights guaranteed to HIV patients which are not being implemented in Africa are: non-discrimination, right to privacy, right to liberty and freedom of movement, right to education (sexual and reproductive health information), and right to health (access to all health care prevention services, including for sexually transmitted infections, tuberculosis, voluntary counseling and testing, among others).

While HIV/AIDS is the disease that gets all the attention in Africa, malaria has indeed been the greatest cause of deaths in Africa. Every year malaria, spread through mosquito bites, results in 300 to 500 million clinical cases and causes more than one million deaths in Africa. 90 percent of annual deaths from malaria occur in Africa. It is mainly children under the age of five who have not yet built up a strong immunity like the adults, who die of this disease, which kills about 3000 African children every day. Malaria also contributes to high maternal morbidity and mortality, and leaves most children and mothers who survive the sickness with other related ailments that hinder their healthy growth and well-being.

GLOBALIZATION AND AFRICAN DEVELOPMENT

> *Three years ago, former Tanzanian President Julius Nyerere asked the question "Must we starve our children to pay our debts?" That question has now been answered in practice. And the answer is "yes." In those three years, hundreds of thousands*

of the developing world's children have given their lives to pay their countries debts, and many millions more are still paying the interest with their malnourished minds and bodies . . . Today, the heaviest burden of a decade of frenzied borrowing is falling not on the military or on those with foreign bank accounts or on those who conceived the years of waste, but on the poor who are having to do without necessities . . . on the women who do not have enough food to maintain their health, on the infants whose minds and bodies are not growing properly . . . on the children who are being denied their only opportunity ever to go to school.

—Peter Adamson, *The State of the World's Children,* 1989.

There is no clear definition of the meaning of globalization. A workshop organized in June 2004 by the Center for the Study of Globalization and Regionalization of the University of Warwick, United Kingdom,[52] came out with some very interesting conclusions. In the first place, different disciplines have had different trajectories of globalization studies. In sociology, globalization studies developed as a reaction against world-system theory as a framework of thinking about trans-national social structure and world-scale social change. In international relations, globalization would entail a study of the state-centric orthodoxy of political realism. In economics, the concern in engagement with globalization is on the dynamics and operation of the forces of international trade and finances buoyed by neo-liberal currents.

As Jonathan Sacks points out, "Global capitalism is a system of immense power, from which it has become increasingly difficult for nations to dissociate themselves. More effectively than armies, it has won a battle against rival systems and ideologies, among them fascism, communism and socialism, and has emerged as the dominant option in the twenty-first century for countries seeking economic growth. Quite simply, it delivered what its alternatives merely promised: higher living standards and greater freedom."[53] According to Sacks, today the time frame is considerably shorter than a single life span. Change has become the texture of modern life. This change is often interpreted in some circles as progress, which gives credence to the charm and power of neo-liberalism to order the world in a certain

52. This study could be found in www.csgr.org.
53. Sacks, *Dignity of Difference,* 25–26.

way. However, many Western thinkers and the harbingers of the glories of globalization have not often interpreted the intentionality of the forces of globalization. What does one understand as progress in a world where over twenty-two million children go to bed without food and 840 million people are starving; in a world where over a billion people lack water and 1.2 billion others lack adequate housing; where the wealth of three richest individuals on earth surpassed the combined annual GDP of the forty-eight least developed countries of the world; where fifteen richest individuals in the world enjoy a combined assets that exceed the total annual GDP of Sub-Saharan Africa[54]; in a world where millions of women do not have a right to authentic human existence; and in a world where there is an inversion of morality in politics, international relations, and in economics? Neo-liberal capitalism with its profit above people, unrestrained competition and the iron rule of uncontrolled free market is in dire need of reform the kind that Pope Benedict calls for in *Charity in Truth*.

Competition for profit and wealth-creation for the strong nations and companies of the world, have become blind to the millions of people who have been permanently destroyed because of the unrestrained forces of the free market economy. Protectionism has become a replacement for solidarity. Many poor countries of the world, as a result, will have to survive by eating the crumbs that fall from the tables of the rich. We need to pull down the idols of capitalism scattered all over the world. These idols make it possible for the lives of millions of people to be governed by a few companies and national interests. These, out of their greed inflict pain and suffering on millions of people around the world. According to the document, *There are Alternatives to Globalization*, prepared by the Justice, Peace and Creation Team of the World Council of Churches:

- The top three billionaires in the world hold asserts worth more than the combined GNP of all forty-eight least developed countries, with their population of some 600 million.

- The assets of the 200 richest people (over US$1 Trillion) are higher than the combined income of 41 percent of the world's people.

- The income gap between a fifth of the population in the world's

---

54. Quoted in Kobia, *Courage to Hope*, 207.

richest countries and a fifth in the poorest is growing at an ever-increasing rate. It took thirty years for the ratio to double from 30 to 1 in 1960, to 60 to 1 in 1990, but it jumped up to 74 to 1 in 1997. The wealth gap is also widening in the rich countries too.

- About 1.5 billion people live in absolute poverty at the beginning of the new millennium. It would take just 55 percent of the wealth of the richest 225 people in the world to provide food, shelter, basic health care, and education to every one in the world who lacks access to these basic needs.

- Just 100 trans-national corporations based in the highly industrialized countries are the driving force for economic globalization. Of all trade 70 percent takes place within and between them. They generate 80 percent of foreign direct investment and own one fifth of all foreign-owned assets; however, they employ less than 3 percent of the world's labor force.

The free market will not save the lives of millions who are dying of poverty and suffering in many parts of the world especially in Africa. The end result of the free market should constantly be scrutinized to see that it meets the requirements of the common good. Indeed, the international free market regime that has elevated private property and capital over the human person does not meet the requirements of natural law, social justice, and the universal common good. Africa is one continent that is being suffocated in the heat of capitalism. Her life and history within the last four centuries have been defined by the pain brought upon her by capitalism. This destruction is ongoing through privatization of public services, the contagion of globalization, the debt burden, and trade restrictions among others. This makes even fellow Africans allies in the conspiracy of destruction of the ordinary people and their national wealth. Many Africans believe that the traditional African sense of community has some elements of capitalism because it allows for competition. However, it has a deep sense of solidarity, communalism, social conscience, and morality that saves people from the blunt edges of capitalism. Capitalism is the mother of corruption in Africa and it is the father that sired the negative attitude of distancing on the part of the Western world to the plight of Africa. The truth is that helping Africa does not make sense in the capitalist calculation of the hawks and priests of the free market economic god in the industrialized world. This is because such help and generosity do not immediately translate into any financial profit.

It is a shame, for instance, that some Western companies, supported by their national governments, will supply weapons of war to rebel groups in Africa and then cry out against the killings at the same time. How did the rebels in most African countries get their weapons and bombs (which are not made in Africa)? The obnoxious trade in diamonds between Sierra Leone, Liberia, and some Western companies was the main stay for the weaponization of sub-Saharan rebel groups in places like Liberia and Sierra Leone. The people of Rwanda and Darfur would have been saved from self-destruction if they had oil like Iraq or if they were strategically positioned like Pakistan or Afghanistan. Available statistics show for example that Iraq, Afghanistan, and Pakistan are among the U.S top ten recipient of aid because of their central role in the war on terror and not because of their poverty.

The debt burden, which hangs over African nations, has remained one of the greatest obstacles to any meaningful economic development in Africa. Sub-Saharan Africa's debt represents 180 percent of exports; debt-servicing drains 12–13 percent of export receipts on average. The failure of most Western nations to forgive these debts is only a sign of the destructive nature of unbridled capitalism. These debts cannot bring any real boost to the economies of the Western countries if they were repaid—they would not make any tangential bearing on the GDP of Western countries—while servicing them alone is squeezing Africa of over 71 percent of her GDP! Africa's debt burden is unsustainable given the fact that it has grown from 30.7 percent of Africa's GNP in 1980 to 82.8 percent in 1994. Most of the African countries are bankrupt and cannot kick start any kind of development initiatives without some major commitment of aid from international agencies and governments. Unfortunately, the official development assistance (ODA) from most of the G8 countries to Africa averages a little above 0.30 percent of their GDP and has gone down in the 1990s from $28.6 billion to $16.4 billion a year. If capitalism, as it is conceived and practiced today, continues to set the tone for the process of world history, we risk destroying our species in the blaze of competition. Those most likely to suffer from brazen competition are the poor, vulnerable, powerless, and defenseless people all over the world, the majority of whom live in Africa. Most of them are dying everyday because their governments daily pay $100 million to Western creditors in a world where an elite of fewer than a billion people controls 80 percent of humanity's wealth. So how can we claim progress in this kind of world?

Progress could only be found in such a world through the lenses of autistic thinkers, who do not feel the pain of millions in Africa and Asia; and the minority and disempowered groups and peoples in Western industrial nations, who suffer because of historical factors and the presence of unjust structures globally and locally. According to Taye Assefa et al., "Rather than benefit all actors relatively equally, by its very nature, globalization tends to produce gains for the powerful at the expense of the relatively weak. The economic inequalities and power imbalances among different actors in the global economy, translate into the uneven distribution of opportunities, constraints and vulnerabilities. Side by side with the inequitable distribution of wealth and power is the inability of the poor and weak to influence world affairs since the decision-making arena is usually a monopoly of the powerful."[55]

The hegemony of globalization has become increasingly questioned in many forums. The optimism engendered by this phenomenon in so many parts of the world and the predominant ideology of neo-liberalism (e.g., science, technology, rationality, wealth, power, and human triumph), which is the propelling shaft around which globalization revolves have come under increasing scrutiny. This has been pioneered, especially in groups like the World Social Forum, Jubilee Coalition, Global South movements and counter-globalization voices in the West, who argue that an alternative world is still possible. This alternative world will be one that rejects the ideologies of a free market that has left African countries with over $345.2 billion debt representing a daily repayment value of $379 for every man and woman living in Africa.[56] Given that most Africans live on less than $1 a day, it would take over 400 years for Africans to repay these debts to the multilateral or bilateral lending institutions and governments. Africa's debt represents 180 percent of her exports; for every dollar that Africa receives in foreign aid, the continent sends

55. Assefa et al., "Introduction," vii.
56. See Collins, "Jubilee," 15.

back $1.51 in debt repayment. The quantum debt servicing profile of most African countries has gone beyond the money they borrowed in the first place. Nigeria, for instance, borrowed $5 billion and has paid by mid-2004 $16 billion and still owes $32 billion.[57] The idea of progress brought on as a result of globalization does not make sense to me as an African, nor does it offer any hope for a better future for Africans, as we shall demonstrate.

As Noreena Hertz has argued so well, African countries like other developing countries cannot make any significant progress with the albatross of debt hanging around their neck:

> Botswana, in which 40 percent of adults are now HIV-positive, pays more today on debt servicing than it can afford to pay on health care or provision. Niger, the country with the highest rate of child mortality in the world, continues to spend more on debt servicing than on public health. Countries that can't afford to provide basic health care, education, or shelter to their people have to use their pitiful resources, including, in many cases, all their aid flows, to repay debts typically racked up by authoritarian, unelected regimes long since gone. Children in Africa die every day because their governments are spending more on debt servicing than they are on health or education.[58]

One cannot engage globalization discourse without understanding its claims and inner logic. That means understanding its various manifestations; the sometimes-deceptive logic around this phenomenon and its unjust structural rough edges. According to Stackhouse, globalization is not only an economic phenomenon, "globalization is in fact a vast social, technological, communications, and structural change laden with ethical perils and promises as great as those brought about by the ancient rise, and subsequent fall, of the ancient empires, the later development and then demise of feudalism, the still later rise of modernity with its nationalisms and recent industrial revolutions, and their decline."[59]

Globalization as a phenomenon cannot be easily defined—references to it are often connected with its manifestations. Globalization is not, for instance, a policy of any organization, nor does one read a

57. See Wiwa, "Money for Nothing," A19. See also the online African social justice online news channel, www.pambazuka.org.

58. Hertz, The Debt Threat, 3.

59. Stackhouse, "Social Gospel," 151.

blueprint on globalization by governments (even though policies of empire-building can reflect underneath them a globalizing tendency as could be seen in the unilateralism of the administration of George W. Bush). There is no given definition of the content of globalization by organizations and agencies and the powerful financial institutions like the World Bank, World Trade Organization (WTO), and the International Monetary Fund (IMF) described by Richard Peet as "unholy trinity."[60] International conglomerates that spread the evils of neo-liberal capitalism around the world also offer no definition of globalization.

Globalization could only be described as the reality that is emerging in which the whole world in the words of Roland Robertson *is becoming one place.* This goes beyond economics. Globalization currents generate a vast, world-wide complex of extremely diversified, highly unpredictable, rapidly changing dynamics that comprehend and transform every particular contextual reality and creates the fragile prospect of a global civilization, one more complex and differentiated than the world has ever known, one that adopts traditional diversities into its ever-extending net, one that has no obvious singularly, coherent center.[61]

In the light of the foregoing analysis, we should adopt a hermeneutics of suspicion in interpreting this phenomenon in Africa. I do not think that globalization is the cause of all the problems of Africa. However, there is no African problem today that can be understood without engaging globalization discourse. The man or woman on the streets and village alleys of Africa would blame the run-away inflation that is squeezing the life out of the populace on the government of the day. While one should hold African leaders responsible for their failed leadership, one should also observe that some of the factors making it possible for African leaders to be the kind of leaders they are can be traced to the forces of globalization. The kind of harsh economic conditions that the IMF and the World Bank impose on African economies can only be applied in dictatorial regimes that are not accountable to the people.

There are six main claims of globalization in Africa, which have shaped the direction of African development since the post-colonial

60. Peet, *Unholy Trinity.*

61. Stackhouse, "Globalization."

era. I will outline these claims and then focus on how these claims have been framed into economic policies in Africa, using Nigeria as an example, while engaging other African voices in the dialogue. I will further do a hermeneutics of these claims.

1. *Integration into the Global Market.* Africa needs to be integrated into the global market so that she can claim her place in the new world order. To this end, the economic recommendations of the *Washington Consensus* are applied with determination by the World Bank and the IMF in Africa. These recommendations include privatization, lower tariffs, devaluation of national currency, increased foreign investment, less inflation and tighter budgets. M. A. Mohamed Salih points out that this kind of reasoning is built on a neo-liberal capitalist paradigm, which holds that the global economy, regardless of social or political consequences, will be most efficient in the long-term if dominated by free market forces. He points out four characteristics of the neo-liberal economic globalization[62]: (1) a relentless advocacy of market efficiency as a foundation for social order, conceiving market forces as more objective than social values; (2) an apparent unease with social justice and welfare, which it views as a hindrance to market freedom; (3) a critical posture of state intervention to correct market failure, which it considers a limiting factor to what it perceives as the more efficient market forces; and (4) a disenchantment with subsidy, which does not allow for the control of the prices of basic needs making it impossible for the poor and vulnerable to suffer from the run-away prices of essential goods and services, which are left to the insensitive free market pricing regimen.

These characteristics are framed into all forms of attempts to enthrone a privatization policy that effectively destroys the possibility of survival for the weak and the poor, while maximizing profits for corporate interests and global financial institutions. Salih argues that the interest of Africa is not protected by these economic proposals. On the contrary, free market competition within the global market is structured to protect the interest of the formidable regional trading blocs like the European Union, the North American Free Trade Agreement (NAFTA) and the G8, with their UN-based major multilateral actors normally referred to as the international community. He concludes by noting that the attempt to integrate Africa into the global economy

62. Salih, "Globalization," 63–65.

has adversely affected African economies and societies leaving it with, "worsening living standards, high and rising poverty and malnutrition levels. In human terms, Africa's economic crisis also meant declining social sector expenditures, falling schools enrolment ratios, and the persistence of a high rate of infant and maternal mortality."[63] Africa can only be integrated into the global market when it can promote the human security of her people and when she meets these three prerequisites: when she can sustain a high level of economic and industrial development satisfying the basic human needs of her populations; when she has developed a global economic and technological reach; and when she has acquired the capacity to compete in the international market, because her economies are no longer susceptible to the crushing power of economic pressure exerted on the global market by the big powers.[64]

At the G8 Summit in Gleneagles in the summer of 2005, it was agreed that successful development in Africa requires sustained and consistent progress across a range of areas, which were identified as impeding the integration of Africa into the global market. The core areas include strengthening peace and security, better governance, improved healthcare and education, enhanced growth, access to markets and capacity to trade.

Unfortunately, the G8 has always been long in proposals and short in concrete action. Since the Birmingham Summit in 1998, the G8 has always presented itself as addressing Africa's problems and that of the developing world, but it has failed to address the structural basis of poverty and inequality in the world, which is rooted in the various agencies that serve the interest of the G8 (IMF, World Bank, and WTO). The G8's call for good government in Africa is always an attempt to divest the control of basic services like water, healthcare, agriculture, and manufacturing into the hands of private Western companies or the propping of dictators in Africa as long as they danced to the tune of Western powers. Many Africans have not forgotten that great African visionaries like Patrice Lumumba of Congo-Kinshasa, Kwame Nkrumah of Ghana, Murtala Muhammed of Nigeria, Thomas Sankara of Burkina Faso, and Sylvio Olympio of Togo were all assassinated by Western agents working with their African turncoats, who

63. Ibid., 65.
64. Ibid., 69.

in turn replaced them with dictators. In the case of Patrice Lumumba, his body was melted in acid as a reminder to future African revolutionaries of the fate that awaits an African leader, who stands in the way of Western economic interest, which are introduced into Africa under different guises.

In an impressive article in *The Guardian* (London), George Monbiot decried the deceptions of the G8 (now G20) with regard to the African condition. He exposed what many Africans are long convinced of: The West does not care about true and lasting peace, progress, and development in Africa whether with regard to debt cancellation, trade promotion, immigration restriction, industrialization, or capacity-building. According to Monbiot, nine days after the G8 Summit in July 2005, the United States announced a pact with Australia, China, and India which undermined the Kyoto Protocol on climate change; on August 2, 2005, leaked documents from the World Bank showed that the G8 had not in fact granted 100 percent debt relief to eighteen countries (fourteen of which are in Africa), but had promised enough money only to write off their repayments for the next three years. On August 3, 2005, the UN revealed that only one third of the money needed for famine relief in Niger, and 14 percent of the money needed by Mali had been pledged by the rich nations.[65] The underlying truth here is that Africa should not be blamed for her failure to prosper like the rest of the world, when there are structures of sin and injustice in the global market that make it impossible for Africa to stand before she can even walk and work with the international global hawks.

2. *Institutional Reform*. This claim holds that internal factors in Africa are largely responsible for Africa's underdevelopment. Africa, therefore, needs a radical reform of her institutions at all levels for her to "catch up" with the rest of the world.[66] This is perhaps one of the most deceptive claims of neo-liberal capitalists. Many Africans and non-Africans have also bought into this kind of mindset that Africa's institutions are largely to blame for the failed development models in Africa. The New Partnership for Africa's Development (NEPAD), for

---

65. Quoted in *Guardian* (6 September 2005) 21.

66. This point of view is strongly promoted in African countries that many African countries are denied loan facilities and are not allowed access to the so-called debt relief program of the Heavily Indebted Poor Country (HIPC) initiatives.

instance, is conditioned on both institutional and economic reforms—another word for structural adjustment. However, these institutional reforms being recommended are often interpreted as Western-type democracy or economic orthodoxies of the World Bank and the IMF. These political models are proposed to Africans without regard to contexts and with utter disregard of established patterns of politics and economics.

Globalization is a continuation of Western imperialism that goes back to the slave trade. This becomes more painful when it has ramified into cultural and anthropological discourses that deny African identity and an authentic and differentiated African way of life. Globalization is based on a wrong anthropology that the human person is what he consumes, produces, or possesses. The African institutional structure advances the whole community and is built on a *universal-specificism* that accepts the primacy of the community (universal) but respects the particular.

The kind of governments that we have in sub-Saharan Africa is not built on participatory democracy as we have argued. Institutional reforms cannot come about with the emergence of *constitutional democracy* but a *participatory popular democracy*. Such democracy has to be worked out in African countries through dialogue and not by any Western blue print. African countries all had constitutional democracies after independence, but they all failed, because they were not participatory democracies. The kind of constitutional democracy that is being proposed in most African countries by the international financial institutions is the one that disempowers the people. Thus, the government is neither accountable to the people, nor do the people take part in the formation of policies that affect their lives. It is this kind of constitutional democracies that produce capitalist champions in governments who can literally buy their respective countries, and parcel away their national interest and wealth without due consideration for the suffering of the people and the future of the children. The same could be said of the economic reforms being proposed by the IMF and the World Bank.

According to *Trans-Africa Forum on Globalization Monitor,*[67] all economic reforms proposed in Africa within the last two decades by SAP, the Heavily Indebted Poor Country program (HIPC), the

67. *TransAfrica Forum,* 2.

Poverty Reduction Strategy Papers (PRSP), and the US Africa Growth and Opportunity Act (AGOA) have the same kind of logic: a tread-mill of endless structural adjustments and debt burden; the belief that Africans do not have the sophistication to draw sound policies and so need to be helped by the IMF and the World Bank; and a glaring disregard for the local conditions and cultural life. The result has been that young people are being pushed into working as unskilled, low-income earners for Western companies in Africa; the best land in Africa is being used to grow cash export crops like cotton, cocoa, tobacco, and flowers and not for growing much needed food crops. According to Jean-Marc Ela, it is this kind of situation that makes it possible for Cameroonian peasants to become mere objects in the hands of international conglomerates:

> In that tropical region where farmers reap but one harvest a year, where sowing is always difficult, and where women and children live in a state of chronic famine, thousands of peasants are being forced to pull up millet that is just sprouting and to plant cotton in its place. In societies where millet is the staple, that deed forced upon landless peasants is a veritable dagger in the heart. It is all done so quietly, under the watchful eye of the agricultural monitors employed by a large development company investing in cash crops.[68]

Governments in Africa, in order to meet their debt obligation and earn some foreign exchange to maintain the barest basic services, have to promote this kind of economic order in Africa. Africans are then blamed for failed economic policies, while in effect these policies, in their conception and execution, were doomed to fail, because of their inherent contradictions and unjust superstructure. All Western-induced economic policies in Africa are doomed to fail because they are not development paradigms directed at grassroots development, but are top-down policies that are aimed at redressing economic imbalance and forcing Africa into the global market to "be like the rest"[69] of the world, when she is not yet ready for such integration. They do not address the development needs of Africans, nor do they have any

68. Ela, *African Cry*, v.

69. The Oversea Development Council (ODC) of the United Kingdom commissioned some African writers and foreigners who buy into this kind of thinking to produce series of publications that try to argue for a new African institutional configuration for development. See Van De Walle et al., *Beyond Structural.*

relevance to the integrated vision of development, which the total picture approach model that we proposed in the last chapter advances.

3. Globalization is an irreversible process that needs to be confronted not by withdrawal but by engagement if Africa is to progress and "be like the rest of the world" and, as a result, reverse the marginalization that she has endured since the late 1960s.[70] This is perhaps one of the strongest and most unrealistic claims of the agents of neoliberal capitalism. There is no economic process in the world that is irreversible or perfect. Capitalism has a history that is rooted in the triumph of property and capital over the human person. Ownership of property and capital conferred power over those who did not own much. Feudalism and monarchy thrived well under capitalism. David Hume, who advocated the existence of government in order to guarantee the rights of people to property and capital, and avert the "war of all against all" in the battle for survival, would be turning in his grave to see how most international financial institutions and conglomerates squabble with each other for interest, without any governmental control, to the detriment of the ordinary people. The most undemocratic institutions in the world are the Security Council, the IMF, the World Bank, and the WTO, because they make decisions that affect the lives of a majority of the people in the world, with no semblance of democracy or participation of the people whose fate they shape. Unfortunately, many governments in Africa have bought into this argument and are mortgaging the future of the continent by joining an international market system that has no place for Africa except to be "hewers of wood and cutters of grass."

4. Setting Goals for Development. The United Nations Millennium Development Goals (MDG) are aimed at bringing the gains of globalization to all countries of the world, especially in Africa. I would say that I find it hard to fit the UN into one trajectory of globalization or another. Viewed in one light, it has been the greatest sign of the possibility of humanity to work together for the common good of all. It has been a center for the articulation of shared concerns and for mutual action for the poor and weak against the wealth and the strong. However, viewed in another light, it represents the negative side of globalization because the main decisions of that body is made by the Security Council, especially the five permanent members, whose

70. See Elbadawi and Geleb, "Financing," 36

decisions on war and peace, trade and security are determinative of the shape and movement of the world. The UN is largely to blame for the failure of humanitarian aid during conflicts in Nigeria in the late 1960s, in Saharawi Arab Republic and Chad in the 1980s, in Rwanda and Congo in the 1990s, and in the Sudan in the past four decades. The scandals that rocked the UN in early 2005, exposing the corruption in the Oil-for-food Program for Iraq, the acts of rapes carried out in Congo-Kinshasa by UN peacekeepers, and the sexual scandals that rocked the UN's humanitarian agency, show also that the UN, like all other human institutions, is not error-proof. Its proposals for Africa should always be chewed carefully before they are swallowed by Africans.

The UN has failed to stem the rampaging devastation of the IMF, the World Bank, and the WTO. It appears that the UN was not formed with Africa in mind, because by the time it was established most African countries were under the domination of the same Western powers who use the UN to advance their national interests. The war in Iraq, which the US carried out without a UN mandate, is a clear example of the weakness of that international body. Unfortunately, as Robert Kagan rightly observes,

> This enduring American view of their nation's exceptional place in history, their conviction that their interests and the world's interest are one, may be welcomed, ridiculed, or lamented. But it should not be doubted. And just as there is little reason to expect Europe to change its fundamental course, there is little cause to believe the United States will change its own course, or begin to conduct itself in the world in a fundamentally different manner . . . Absent some unforeseen catastrophe . . . it is reasonable to assume that we have only just entered a long era of American hegemony.[71]

Globalization appears to have found its home in North America as well as in Europe and the emerging Asian economic bulldozers, i.e., China, Japan, Indonesia, Malaysia, India, and Taiwan.

In Africa many agents of international financial organizations and their African sympathizers frame UN Millennium Development Goals within the terms of globalizing forces. The UN goals are sometimes unrealistic, but they help to energize nations to work for some

---

71. Kagan, *Paradise and Power*, 89.

positive changes in their countries by establishing some benchmarks. How this is worked out is often a big challenge in Africa, where no real progress could be made, because of the structural injustice of the global economy. This is a very fundamental issue. Trade barriers against Africa and government subsidies of local goods in the industrialized nations make it difficult for African countries to compete in the international market. African countries have to devalue their currency and lower the prices of their products, which in turn destroy their economy. The redemptive infusion of capital into the African market by the IMF and the World Bank has been a chimera of economic recovery.

5. *Implement Effective Systems of Support for Development.* This claim holds that the decline in aid to Africa has been brought about by the failure of African countries to build an appropriate framework and system for working with the international development agencies. Africa is a failed partner with the international financial markets and donor agencies. There is no attempt made to expose the failure of these institutions, their lack of accountability, and their institutional framework vis-à-vis Africa. The IMF, the World Bank, and the WTO have internal structural incoherence; their modus operandi is flawed with regard to cooperation with African economies. However, the argument is aggressively pursued that they should be directly involved in private and public capital flow and supervising domestic policies in Africa. There is no single nation in Africa whose economy has been saved by these institutions and the blame should not be laid solely on the doorsteps of African countries.

6. *Legislate Long-term Economic Policies.* Africa needs a long-term economic policy, which would offer her sustainable economic development. Globalization offers African countries the opportunity of broadening their vision beyond the limited scope of immediate needs and disengagement from African regional groupings, which are collapsing because of the forces of globalization. African economic groups are indirectly stymied by these international financial organizations.

Globalization presents a lot of challenges to African countries. There is the mind-pollution through the internet and the cable systems; there are the cheap encryption programs on the internet that make trans-national crimes a seething cesspool. Many people are worried at many phony emails purportedly originating from Africa, offering fake contracts and money transfers. Globalization has also wiped out the middle class in Africa and destroyed the moral fiber of young Africans, as it has spread unwholesome Western tendencies like pornography, online prostitution, and impersonal life styles to most of Africa's young people. Globalization[72] has not provided answers to a universal social justice agenda, the growing illiteracy in some developing countries, especially in Africa, or to the existence of dictatorial regimes in Africa and how to resuscitate decrepit state economies. There is also the challenge of curbing the power and magic of the media and the issue of threatened cultural traditions of people and disappearing national identity in many Africa countries and how to lift up the millions of Africans suffering from the time-crusted mud of poverty.

African governments and people must pay attention to the intentionality of this new reality, which is based on a superstructure of deception and on an anti-African ideology, which goes beyond the economic. Globalization and the debt burden in Africa are structures of sin, because they are invisible forces that promote unequal development; they take away the ability of African peoples to take control of their lives; and they sustain a well-tailored pattern of economic, political and cultural enchainment of the African peoples. They also destroy, invisibly, the lives of millions of Africans and spread poverty and suffering to peoples by subletting human needs for economic profits, making the rich richer and the poor poorer. Globalization has become a kind of monstrous behemoth defying control, rampaging economies of Africa and other developing countries in what Claude Ake calls "antinomies of peripheral development." It has become a giant spider at the hub of an inter-continental economic web of wheeling and dealing, with an over-weaning suction pipe placed at the fountain of African economic and cultural life. It has also distorted the aim of knowledge and education globally, making them serve the interest of economics and Western linear-progressive view of history, and undercutting the religious and cultural life of many people.

Globalization is not the measuring rod that will equalize the economic imbalances in the world, nor is it the moral antiseptic that will salve the decaying moral platform of the world. The trade

---

72. Fergin, "Buzzword."

liberalization and privatization advocated by agents of globalization have destroyed African economies by leaving the fate of millions in the hands of greedy conglomerates. The world is not free from the dangers of an economic meltdown as a result of the absolute faith in the triumph of the free market. Similar financial complacency, in 1929, led to the Depression of that year, with the collapse of the US stock market and Wall Street. The free market cannot sustain a just world unless international financial organizations, multilateral agencies, and international conglomerates are globally held accountable. They should search for new ways that will allow peoples still underdeveloped to break through barriers, which seem to enclose them, and to discover for themselves in full fidelity to their own proper genius, the means for their social and human progress.[73]

In 1989, *African Alternative Framework for Structural Adjustment for Socio-Economic Recovery and Transformation,* a publication of the United Nations Economic Commission for Africa (UNECA), exposed the lies of the World Bank (in her publication *Africa's Adjustment and Growth in the 1980s* which tended to demonstrate the soundness of her economic policy of SAP for economic recovery). This has followed the same pattern in other parts of the world, because the World Bank and IMF have never been favorably disposed to other voices that challenge their neo-classical death-dealing economic theories for developing countries. A critical examination of these claims already reveals its lack of foundation. It does not take into consideration the local needs; it neglects the dynamic character of cultural traditions; it lacks a sense of history and is insensitive to the sufferings and poverty that suffocate the lives of millions of Africans. It is, to say the least, mercenary-motivated.

Claude Ake's *Democracy and Development in Africa*[74] is considered an African classical critique of the claims of globalization. His main argument is that democracy and development in Africa have not started. The institutional context of globalization in Africa is not so much the problem against globalization, but rather the reason why Africa does not need exogenous intervention in her economic life. The development paradigm from Western nations and financial institutions like the IMF and the World Bank fail in Africa, because

73. Paul VI, *Populorum*, 64.

74. Ake, *Democracy and Development*, 31–41.

they have an a priori negative conception of the African people and their economic life. The ideologies of globalization pay little heed to historical specificity and wrongly treat development as a way of connecting cultural, economic, institutional, and political contexts. These claims are the bases for different economic policies like the Structural Adjustment Program, the Poverty Reduction Strategy Papers, and the New Partnership for Africa's Development, which have been offered to Africa. In addition, they interpret the African society in economic categories, without regard to other aspects of life in Africa such as ecological issues, gender equality, grassroots democracy, ethnic diversities, cultural, and religious traditions of Africa, among others

According to the IMF, the Structural Adjustment Program targeted the integration of African economies into the global market as a way of solving the problem of poverty. The argument was that the root cause of poverty in Africa was found in the structural organization of her national economies. Among other things, SAP was supposed to help lower inflation rate, increase export, create an enabling environment for the development of agriculture and industrialization, relieve the debt burden, overcome public sector inefficiencies, and spread rationalization of many unwieldy and unprofitable parastatals.[75] Using Nigeria as a test case, one would immediately see the negative effects of globalization.

According to Ake, the economic policies of SAP reduced local control of the governments of Africa over their economies; it led to the production of primary agricultural products, which were exported while the local people suffered hunger. It reduced access to health care and basic social amenities with the withdrawal of subsidies from the government. It disempowered the small-scale farmers whose credit lines were cut by the national governments in order to check inflation. Basic services like water, electricity, and telecommunications were privatized making it impossible for the ordinary majority to benefit from them.[76] It is also significant that at the time of the implementation of SAP, most countries of Africa were under dictatorial rulers who, as in Nigeria, carried on with the austere measures of the IMF without regard to the groans of the populace. Indeed, this has been a constant tendency in Africa; the exogenous policies of the

75. *Newswatch*, 18.

76. *TransAfrican Forum*, 2.

international financial institutions are often imposed on the ordinary people without their counsel or consent.

Since her attempt to be integrated into the vast expanding global economic network, Nigeria, like most African countries, has experienced the worst policy incoherence of any country in the world. Her external debts have continued to increase, while the oil industry, the main stay of her economy, has witnessed the worst decay ever known since oil exploration started in the country in the late 1950s.[77] By the end of 2004, the Nigerian government came out with the conclusion that the country can no longer sustain her debts and cannot fulfill her debt serving from 2005 and beyond. Ake concludes that the exogenous agents of development conceive it in the framework of the global capitalist economy of liberal democracy. He sees this as undesirable and detrimental to local conditions.

In terms of African development and economic growth, the attempt at integrating Africa into the global economy will continue to be a failure. Neo-liberal globalization has brought destruction to Africa. I agree with Ake and many other perceptive African social scientists that Africa must take some steps away from the globalizing tendencies of neo-liberal capitalism, which tends to vertically connect Africa to the industrialized Western countries. Some of these proposals have already been adopted in the Lagos Plan of Action (1980) developed by African leaders and leading social scientists and economists from Africa (a plan rejected by the IMF as unrealistic). At that critical stage of economic crisis in Africa, this plan was a new development paradigm that was African-woven and grassroots-based and which bears a re-reading because it presents the vision of Africans for African development without Western interference.

According John A. Tesha,

> Although Africa has the potential to be the richest continent on earth, its present and future, like its past, remain the object of international manipulation, exploitation and ridicule. The solution to Africa's development dilemma thus lies squarely with Africans themselves. External partners can only supplement the efforts of the Africans; they cannot replace the initiatives of the African peoples and their leaders. Africa's capacity to address its own problems was clearly demonstrated during the liberation struggles, when African leaders and

77. Guyer et al., *Money Struggles*, xix.

peoples committed themselves and resolved to fight foreign domination in all forms including the dismantling of the racist apartheid regime of South Africa. The same determination and resolve should be marshaled to effectively respond to the contemporary challenges of globalization, marginalization, and exclusion.[78]

We wish to propose the following steps as an alternative route to economic growth and poverty alleviation in Africa:

- A human-centered approach that rejects completely any mechanistic classical neo-liberal economic orthodoxy.

- A holistic approach to socio-economic change. Human development does not subsist only on economic variables; rather change should be situated within the social, political, cultural, and economic values and institutions of Africa. The most solid foundation for lasting socio-economic development and progress is the infrastructure of human capital, especially those anchored on emerging skills midwifed by locally based science and technology.[79]

- The validity of any economic policy in Africa should be dependent on the validity and legitimacy of the structural nature of the political economy of specific African countries. It is also to be amplified by its viability at the village and grassroots level. "The activist groups that are alleviating poverty the most are those working at the local village level in places like rural India, Africa, and China and to spotlight and fight corruption and to promote accountability, transparency, education, and property rights."[80] It must be context sensitive and people-friendly. The application of economic paradigm without regard to context is destructive and defeats Africa's genuine thirst for integrated development.

- There is no "ready-made" economic policy that globalization offers which can solve any of the problems of Africa. Any development in Africa that is not specific to African context will perpetuate the tragedy of Africa, which is the deepest and most

78. Tesha, "Reminiscences and Personal Reflections," 16

79. See Anya, *Re-inventing Nigeria*, 20

80. Friedman, *World is Flat*, 389.

protracted crisis of modern history.[81]

- Africa's liberation from the negative effects of globalization will be in its ability to find its own unique voice and speak its own reality. There is the tendency in us all to lose ourselves and to compromise our identities in the presence of those perceived to be stronger than ourselves. The danger of economic globalization is that it so subtly, yet forcefully, defines for us who we are and what we need.[82]

The search for the common good of African communities and humanity as a whole should be what is primary in Africa's engagement with the global market. Africans should use their experience of globalization as a starting point for a dialogue on a viable alternative to her present crisis generated by globalization. Unfortunately, most Western nations and international lending groups predicate the granting of financial remedies to Africa on the adoption of the economic orthodoxies of these groups. The reason is always that Africa needs to be helped through some of these stringent conditions so that she might repay her debts. What Africa needs is not a rescheduling of debts but unconditional cancellation of her debts so that she can begin a new journey to sustainable development. The world today owes Africa a debt in justice more than Africa owes a debt in capital. Why should the G8, the Paris Club, the IMF, and the World Bank cancel Iraq's $145 billion foreign debt and freeze the debts of Asian countries affected by the Tsunami, while Africa's unsustainable debt burden is upheld with increasingly fiscal severity? Here again, we see the unjust structure of the world and the weaving of issues that deal with the life and death of millions of people around the world on the national interests of a few Western nations.

However, it is important that Africans articulate clearly their worldview and *reject any attempt to be framed into global situations that are destructive of African autonomy and self-understanding.* Globalization is a kind of cultural cloning that makes it impossible for Africans to think "in *concreto*," to explore the inexhaustible and unfathomable mystery of God and creation in Africa, which is always in differentiation and in the plural. Globalization absorbs the individual and communities and makes them faceless even as it

81. Ibid., 158–59.
82. Kerber, "Globalization," 56–57.

despotically determines their fate, without their involvement in the whole process.[83]

Globalization is not inevitable. Rooted as it is in materialism, profit-making, scientific and technological reductionism, with its claims of being a "god" or a merciless behemoth that controls the lives of billions all over the world. A Christian social ethics could join in the counter-voices and convergence on seeking an alternative vision. The terms for this engagement can never be a prior determination, but rather should evolve from the historical conditioning of the people. Christian theology proposes the principles of subsidiarity and solidarity[84] as a response to neo-liberal capitalism. This is a starting point for discussion with other new voices rising in opposition to globalization.[85]

Thomas Rourke[86] drawing from Catholic social teaching reflected in a new way in *Charity in Truth*, has summarized four definite requirements of any social order that is free from the dark forces of structures of sin: The first, that its conception of the common good must be rooted in a strong sense of service and an efficacious desire to realize the good of all members of the community. Economic and political policies, charitable aid and donor initiatives that proceed from self-interest of individuals and groups do not meet the requirements of justice and the good of all. The second, that society should reject consumerism and materialism; and should work to prevent them from becoming structures that shape the way people relate to each other or evaluate each other. The third, that profit making and capital should not be the determining factor of economic policies rather the determining factor should be the good of all, especially the weak and the marginalized, and the environment. *Any economic policy must put the interest of people first and must ask the question: Who suffers and who stands to gain from it?* Fifth, that a healthy society is one that is built around a moral vision which is based on social justice, eco-

83. Bujo, *African Theology*, 160, 166.

84. Pope John Paul II has called for a globalization of solidarity in *The Church in America* (55). See also Rourke, "Contemporary Globalization," 27. This edition of the journal *Communio* was dedicated to discussion of the theology of globalization taking from a broad horizon of discourses.

85. See George, *Fate*; George and Sabelli, *Faith and Credit*; Duchrow, *Alternatives to Global Capitalism*; Sacks, *Dignity of Difference*; Lifton, *Super Power Syndrome*.

86. Rourke, "Contemporary Globalization," 491–92.

systems health, the distribution of goods and services to all, especially the marginalized. It would reward individual initiatives but not at the detriment of the common good and the weak. It is this kind of vision that Pope John Paul II had in mind when he called for the globalization of solidarity[87] and the building of a new kind of world on the civilization of love. Another point that needs to be integrated in dealing with the challenges of globalization in Africa is corporate responsibility, which should be an integral element of corporate business practice. Business practices must be evaluated from the perspective of their impacts on society, economy, ecology and culture of the people. Indeed, the ecological crisis in Africa caused by the exploitation of oil and other minerals is a major cause of poverty and social dislocation among others.[88]

Today, we must emphasize the connection between poverty and human rights, and the relationship between development aid, donor initiatives, and human rights. The Universal Declaration of Human Rights states: "Everyone has the right to a standard of living adequate for the health and well being of himself and of his family, including food, clothing, housing and medical care" (Article 25). "Everyone is entitled to a social and international order in which the rights and freedoms set forth in this Declaration can be fully realized" (Article 28). The connection between poverty and human rights is based on a moral vision and a Christian anthropology on the intrinsic value of the human person, and the inter-connection of human beings on earth. When severe poverty denies another person his freedom to actualize himself, or to live a decent life, the person cannot fully exercise the rest of other freedoms guaranteed them in international covenants and national constitutions. In addition, extreme poverty in many parts of the world diminishes all us. The poverty in Africa and in many parts of the world has led to what Thomas Nigel calls "radical inequality" wherein the poorest party is in direst need.[89]

87. John Paul II, *Church in America*, 55.

88. There is a growing number of literatures on African ecology which offer helpful insight on this challenge. See for instance my lecture "Partnering for Eco-Justice in Africa" at the twelve International Conference of the International Society for Third Sector Research, Israeli Center for Third Sector Research, Ben Gurion University, Negev, March 17th 2009. See also Mugambi and Vahakangas, *Christian Theology*; Wisner et al., *New Map of Africa*; Ike, *Globalization*.

89. See Nigel, "Poverty and Food," 49.

The fact that this unacceptable condition persists in an affluent world shows the poverty of the prevailing global moral vision, and the weakness of the global moral will. It also reveals a lack of courage in addressing the root causes of poverty that is the world economic systems, and the rejection of a transcending ethical and spiritual value base for the world. As Marcelo Alegre passionately proposes; "Poverty is not unavoidable, its eradication is feasible at low cost, and pro-poor policies accelerate and do not slow development. If this is right, this means that in 2005 the human right of subsistence is correlated with duties involving no relevant costs, which in turn means that the violation of human rights implied by extreme poverty is particularly egregious because it is gratuitous and irrational."[90] He notes that more than a billion people are being wronged because they have been reduced to means in a social and economic wheel that oils the accumulation of capital for developing nations and powerful people in the developing countries. In addition, the poor have become objects, and voiceless in a world where the echo of greed, the logic of security, and the fear of tomorrow have become louder and more virulent.

My concern in this chapter is to show that the increasing number of poor people in Africa is unacceptable. African governments and the international community must accept that poverty is an abuse of the rights to human fulfillment in Africa. Development aid and donor initiatives are, therefore, necessary within the African social context. However, it must be borne in mind that development aid are not tokens to be administered randomly and arbitrarily without any accountability to the poor and the people who make contributions either to the voluntary, church, and religious organizations or through taxes to governments. Charity in truth is a high calling that is tied to a moral vision as well as to the ongoing global concern to promote human rights and freedom all of which are assaulted by poverty. I tried in this chapter to show also the extent of Africa's poverty without being exhaustive because of limitations of space, but I think that Africa's poverty seen as an abuse of human rights reveals the full impact of this unacceptable situation.

The African social context is wider than poverty, just as the African story encompasses diverse and emerging narratives. The young people of Africa are dreaming dreams and working hard to achieve

90. Alegre, "Extreme Poverty," 240.

their dreams. There is a new impetus in many African countries to build a new Africa. The African women continue to emerge gradually from the stranglehold of male domination, and are contributing in significant ways to African renaissance. However, one important institution whose growth and influence continue to amaze many people within and outside Africa is Christianity. African Christianity offers one of the most exciting narratives for interpreting and understanding Africa's social context. This is particularly prominent in Sub-Saharan Africa. Christianity in Africa also contains some of the tools needed for the practice of charity in truth in Africa. While the decisive nature of traditional, national, political, and economic structures in Africa's development cannot be discounted, Christian enterprise in Africa can bring an important transformative service for Africa's development by showing how to do charity in truth. They can do this in a co-operative manner with other social capitals in the continent and through critical and discerning partnership with governments and donor agencies both within Africa and outside Africa. In the rest of this book we shall consider some of the socio-ethical, economic, theological, and philosophical proposals that show how this should be done.

4

The Church and Christians at the Service of Charity in Truth

Do you really wish to pay homage to Christ's body? Then do not neglect him when he is naked. At the same time that you honor him here (in church) with hangings made of silk, do not ignore him outside when he perishes from cold and nakedness. For the One who said, "This is my body" . . . also said "when I was hungry you gave me nothing to eat." For is there any point in his table being lade with golden cups while he himself is perishing from hunger? First fill him when he is hungry and then set his table with lavish ornaments. Are you making a golden cup for him at the very moment when you refuse to give him a cup of cold water? Do you decorate his table with cloths flecked with gold, while at the same time you neglect to give him what is necessary for him to cover himself? . . . No one was ever condemned for neglecting to be munificent: for the neglect of others, hell itself is threatened, as well as unquenchable fire . . . The conclusion is: Don't neglect your brother [or sister] in his [her] distress while you decorate his house. Your brother [or sister] is more truly his temple than any church building.

—John Chrysostom

THEOLOGICAL JUSTIFICATION FOR THE CHURCH'S SERVICE AND PRACTICE OF CHARITY IN TRUTH

The role of many church denominations in charitable and development activities has grown in diversity and intensity. Within the Catholic tradition, this role has become very prominent since the end of the Second Vatican Council in 1965. One of the reasons for this is the renewal of the self-understanding of the Church with regard to the social context in which the gospel is to be preached. Evangelization is integral and demands an immersion in the social conditions of the people who receive the good news. This draws directly both from the words of the Lord and his deeds. The command to love our neighbors is a call to be directly involved in concrete acts of love to bring the blessings of the Lord to transform the condition of the poor. The nearness of the kingdom of God which Jesus preached was the closeness of the saving presence of God in the lives of all people especially the marginalized, the victims of inequality and injustice in society, those who are left behind in the broken lower rungs of a decaying and sinful socio-economic ladder in many societies.

The list of the poor and needy in our society is long and worrisome. These are people in our families and neighborhoods, in our churches and town halls, on the lonely path to streams and farms. There are many brothers and sisters who are dying silently on the time-crusted path of poverty and want. We see them in the hospital main foyer turned back at the doors of hospitals in many African countries because they could not afford the admission fee to consult a doctor. How many millions of Africans are dying today because they have no access to basic medical intervention whether in treating simple ailments like malaria or diarrhea, or for simple intervention like appendectomy, etc.? How many HIV positive Africans are dying of AIDS because they have no access to antiretroviral drugs? How many Africans are starving today, and how many poor people all over the world are dying of hunger? How many millions of young and poor African kids are street-children and beggars, victims of rape and violence because instead of going to schools they are being used as child soldiers, domestic servants, hawkers of goods on highways, and prostitutes? These are God's children whose plight and condition should be central to the mission of the Church and Christians at all times.

JESUS CARES FOR THE POOR AND NEEDY

The experience of poverty and suffering among many ordinary people in Africa is similar to the social conditions of many people during the time of Jesus. Jesus was identified as the friend of poor people and shared their company. Jesus had a limitless compassion and empathy for the poor: "When he saw the crowds, he had compassion for them, because they were harassed and helpless like sheep without a shepherd" (Matt 9:36). In all instances, the throng that followed him included sick people, hungry people, troubled people who were afflicted emotionally, spiritually, socially, and economically. The collective term "poor" applied to all these people who came to Jesus: the hungry, the unemployed, the sick, the discouraged, the homeless and the crippled, and the sad, and suffering. They were the subjected and humiliated people, those who were suffering all kinds of oppression and injustice. They represent "the crowd" in the gospel, those who were poor, non-persons, sub-humans, dehumanized, and human fodders[1], who had no name except that they followed Jesus in search of something to eat. The Lord is presented as being moved to compassion at seeing these people and as doing something to help them: "Jesus summoned his disciples and said, 'my heart is moved with pity for the crowd, for they have been with me now for three days and have nothing to eat. I do not want to send them away hungry, for fear they may collapse on the way'" (Matt 15:32).

All the poor who came to Jesus found in him a friend, a helper, and a support as he healed them of their diseases, restored their sense of dignity devastated by poverty, took away their shame and their sins and gave them a new identity, a new image, and a new hope. Selfless love, unconditional acceptance, concrete acts of kindness, practical acts of compassion, sensitivity and understanding to the painful condition of the poor were habitual attitudes of Jesus to the less privileged who came to him in the course of his earthly ministry: publicans, sinners, prostitutes, criminals, immigrants, foreigners, lepers, widows, homeless and nameless children, the sick, the suffering, the possessed, among others. He looked upon them with eyes of mercy and even pronounced a blessing on them and all those who even with some possessions will place their whole trust in God and not on the things they have or lack: "Blessed are the poor in spirit, for theirs is the king-

---

1. Moltmann, *Way of Jesus*, 99.

dom of God" (Matt 5:3). Giving to the poor, reaching out to the needy, and being there for all those on the margins of society and those who are far from God was an essential part of the mission of Christ. It should as a result be central to the Church's mission of proclaiming the kingdom of God and witnessing to the coming of this kingdom in history. This is a mission both for the universal church as well as local churches and all Christians.

Jesus' care for the poor is shown in Scripture to be the necessary consequence of the irruption of God's kingdom. Salvation was both a spiritual and material gift from God since the whole person is to be saved, and restored to full human dignity fitting for a child of God. In the ministry of Jesus, his healing miracles and his outreach to the poor were central to the realization of the messianic reign of God. The liberation from the net of sin and evil, as well as from the clutches of poverty and suffering caused by injustice was central to the proclamation and ministry of the Lord. The kingdom of God as the emergence of the reign of God, and the submission of all things to the lordship of Christ, demanded the toppling of sinful structures, and unjust and unacceptable conditions. This is why the Lord did not stop at simply providing food for the hungry, and healing the sick. He also was concerned with empowering the poor so that they can take control of their lives. He did not preach or practice a dependent charity, but a liberating charity that freed the people on one hand, and gave them the impetus to transcend and change their condition on the other. It was a charity that was concerned with doing justice and confronting the root cause of poverty—the sinful hearts and sinful conditions and structures of his times. The ordinary folks who became his disciples were given a new mission and empowered to do so; the sinners and even the rich who were upbraided for their exploitation of the weak were forgiven and given a new vocation. In many instances of healing and restoration, the Lord ended with giving the liberated man or woman a new impetus and a new vocation often ending with the vocational summons: "Go!"

Here we find the quality and distinctive character of God's kingdom being made manifest in Christ's words and deeds. The liberation from poverty is radically rooted in the transformation of human hearts and human institutions so that there will emerge a new reality characterized by just and fair social conditions. The charitable outreach to the poor is not a dependent chain, but a liberative ministry that empowers people to self-transcend their personal limitations to pursue their missions in life. The Lord reached out to the poor to remove the obstacles that held them down so that they can live fully as children of God and participate in building up and protecting the common good. He also liberated them so that they can become disciples who work in bringing the world to conform to God's plan. It is important that we keep this in mind in our vision and mission for charitable works and aid both locally and internationally. Christian charities today need a christological and trinitarian foundation if they will bear enduring fruits. The words and examples of the Lord should be the foundation of charity in truth for today's Christians and church charities.

THE CHURCH'S MISSION TO THE POOR

One of the greatest signs and splendor of Christianity as a global institution is her heroic efforts in international development and humanitarian activities in the face of rising incidents of wars, and natural disasters, and support for poverty-eradication in many developing countries. These efforts coming especially from the North to the South are the greatest testimony to the power and presence of Christian charity. Having lived for close to a decade in Europe and North America, I can conclude that charity is one of the strongest Christian values that has remained very solid in the West. Hopefully, it will be the path through which the Holy Spirit could reconnect people to God and to one another and bring back to himself many people in the West and in many parts of the world where the Christian message no longer captures the cultural imagination.

The early church set for today's Church the model of the radical and essential nature of the social ministry of the church and individual Christians. William J. Walsh and John P. Langan show in their article on patristic social consciousness that the early church was a church of the poor. Before the *imperium Christianum* introduced by Constantine, the Christian congregations were communities with a social commitment. Strangers and migrants were welcomed and easily assimilated and new works found for them by the Christian community. According to Moltmann, this way of living was distinctive because it showed that the early church was a church that cared for people and lived in simple poverty like the common people. The early church took the words and examples of the Lord to heart and lived it to the full in her outreach to the poor, healing ministries to the sick and the marginalized. With the Constantinian transformation, the Church took on imperial powers and left the service of the poor to the welfare services of the state and confined her ministry to the salvation of souls. "If it had not been for this, the conflict which Jesus initiated with the Gospel for the poor would have remained a living conflict, and spiritual and political power in the Christian empire would have remained unharmonized."[2]

Why did Christianity capture the imagination of the people in a Roman empire where the Church was not only under persecution, but was an invisible minority? Walsh and Langan argue that many theological factors contributed to this, but one decisive internal factor in the astonishing success of the early church was the radical sense of the Christian community which was open to all and insistent on absolute and exclusive loyalty and commitment to every aspect of the believer's life, "From the very beginning, the one distinctive gift of Christianity was this sense of the community. Whether one speaks of 'an age of anxiety' or 'the crisis of the towns,' Christian congregations provided a unique opportunity for masses of people to discover a sense of security and self-respect."[3]

The early church's sense of community was not only sacramental but practical: In the first place, the church's way of being poor was a sign of her identity and self-understanding. In the second place, there was a direct and ongoing commitment to support the poor and pull them out from the pit of despair and suffering. This kind of attitude to the poor is well described in the *Didache*, "Never turn away the needy; share all your possessions with your brother, and do not claim that anything is your own. If you and he are joint participators in things immortal, how much more so in things that are mortal."[4] This way of living was in direct opposition to the practice in the wider society where the poor were treated as burdens and in many cases disabled and disadvantaged people were systematically removed from society.

2. Moltmann, *Way of Jesus*, 104
3. Walsh and Langan, "Patristic Social Consciousness," 113.
4. Ibid., 114

The consequences of the theology and praxis of the early church with regard to the poor were multiple and enriching: it transformed the worldview of the environing social context in which the Gospel was preached. In the first place, it showed the primacy of charity in truth as being truly divine and truly human. Secondly, it led to the transformation of the pagan world in which the gospel was preached by showing the distinctive quality of Christian community in their attitude to those on the margins of society. It also transformed the inner life of people by offering a criticism of the selfish desires of the heart that will turn away at the pain of the other. The early church in the writings of the early fathers showed through charity the ordination of material goods, and the ultimate destiny of all things towards Christ. They also identified the poor with Christ, so that reaching out to the poor in the community was intimately linked to our attitude to Christ. More importantly, they showed that love and sharing in the Christian community is the only way of being church and that this internal act of mutuality and sharing in all things is a credible way of showing the power and presence of the Lord in the Christian community.

The early church was also following the tradition of the Old Testament where the poor were treated with love, compassion, and care. Also the conditions that promoted poverty were considered sinful and aggressively removed from the midst of the community. Jill Jacobs has demonstrated that the Old Testament and other Jewish religious laws and tradition have one basic mandate for the Assembly of God: there shall be no needy in the land. This vision is summarized in Moses' final exhortation to the people of Israel: "There shall be no needy among you . . . If there is among you a needy person, one of your brethren, within any of your gates, in your land which *Adonai* your God gives you, you shall not harden your heart, nor shut your hand from your needy brother; but you shall surely open your hand unto him, and shall surely lend him sufficient for his need in that which he wants. Be careful lest there be a hateful thing in your heart, and you say, 'The seventh year, the sabbatical year, is coming' and you look cruelly on your brother, the poor person, and do not give him, for he will call out to God and this will be counted as a sin for you" (Deut 5:4–15).[5]

---

5. See Jacobs, *No Needy*, 11.

If in the past there was doubt whether the church should become involved in social justice initiatives and works, today the question is no longer "Why?" but "How?" We do not need today to defend the Church's involvement in changing the social conditions of people. In our times, the Church's involvement in the life of the poor, the needy, the suffering, and those on the margins of life is perhaps the greatest defense we have about the validity of our gospel. Christian realism thus demands the intimate immersion in the whole condition of the human person to whom the good news is to be preached. It also demands involvement in a direct manner.

Flying to South America in 1987, Pope John Paul II was asked by a reporter whether he would press the dictatorial regime of Pinochet to return Chile to democracy and respect human rights. The Pope said: "I am not the evangelizer of democracy; I am the evangelizer of the Gospel. To the Gospel message, of course belongs all the problem of human rights, and if democracy means human rights then it belongs to the message of the Church."[6] Pope John Paul II in effect was saying that the Church is concerned about everything that conduces to the common good. The mission of the Church is the salvation of the whole person. This is why central to the message of the Church is the presentation of the truth of salvation, which is incarnated in the person of Jesus Christ. This truth has the power to save and change societies so that it shines with the splendor of God. The truth of faith can penetrate every sphere of life including politics.

However, in contemporary society—whether in Africa or in other parts of the world—the mission of the Church in development, in promoting good governance, and in the social sphere in general has come under scrutiny. On the one hand, there are many who argue that the Church has no role in the public square beyond the formation of conscience and preparing men and women for eternal life. Also in this group are those who accuse the Church of lacking the credibility to play such a socio-political role when she lacks the very democracy and equality that she advances for the wider society. In many African countries, many people also point to the poor working conditions of many church workers as another reason why the Church is not qualified to speak out for the poor. During the Second African Synod in October, 2009, Cardinal Arinze of Nigeria said that most church

6. Quoted in Weigel, *Truth of Catholicism*, 155.

workers in the African churches go home at the end of the month with only a cup of holy water instead of a fair and meaningful wage: "It is a scandal when these humble workers have only holy water to take home at the end of the month."[7]

On the other hand, those who advance the involvement of the Church in the political and public square make appeal not only to the words and deeds of the Lord, but to the laicity of the Church. Bruno Forte describes it this way: "In terms of the temporal order, the laicity of the Church means ordination to the service and mission inherent in the anthropology of grace and, therefore, the responsibility of every baptized person in the work of mediating between salvation and history."[8] This needs further theological elaboration.

TOTAL ECCLESIOLOGY AS JUSTIFICATION FOR THE MISSION OF THE CHURCH AND CHRISTIANS TO THE POOR

One of the developments in the self-understanding of the Church in post-conciliar times was the re-appropriation of "total ecclesiology." This involves the richer appreciation of the "in-between" or "between times" status of the Church; the Church is embedded within history and is at the same time an eschatological community on its way to its full destiny. The reality of its trinitarian origin gives the Church an identity as the people of God in the order of grace, communion, and friendship. However, her being "inter tempora" gives her the unfulfilled mission of being touched profoundly by the joys and sorrows of the people of God and the groaning of creation in their search for abundant life. This is opposed to the dualism which separated the Church from the world. Ecclesial dualism, according to Avery Dulles, bears certain analogy with Platonism in which the realm of appearances was superficial and unimportant. Sometimes, in order to escape from this dualism, Henri de Lubac argues that the Church fell into some monism.[9] Holding these two tendencies together requires a proper understanding of the nature of the Church, and the goal of the Christian journey. Christianity proclaims an order that is not timeless.

7. Allen, "African Bishops."

8. Forte, *The Church*, 35.

9. See the analysis of Lubac's theology on our double citizenship in Schonborn, *Death to Life*, 111–14.

Eternal life has a beginning in time, even though in principle it has no end. The kingdom of God which Christ preached exists not simply in some super-celestial realm, but as a real promise for the future of this earth. With the Resurrection, the new era of transformation has already begun. The Church is the herald of what is already won; she works and walks towards and anticipates in her life especially in the Eucharist that which is not yet here. Christians are those who in faith already belong to the ultimate future that lies hidden in God.[10] Indeed, as Schonborn so eloquently put it, "True 'responsibility for life here on earth' is generated only by the genuine 'hope in life after death.' But the opposite is true likewise: only responsibility for eternal life gives the right joy in this life: 'responsibility for life after death generates the genuine "hope for this life here on earth."'"[11]

Total ecclesiology also helps to integrate the ministries of the hierarchy and the laity as one mission of evangelization instead of creating a dual or binary identity which leaves the laity lacking creativity and dynamism in their secular mission, and the hierarchy lacking a better understanding and respect for the autonomous value of earthly realities, and attention to and engagement with the secularity of the world. What it signifies in a more concrete sense is the idea of the Church of communion in which there is a symbiosis between the visible and the invisible, the communal and the personal, the hierarchical and the charismatic, the local and the universal in which all diversities and dimensions of being Church are tied together in the depth of communion created by the Holy Spirit (Pascal).[12] In this communion, is reconciled all things in Christ through the love of God. Such an image already validates, justifies, and obligates the radical nature of Christian charity, and total gratuity for the sake of God and our neighbors.

What total ecclesiology proposes is that it is not "the Church" and "the modern world," but "the Church in the modern world." This has profound implications. In the first place, the Church is not a sociological concept, but a trinitarian communion. Yet at the same time she is not held hostage by the world, nor does she have to conform unreflectively to the world, nor flee from it. The involvement of the Church

---

10. See Dulles, *Reshaping of Catholicism*, 156–57.

11. Schonborn, *Death to Life*, 124.

12. Tillard, *Flesh*, 136.

and Christians in the world is missionary and evangelically driven by faith, inspired by love, and directed by hope. In this regard, the activities of Christians and the Church in the world is not simply a social or welfare service but a spiritual service, through well ordered and concrete acts which are faithful to the commandment of the Lord that we love one another. Charity is constitutive of the very identity and mission of the Church at all levels. Based on this, any parish, diocese, or church which does not integrate charity as essential to her ministry is lacking an essential dimension of being Church. The ministry of preaching the Word of God, the celebration of the Sacraments, and the ministry of service are three essential responsibilities of the Church; they presuppose each other and are inseparable from each other. If I preach wonderful homilies to hungry people in the pews what good news does that offer if I am not concerned about how to give them something to eat? If I bring the sacrament to homeless people without seeking to help them find a home, how will the sacrament bring them succor? If the poor bow before me as a priest or bishop while poverty has bent them down under the iron wrought mercilessness of hunger and suffering, while denying them of authentic humanity and dignity what benefit does that bring to them?

Total ecclesiology seeks to bring these three dimensions of Church life together: a Church preaches the good news which she has received from the Lord, celebrates the liturgy with dignity and respect, and also and more significantly is open to and concretely involved in the service of charity to the poor especially those within her immediate community. All of them mutually nourish and inspire each other. Indeed, abandoning the social context will tantamount to abandoning her mission because she is in the world as both sign and mission. However, in this complex world where the lines of identity are becoming blurred, the Church's role in charitable works has gone beyond addressing the needs of her members to being open to all. In many hospitals and schools established and run by the Catholic Church in Africa and other parts of the world the doors are open to non-Catholics and non-Christians as well. The social ministry of the Church even though tied to her mission of evangelization is not actively directed at proselytizing. However, the words of Francis of Assisi are still a guide here: "Preach always when necessary use word." The poor need our love, and if in showing them the face of Christ who is love, they come to love and embrace Christ, they are received with love into the Church. However, the primary goal here is to give the love of Christ and meet the immediate human needs of the poor in a world where human suffering has become inexcusable given the measure of wealth and prosperity in the hands and under the control of a few. Summarizing this position, Pope Benedict writes:

> A Christian knows when it is time to speak of God and when it is better to say nothing and to let love alone speak. He knows that God is love (cf. 1 Jn 4:8) and that God's presence is felt at the very time when the only thing we do is to love. He knows that disdain for love is disdain for God and man alike: it is an attempt to do without God. Consequently, the best defence of God and man consists precisely in love. It is the responsibility of the Church's charitable organisations to reinforce this awareness in their members, so that by their activity—as well as their words, their silence, their example—they may be credible witnesses to Christ."[13]

According to Pope Benedict XVI, "The entire activity of the Church is an expression of a love that seeks the integral good of man: it seeks his evangelization through Word and Sacrament, an undertaking that is often heroic in the way it is acted out in history; and it seeks to promote man in the various arenas of life and human activity. Love is, therefore, the service that the Church carries out in order to attend constantly to man's sufferings and his needs including his material needs."[14] Pope Benedict points out that this is the normal way of being Church from the time of the early church. The Church's mission has always centered on the practice of charity and direct involvement in ordering society to meet the challenging and changing conditions of people. It was because of this essential aspect that the early church set up the diaconal ministry: "All who believed were together and had all things in common; and they sold their possessions and good and distributed them to all, as any had need" (Acts 2:44–45). In these we find a definition of the Church whose constitutive identity includes: communion (*koinonia*), sharing (*diakonia*), breaking of bread, prayer, a common life, and the lack of distinction between the rich and poor as every one in the community was provided for through the charity

13. Benedict XVI, *God is love*, 31.
14. Ibid., 19.

and generosity of the rest of the community. It could be said of the early Church that she organized her life in such a way that there were no needy in the community who were not made to feel the charity, and kindness of the community through acts of solidarity. "As the Church grew, this radical form of material communion could not in fact be preserved. But its essential core remained: within the community of believers there can never be room for a poverty that denies anyone what is needed for a dignified life."[15] The examples of the early Church show to today's Church and Christians that concrete acts of kindness and charity are fundamental to a total ecclesiology in which the sacred and the profane are to be held in harmony. "If the Spirit blows where it wills, it is not possible to limit his action with extrinsic categories. If the lordship of God embraces the whole person and life itself, every worldly situation is capable of being lived in relation to the promise of faith and, therefore, assessed and guided by the "eschatological reserve" proper to the Christian. There are no separate spheres—the sacred and the profane, God and Caesar—for which each person has recourse to specialists (sacred ministers and lay people). There is one sphere of existence with a complexity of definite relations that make up history."[16]

RENDER TO CAESAR . . . RENDER TO GOD

Is the Church's involvement in practical acts of charity in truth inter-ference in politics and the state? In assuming a prophetic stance against the structures of sins that sustain poverty and human suffering, is the Church over stepping her bounds? In contemporary discourse, this has become a pertinent question especially in Western societies where a distinctive Christian voice in increasingly being questioned. There are some who will propose in many Western societies that the Church has become moribund, they also make appeal to the separation of Church and state. There are some who like Jean-Jacques Rousseau will argue that the Church is "actively opposed to the social spirit" and subverts the very basis of the social contract. Thus, in many instances some argue that the Church has no right to call the state to account

15. Ibid., 20.
16. Forte, *The Church*, 58–59.

for laws and policies it makes, which threaten Christian values and tradition, perpetuate injustice, and pauperisation of the vulnerable, and endanger the health of society? In many instances, challenging the hegemony of corporate moguls and interests and calling for equal participation of all in promoting and in drawing from the common good as was done in *Charity in Truth*, is seen as the endorsement of one form of social order by the Church. The question is: How can Christians and the Church be the light of the world and the salt of the earth if they are not active in public life? How can Christians renew the face of the earth, and bring joy and comfort to the lonely traveler who has nothing to eat?

If we look at our society today we will observe that Christian values appear to be increasingly under threat. Humanitarianism has become universal but driven in many instances by ideological and secondary goals. In many cases, secular humanists have built a global coalition of a kind that preaches and promotes this-worldly humanistic ethos of salvation through charitable works. Christians must work with these groups but at the same time show the moral and spiritual vision that should govern charity in truth. It is important, as Tillard rightly proposes, that we do not fall into the temptation of reducing the Church's role in the modern world to that of a teacher of ethics, an agent of philanthropic endeavors, and a creator of magnanimous ideologies, and a business-type modern day secular messianic champion. He argues further: "the church is essentially the presence of a space in which the fabric of the 'humanity-God-wants' is restored, an ideal for which men and women of today yearn, often, without realizing it. In fact, the generous commitments to justice, freedom, equality of opportunity and rights remain incomplete, sometimes even ambiguous if an authentic, entirely gratuitous fellowship is not re-established."[17]

Christians must understand the source and destiny of the Church and the Christian life. This way, these values will direct the activity of the faithful and the Church in temporal affairs. Jesus warns us of the danger of separating the Church and the state in such a way that the state suppresses religious values: *Give to Caesar what is Caesar's and to God what is God's*. He also taught that we cannot serve two masters at the same time. Jesus here sets a principle that is valid for all time. It is on this principle that the Church builds her teaching on the secu-

17. Tillard, *Flesh*, 137.

larity of the state, which is, that the state and the Church should be *independent* and that both should *work together* for the promotion of the common good. The secular state is to be perceived, as a country in which the politics and the government are not an extension of the governance of an institutional religion. It means the autonomy of the secular realm free of any religious creed and any leaning to any particular faith. It means also that government should not be controlled by religious organizations.

However, this should not be construed to mean that politicians should not publicly profess their faith and apply their moral convictions in their involvement in government. Nor does it mean the rejection of religious signs and symbols or, more deeply, the place of religious values in the state and public square. The autonomy of the two realms is at the heart of the teaching of the Church on secularity. Christopher Dawson captures this well when he argues that Christianity gave birth to true liberalism, because "at the root of the development of Western freedom and Western democracy there lies the medieval idea that men possess rights even against the state and that society is not a totalitarian political unit but a community made up of a complex variety of social organisms each possessing an autonomous life and its own free institutions."[18]

Jesus did not say "Caesar alone" or "God alone" but to both, each one on his plain. The Second Vatican Council's Pastoral Constitution on the Role of the Church in the Modern World, *Gaudium et Spes*, was an attempt to overcome the so often monolithic logic that saw the Church as opposed to anything earthly; the Church was only there to judge the world and the world had nothing to give the Church. Christians being citizens of heaven should distance themselves from worldly concerns as much as possible. This view is typified in the words of Thomas à Kempis in *The Imitation of Christ* when he writes; "the more I go into the world, the lesser a man I become." The Church became a fortress impenetrable to the world, and the world was seen as an obstacle to the eschatological pilgrimage of God's people. Cardinal Walter Kasper points out that this mindset helped to widen the gap between the Church and society and facilitated the process of secularization set in motion by the liberating rationality of the Enlightenment. The reality of a Godless world that we now face in

18. Dawson, "Failure of Liberalism," 862.

our society is the consequence of a 'worldless' God that the Church sometimes presented.

Herein lies the need for the Church and Christians, under the inspiration of the Holy Spirit, to engage in the movement of history, to listen to and read the signs of the times so as to offer the leaven the world so urgently needs. All Christians have a role to play in the evangelization of our culture and the transformation of our communities. Every worldly relation, as Bishop Bruno Forte argues, is capable of being lived in relation to the promise and power of faith. Through the grace in Christ, secular life can be assessed and guided by a Christian vision that is critically enlightened by the Church in her prophetic calling. The gulf between the secular and the sacred has been bridged by Christ, who has drawn all things to God. In a sense, every secular reality is open to redemption in Christ and every secular event-politics, globalization, environmental initiatives, global social networks for a better world etc-is inseparable from the concerns of the Church.

Today, unfortunately we have given so much to the modern Caesars represented in our day by the government, international businesses, multi-national companies, and agents of neo-liberal globalization who most times do not have a moral sense for carrying out ethico-social responsibility in the civil realm. We are facing new forms of dictatorship aimed at suppressing the distinctive quality of Christian worldview and engagement in the world. The call for a revitalization and spiritualization of the social ministry of the church and Christians by Pope Benedict's *Charity in Truth* could not have come at a better time. It is a call to return to the origins again and discover the sources, the means, and goal of authentic human development and Christian activism based on a sound Christian anthropology, Christian realism, and social gospel. It must be said that a *Christian faith professed only within the walls of the Church and which is not lived outside the Church precincts through credible life styles and acts of love, and defended in the public domain, is empty. If the values of the Christian faith will ever capture the imagination of our people again; if the values of the Christian faith will ever change the inner center of our cultural life today, it must begin from the kind of Christians that we have out there in the public square. It must have an external reference and a socio-ethical responsibility majestically or simply validated by charity in truth.*

"Render to Caesar what is Caesar's and to God what is God's" indicates that the Christian has a double citizenship: we are citizens of heaven and citizens of earth. The claims of the earthly city and the claims of the heavenly city should not be at war with each other but mutually reinforce each other. We are here on earth in expectation of the Lord's coming, and the Lord's coming is already anticipated here on earth through the coming of God's kingdom which we pray should be incarnated here on earth as it is done in heaven. In the same vein, the claims of the state and the claims of the Church do not and should not conflict because both are in history as partners in bringing about the reign of God. Pope Benedict underlies these relations by making two important clarifications. In the first place, it is to be noted that the social order must be governed by ethical principles of justice and right order. Augustine is quoted to have said that a state not governed by justice is nothing other than a bunch of thieves. In the *City of God*, he underlies the need for morality as the foundation of a just social order when he wrote: "When a man does not serve God, what justice can we ascribe to him, since in this case his soul cannot exercise a just control over the body, nor his reason over his vice? And if there is no justice in such an individual, certainly there can be none in the community of that person."[19] The Church as the social expression of the Christian faith has her own autonomy just as she recognizes the autonomy of the temporal sphere personalized in a concrete way through the state and political bodies.[20] The activities of Christians and the Church in the world is structured by their faith and directed by their Christian consciousness which are not in opposition to the goal of the state which is the ordering of society through just laws, principles, and policies which bring about the common good.

The Church's role in the public square is similar to that of the state in some sense which is to bring about a just order; "This is where Catholic social doctrine has its place: it has no intention of giving the Church power over the state. Even less is it an attempt to impose on those who do not share the faith ways of thinking and modes of conduct proper to faith. Its aim is simply to help purify reason and to contribute, here and now, to the acknowledgment and attainment of what

---

19. Augustine, *City of God*, 700.
20. Benedict XVI, *Charity in Truth*, 28.

is just."[21] Both concerns for justice proceed from reason and natural law in accordance with what is proper to the human person. For the Church, on the other hand, the means through which this is to be brought about is the purification of reason, and the sharpening of the moral sense through faith that comes from close contact with the Lord Jesus. The state might make appeals to justice through the coercive power of state agencies and apparatus to maintain law and order and to reward or punish those who do not conform to what may be called the social contract, which is embodied in national constitutions and legal codes. However, the state cannot of its own bring about the inner transformation of individuals, or create the spiritual environment in which morality and virtuous conduct are developed and maintained.

The Church thus provides a critical framework for evaluating the actions of the state through rational and moral arguments. This is what the Church offers to humans and every state in order to awaken the spiritual sense of the people, and the strength to make sacrifices for the good of one and all. Pope Benedict points out that a just social order is the achievement of the state and not of the Church.[22] However, he teaches that "the direct duty to work for a just ordering of society, on the other hand, is proper to the lay faithful. As citizens of the state, they are called to take part in public life in a personal capacity."[23] Being, for instance, a good Zimbabwean *citizen* is not incompatible with being a good Zimbabwean *Christian*. We must fulfill our civic duties as well as our religious commitments. The participation of the laity in legislative, cultural, administrative, economic, and the social lives of their communities is decisive for their salvation. This is the major way in addition to the family through which they bring the good news to the ends of the earth. Their lives and mission are to be lived out in the thick of daily life and in helping to bring charity in truth to their neighbors.

But how often have we heard Christian politicians say that their Christian faith will not guide their sense of judgment in carrying out their public duties or that the demands for charity made by the Church is intrusive. The question is: Can we separate our faith from our life? Can we live our lives as Christians solely in the confines of

21. Ibid.

22. Benedict XIV, *God is Love*, 28.

23. Ibid., 29.

our churches, and not care about the insecure existence in which our neighbors are weather-beaten by poverty and suffering? Anyone who really has the Christian faith coursing through his or her life—veins and shaping his or her mind, vision and action cannot separate his or her being on the pews on Sunday from his being in parliament on Monday or in the homes for HIV/AIDS orphans on Tuesday. There should be no separation between the sacred and the profane. *The Christian lives as he or she believes; believes as he or she lives; and professes, confesses, and witnesses in concrete life situations and diverse contexts what he or she believes.* Faith and life can never be separated. The former gives life to the later and the later confirms the validity of the former. Why should the Christian have two personalities: the Christian personality on Sunday and non-Christian personality on Monday in the office? Christians should heed the demand of the Lord to give the poor something to eat, to help change the global or local unacceptable social orders through acts of solidarity and love.

Christians should be concerned for instance about issues of justice and poverty in our society and suffering in the world; we should care about the abuse of human rights and the plight of minorities and the weak. It is our duty as Christians to pay our taxes and not cheat on the government through the falsification of our income tax returns. It is our duty also to work hard in our different work stations so that we can promote the common good and justify our pay package from the state or our employers. We as Christians should be in the forefront in the defense of the rights of workers among other things and shun all kinds of laziness and consumerism. Charity in truth also demands as Pope Benedict points out living a simple life style. More importantly, we should, as Christians, be active in politics and hold the government accountable for the promises they make and the policies they formulate. Christians have a moral responsibility in taking part in shaping the moral vision and the ideals that we are leaving behind for our children, and confront seriously and consistently the unacceptable situation of suffering and poverty which face humanity in contemporary times.

God has first claims over us, over and against any other allegiance on earth. We must give to God what is his: *our whole life.* The reason Christ came to earth is to subject all things under the dominion of God; to establish God's kingdom. On the Feast of Christ the King, the Church prays in the preface this way; "As king he [Jesus] claims dominion over all creation, that he may present to you, his almighty Father, an eternal and universal kingdom: a kingdom of truth and life, a kingdom of holiness and grace, a kingdom of justice, love and peace." In Christ, we all have become the subject of God's love because through him and in him God has conferred on us an image and dignity that is beyond comparison. The Church on earth is the instrument for building this kingdom and that is why the teachings of our Church are aimed at bringing out the best from every man or woman and offering a healthy leaven for our society. Christian activism and witnessing in the world will lack credibility and force, if they do not stem from a unified and clear perception of truth as revealed, received, and lived by all faithful. This is why Pope John Paul II taught thus in an address, "The only true freedom, the only freedom that can truly satisfy, is the freedom to do what we ought as human beings created by God according to his plan. It is the freedom to live the truth of what we are and who we are before God, the truth of our identity as children of God, as brothers and sisters in a common humanity. This is why Jesus Christ linked truth and freedom together, stating solemnly: 'You will know the truth and the truth will set you free' (John 8:32)"[24] Charity is linked with truth in all the actions and works of Christians and the Church. It is necessary to underlie some fundamental principles that should govern the social ministry of churches, Christian charities, and Christians in addition to the ones we have outlined in the foregoing theological analysis. These principles are drawn from Pope Benedict XVI's first encyclical, *God is Love*. I also have added further insights from personal theological reflection and other Christian theological sources to enrich these principles. We shall proceed to apply them in practical terms to aid and development in the challenging social context of Africa.

PRINCIPLES FOR DOING CHARITY IN TRUTH FOR CHRISTIAN CHARITIES AND INDIVIDUAL CHRISTIANS

The first point to be made here is that the Christian charitable work is not simply aimed at offering material help to people suffering, but re-

24. Quoted in Dulles, *Church and Society*, 122.

freshment and care for their souls as well. The human person is more than the sum of his or her parts. Thus, advocacy and initiatives for freeing people from poverty should also be concerned with the sinfulness which creates ugliness of soul and which causes the festering of most of the social sins that create structures of sin, injustice, and social disorder and dislocation. The Church's charity as well as individual Christian's acts of love to those in need should address the whole person in his or her totality of existence. It must proceed from embracing the whole story and the truth about the person or the situation that has caused the painful condition.

The second point is that the rights of church groups to do charity is intrinsic to their character as faith communities celebrating the love of God in Christ in the power of the Holy Spirit. It is the love of Christ that inspires Christian charity (2 Cor 5:14). As a result, it should be animated by an evangelical spirit of poverty, deep Christian love, and driven by sound Christian principles. Evangelical poverty demands that we give of ourselves fully in our charitable works, being present to the poor. It also calls on Christians to share in the suffering, and poverty of our brothers and sisters and thus be with them in the place of shame or pain. Charity is not an armchair or arms-length act where we treat the poor as if they are a contagion to our sense of social standing or humiliate them by our condescending attitude to them. The poor are not a burden to us nor is poverty and human suffering strictly speaking the consequence of people's positive choices. Charity in truth demands humility and poverty of spirit: "Those who are in position to help others will realize that in doing so they themselves receive help; being able to help others is no merit or achievement of their own. This duty is a grace. The more we do for others, the more we understand and appreciate the words of Christ: 'We are useless servants.'"[25]

Charity is the mission of the Church and all Christians; it is not optional but is a divine mandate. All Christians are called to embrace the mission of serving the poor. Thus, establishing structures and organizations to help her carry out her charitable mission on the part of the Church is a right. She can, however, work in collaboration with the state and other organizations to coordinate and effectively bring a better charitable services regime in differing social settings. However, the Church's charitable works are not social services, but are Christian

25. Benedict XVI, *God is Love*, 35.

and ecclesial charity carried out in truth and fidelity to Christ. It is aimed at bringing love to those in need in the full range of a Christian humanism on the dignity and rights of everyone, which are debased by poverty and unacceptable living conditions.

Thirdly, those involved in the Church's charitable activities must be professional who are competent in their fields. They ought to be driven by the right Christian attitude towards the poor like the Good Samaritan. They need to be trained in the affairs of the heart so that authentic Christian love, compassion, respect for everyone no matter their status or condition in life will govern their actions.

Fourth, Christian charity is not driven by secondary motives, ideological ends, political stratagem or economic objectives. It simply aims at making concrete and incarnate God's love to everyone. It is sensitive enough to see where love is needed and goes out to give love. It is critical enough to see where justice is lacking and causing poverty, and works hard to change the unjust order through the faith and con-science formation of Christians. These ways, all Christians through Christian activism and good works will be helping to bring this world with its ambiguities to conform to God's plan.

Christian charities are not, therefore, to be run on a busi-ness model aimed at making profit for the Church or for individual Christians who run them. This is not to say that charitable organiza-tions should not be involved in business, but clarity is required so that the end is not profit-making but the good of the poor. It is painful to observe in many African countries that Church owned educational institutions (day cares, primary, and secondary schools, and colleges) are so expensive that poor people cannot enroll in them. In many instances in Africa, church schools are seen as elitist offering little as-sistance to the poor, but actively training the children of rich people. There should be a balance in supporting the poor as well as the rich. Even though these institutions need money from the wealthy to keep afloat, the mission of the Church is negatively affected when its ser-vices are perceived as exclusive to the rich. This could be scandalous in poor communities in Africa.

Five, every ecclesial body must have a charitable arm. This means that every parish, church congregation, and denomination should have an open and ongoing ministry to the poor as well as so-cial justice advocacy. There are questions about who should manage the Church's charitable ministry whether it is the priests, ministers, religious, or bishops. What is important is that all administrative obstacles and hierarchical bottlenecks should be removed in doing charity through the Church. While one admits the need for account-ability, organization, proper coordination, and monitoring, it seems to me that an over organized and regulated charitable mission denies the church and Christians the spontaneity and directness to which charity and human needs demand. Pope Benedict draws attention to this in *CIV* 60 when he writes: "A more devolved and organic system of social solidarity, less bureaucratic but no less coordinated, would make it possible to harness much of dormant energy, for the benefit of solidarity between peoples."

In a more concrete sense, I think that it is more fitting for the la-ity and religious to run the administrative and organizational aspects of the Church's social ministry. In proposing this, I am inspired by the laicity of the Church and the secularity of the Church as properly oriented towards the ennobling of the secular sphere through lay and active religious. In many African dioceses, bishops and priests control the social services and charitable donations coming from abroad and other internally generated charitable fund. In some places, working for development and peace commissions is seen as juicy positions be-cause it gives one unlimited access to foreign contacts, travels abroad, and money. In some instances, those in these agencies live above the level of the other priests and the ordinary people. However, it is obvi-ous that many church leaders are not experts in development work and social and charitable ministries. Therein lies the need for them to leave in the hands of competent and well-trained laity and religious this very important ministry to the poor.

It must be stated again that doing charitable work is not a means for social progress. It is a counter witness when the agents of char-ity and social ministry in the Church display materialistic tendencies or use the plight of the poor as a platform for economic and social progress. It is important to structure the social ministry of the Church in Africa in such a way that it is prophetic, sacramental, credible, ac-countable, simple, and procures immediate and direct benefit for the poor. It should also be open to all people including non-Catholics, Muslims, practitioners of African Traditional Religions, and all who are in crying need of God's love. The Catholic dimension of Christian charity demands listening to, and coming to the aid of all poor people no matter their sex, ethnic group, nationality, religion, or political leaning. If a Muslim is hungry and abused, Christ suffers hunger and abuse in him or her; a Hindu is no less worthy of my love as my fellow Christian. However, my charity always begins from the need immediate and direct to my world of family, faith, and friends.

The Catholicity of the Church's social ministry also requires charitable initiatives across and between nations and dioceses, across races and climes, and across denominational divides. The Catholic dimension here also implies that Christian charities should be open to collaborating with other charities in promoting the common good, in effectively reaching out to the poor, and in advocacy and activism for a just social order. However, it must be noted that working together with other NGOs or across nations and diverse cultural frontiers must be carried out with discernment so that Christian charities are not seen to be supporting ideologically-driven organizations and groups who are actively promoting abortion, anti-population ideologies, political goals, and anti-life message among others.

Six, is the principle that all charitable activities are extensions of our spiritual life. They are, therefore, to be driven by prayer and praise. Christian charity driven by prayer helps us to see and read correctly the signs of the times; it also gives us the hope for a better tomorrow, and patience to appreciate our little acts of love as an incomplete offering. At the same time, it gives us grace and endurance to wait upon the Lord especially when we feel apathy, and despair because our little efforts have not contributed in changing the condition and plight of the poor. In doing charity, we all realize as Christians and as a Church that we are not Messiahs, we need to only light a small candle, knowing that a drop of water gradually makes an ocean.

Prayer helps to connect us to God and to the poor and everyone. But more importantly, it helps us to discern the will of God or the lack of it in the social order and the power and presence of sin and evil which wars against the divine governance of the world. When we cry out in prayer to God as we do sometimes as Christians in Africa, we do not presume to accuse God for being silent to the cries of the poor and the plight of Africa. What we do is to affirm with faith and conviction that if we co-operate with God, if we submit to his laws, and live according to the way of the Lord Jesus, we can change the world. We are also noting at the same time our limitations in bringing this about ourselves through our human plans and projects. Poverty, injustice, suffering, diseases, wars, pain, and social dislocation are all indications of the presence of evil in our human world and not necessarily the result of the silence or absence of God. Indeed, in doing Christian charity we are affirming our rejection of these evils as relative and our co-operation with God in bringing about the signs of God's kingdom in the present history of our world.

Pope Benedict's conclusion of his teaching in *God is Love* on the charitable mission of the church is very deep and hopeful: "Faith, hope and charity go together. Hope is practiced through the virtue of patience, which continues to do good even in the face of apparent failure, and through the virtue of humility, which accepts that God has given his Son for our sakes and gives us the victorious certainty that it is really true: God is love! It thus transforms our impatience and our doubts into the sure hope that God holds the world in his hands and that, as the dramatic imagery of the end of the Book of Revelation points out, in spite of the darkness he ultimately triumphs in glory."[26]

26. Benedict XVI, *God is Love*, 39.

5

Transforming Africa
through Charity in Truth

A Creative Appropriation of the Social gospel

THE ROLE OF THE CHURCH IN AFRICA IN THE SERVICE OF CHARITY IN TRUTH, JUSTICE, PEACE, AND DEVELOPMENT

How should the Church in Africa fulfill her mission of charity in truth today? How should international Christian charities
support the churches, social capitals, and third sector organizations
in Africa in the work of development, justice, and peace? These questions have been raised in African Christianity and in different African
contexts within the last two decades. It was also a central concern in
both the First African Synod (1994) and the Second African Synod
(2009). Both synods were concerned with the evangelization of Africa
as well as how the presence of Christianity in Africa could lead to justice, peace, reconciliation, and development in the continent. A central concern of these synods was the troubling social context of Africa,
and how the presence of Christianity in Africa can help offer concrete
and practical solutions for a transformative praxis for this beautiful
but troubled continent. Indeed, building God's kingdom in Africa was
the goal of these two synods. Evangelization is about building God's
kingdom on earth within diverse cultural and social contexts. Thus, an
integral evangelization stems from, responds to, and transforms the
social context and makes available to peoples and nations the abundant life that Christ offers to all.

My goal in this chapter is an effort at a transformative theological praxis. I will creatively appropriate Catholic social ethics, the social gospel, and some of the conversations that have taken place in Africa within the last two decades on the place of Christianity, cultures, and churches in bringing about abundant life for Africans. I will also show how this can be possible in a concrete way. There has been a substantial theological corpus coming from African theologians on this question, some of which I will reference in this chapter. What I will offer here is a fresh and creative insight on principles and practices drawn from theological, ecclesial, and social scientific and historical sources for assisting churches and Christians in their charitable works in Africa. In a sense, this chapter is an attempt to creatively appropriate Catholic social teaching on one hand, and, on the other hand, to concretely show how the message and vision of the two synods on Africa can be realized. The challenge of charity in truth has become very pressing because Africa is at the crossroads today. At the same time, there is a new and resurgent Christian consciousness, which could be tapped into to create the suitable environment and lay the foundation for African development and abundant life for God's children in the Black Continent.

Until recently, African theologians have dealt with the question of the Church's involvement in the social questions of the day from the perspective of liberation theology.[1] Theologians like Jean-Marc Ela, Mercy Amba Oduyoye, Laurenti Magesa, Engelbert Mveng, Benezet Bujo, Uzukwu, Emmanuel Martey, Tinyiko Maluleke, and Desmond Tutu—to mention but a few—belong to the liberation theology school. They proceed from a Christology of liberation, and show how Christ liberates African society in a concrete sense through the offer of abundant life. Other theologians like Nyamiti, Kato, Vincent Mulago, Kwame Bediako, John Mbiti, are identified, on the other hand, as theologians of inculturation who, in many cases, pursued the translation model of contextual theology. As a result, there has been a theological dividing line between these two approaches to theology. The inculturation theologians were interpreted as those who were concerned with orthodoxy and the integrity of the gospel message and its appropriation in its "pure" form in Africa. In the other camp, are

---

1. Some of the references here will include: Bujo, *African Theolog*; Magesa, *Church and Liberation*; Martey, *African Theology*, etc.

the liberation theologians who seek contextualization in Africa, which would inevitably lead to engagement with the social context. While the inculturation school had a normative understanding of Christianity, the liberation school applied a more critical and historical approach to Western Christianity, and advanced a contextual, post-missionary Christianity in Africa that draws from missiological cultural hermeneutics of the concrete and local.

I believe that social analysis and the critique of the power-play and unacceptable social contexts and unjust structures all of which lead to poverty and unnecessary human suffering is vital for doing any kind of theology, especially in the challenging contexts of Africa. Indeed, the authenticity and relevance of any theology depends on the interpretation and judgment it brings to bear on the social context as it impacts on Christian faith and praxis. The warrants for judgment are determined by the presence or lack therein of the eschatological fruits of God's kingdom, which must be found within any social context that is informed by the Christian faith. While we do not have the space to deal with the merits of these two positions, it is necessary to theologically highlight the danger of an African theology that creates a polarity between an ethos of salvation and an ethos of liberation. In addition, preoccupation with tagging or stereotyping theologians and theologies based on *a priori* generalizations is an unhelpful approach in the construction of African theologies. Therein lies the need for a new kind of theology that will bring the social gospel and theological ethics in conversation on how Christianity can help bring about the establishment of the kingdom of God in Africa and removing the obstacles on the road to its emergence. This demands both a clear and critical theological reflection, and pastoral praxis informed by a relevant theology.

There is certain uneasiness with the term "liberation" in theology in the Catholic Church in general. This is especially evident among the hierarchy in Africa whose commitment to fidelity to Rome has assumed a life of its own and often paralyses their pastoral creativity and dynamism. The suspicion is that liberation theologies are borrowed from Latin America and use Marxist dialectics of material determinism to interpret history. The conceptual framework that this approach appropriates for interpreting history, according to its opponents, has already been rejected by the institutional Church. In addition, there are some fears that using social analysis to gain the data for theologizing in Africa is somehow "untheological" because theology should draw from the Bible, tradition, and magisterium.[2]

The strong appeal to traditional theological method with its limitations with regard to history and context poses serious challenges. This is because the theologian is not simply a pipe for mediating the truths and realities about God, faith, morals, social ethics etc. He or she is an agent of mediated truth. The theologian is a dynamic subject of relations and not an object into which God and the Church pours the deposit of faith. Quite to the contrary, the theologians needed today in addressing the exciting frontiers of the Christian faith in Africa, and in arresting the heart wrenching social conditions of Africans are those who seriously engage the historical nature of faith. They must draw from their own history and experience, and appropriate the Christian faith as a mediated truth in conversation with traditions, histories, contexts, existential pathos and joys of the people who are seeking faith's answers to their troubling social context. The cries of Africans today have become in a very real and concrete way, the direct source of faith and the phenomenological hermeneutics for reading faith's demands and goals for our people. It is important to briefly sketch what I understand as African theology. This will enable me to propose how the message of *Charity in Truth* fits into such a theology, within the concerns and questions raised from the African social context and the role of the Church and Christian charities.

African Christian theology, in the first place, is the naming of the inner enrichment of African history as well as the external forms and manifestations of this history in its cross-cultural relations. The data for this task is drawn from a Christian consciousness discoverable in the practice of the Christian faith in Africa. At the second level, African Christian theology plays a critical role. This is achieved through an analysis and critique of the socio-cultural context by an

---

2. See for instance Charles Nyamiti's criticisms of Orabotor's work *From Crisis to Kairos* in Nyamiti, *Studies in African Christian Theolog*, 203–30. Orabotor's latest work also addresses the priority of an inculturated ecclesiology of the Church as family of God in Africa, which was the image chosen by the First African Synod of 1994. This work shows that the image of the Church is open to new understanding in African culture through a new grammar from the African context. See *Theology Brewed in an African Pot*, 81–93. A comprehensive study of some African ecclesiologies being developed on the model of *Lumen Gentium* could be found in McGarry and Ryan, *Inculturating the Church in Africa*.

interpretation and application of the Christian message to African Christian experience within the wider African history and Christian history. This critical role extends to the Christian message itself since it is always carried in the vessel of cultures that are always in need of redemption. The Christian message and the Christian experience in Africa should be the constant frames of reference in the hermeneutical task of the African theologian as he or she searches for the eschatological fruits of God's kingdom within history. The naming of these experiences should be governed by the search for abundant life, that is, the irreducible offer Christ has made to all Christians and which is analogically related to the goal of African Traditional Religions.

The goal of African theology is accountability both to African and Christian histories. At the same time, it must integrate the full range and phases in African history as they impact on the African condition, African Christian experience, and the future of Africans. This is why cultural hermeneutics that mediates the data of the inner enrichment of African history in its totality, and engages the cross-cultural currents that impact on this history, should be the starting point of African Christian theology. Any theology then which is to be considered African will shed light on the diverse histories of African peoples in their antiquity, uniqueness, diversities, complexities, and ambiguities in order to discover what is enriching or harmful to human and cultural good within Africa. The search for human and cultural development as constitutive of human fulfillment should be the concern of African theology using the categories, terms and relations offered by the Christian message and African cultural and religious history, as well as African social context.

The African condition can best be explained through a commitment to African history in its richness and diversity (African traditional religion, African cultural traditions, African worldview, African Christian experience, African Islamic experience, African political history, etc.). African theology cannot do without history nor should it be concerned with an abstracted Christian history or Christian gospel. This is because Christian consciousness in Africa today is a rich hue of the convergence of an appropriated Christian message with African culture and religion which continues to draw its data from Africa's cultural past and present, Africa's richly varied worldviews, and challenging social context. African Christianity today contains both missionary elements, and post-missionary elements: there are traditions that were introduced into African Christianity by missionaries, which continue to enrich the practice of the faith. There are also many elements found in today's African Pentecostalism, Catholicism, African Independent Churches, and Anglicanism, etc., which emerged spontaneously from the African appropriation of the faith through their own cultural momentum.

It is, therefore, wrong to impose on African Christians an essentialist understanding of the Christian message or to judge African condition by those canons. It is also unhealthy for Africans to look outside Africa for the rich harvest of the social gospel that has the very quality and character for the imaging of a new Africa, which is within the realm of God's plan for Africa. It is important to note that the Christian message is not a normative canon that has to be applied to various cultural and historical settings without some critical hermeneutics both of the gospel message itself and its application and actualization in various historical settings (Christian doctrine, faith, morals, liturgy, structures, laws, etc).

Since the person of Christ is central to Christian consciousness, and at the core of the Christian faith, since Christ is also central to the Christian understanding of history, human and cultural fulfillment, African theology must show how the centrality of divine revelation as the center of history in Christ integrates and transforms African understanding of history, anthropology, cosmology, and eschatology. The revelatory content of African religious traditions in its relation to and difference to Christian dogma of the triune God is also essential in articulating theologies in an African worldview. In doing this, African theology will be providing an analytical compass for African Christians to understand themselves, their religious worldview, to see the meaning or the lack thereof of meaning in their present history, and name how Christianity is contributing to the shape and texture of their present condition and showing the path for a better future. This is why I think that African theologies are mission theologies, and must be richly grounded in the social gospel to give answers to how charity in truth should become the dynamics of today's African Christianity and African societies. In this light, the task of African theology is more analytical than synthetic, and more descriptive than prescriptive.

A sharpened sense of history gained through a cultural immersion in the totality of African condition which yields a fuller picture of the African world, is a required basis for doing theology in Africa. African Christian consciousness should be *thickly described* as a construct and not a single reality or an isolated reality from the wider existential and historical leitmotif of the African. African theologians must name what they see in African history; and the African Christians should be able to see themselves and their experiences in the theological formulations that African theologians are proposing. This, I believe, is the ongoing question of history which every theology incessantly wrestles with whether it is inculturation or liberation or reconstructive, restorative, ecological, or feminist in shape and intention.

From the foregoing, it is obvious that there is no theology which should be proposed to Africa today which will not first show how the gospel has become good news indeed to Africans in their present challenging social context. What has Christianity brought to Africa? Why should Africans continue to embrace Christianity even though their communities continue to experience serious tension and instability? By taking up the social question of the day, Pope Benedict is leading in the way by calling the Church's attention to the ever-widening horizon of her social ministry in a globalized world of today.

Secondly, African theology today will not fit into any apodictic theological system. It will be a different theology because the African situation is different and also in many points unexplored and unknown. Thirdly, African theologians who integrate a historical approach to their theologies will achieve better success in pastoral appropriation because their theologies will be drawn from, be informed by, and lead back to the living condition of the people and their dynamic Christian consciousness. Fourthly, in place of the polarity between liberation and inculturation theologies, I am proposing a missional, cultural hermeneutic approach in doing African theology. This approach is concerned with how the reign of God is being established in African Churches, how the fruits of the reign of God are being reaped in Africa, as the Church engages with and crosses different cultural frontiers and social contexts in Africa. Thus, the role of theology in Africa will be accountability in terms of how a regenerative ethics of communion, mutuality, and friendship has become active and dynamic in the different settings of the Church and in the public square. Accountability here will also relate essentially to the core elements of the Christian message (the Trinity, the identity of the Church and Christian identity, revelation and the sources of revelation, the sacramental economy, human nature and destiny, and morality). It will also be concerned with how the dynamic nature of African religious consciousness is appropriating these core elements for the enrichment of the African Christian consciousness amidst the diversity of a global Christianity. Fifthly, African theology of development will not be different from an African Christology or an African Trinitology. On the contrary, it will be the natural extension and consequence of such theologies.

One of the challenges of doing theology in Africa is the pervasive influence of Western theological categories and frameworks that constantly lurk on the horizon for most African theologians. African theologies are still done with foreign languages, as many African languages continue to recede in usage. This is a serious limitation in every sense of the word. As a consequence, most African theologians attempt to use foreign categories to explain African cultural grammar, which obviously limits their meaning. In addition, African theologians also accept as given Western distinctions and divisions of theologies, which lead to specializations into for example a dogmatic theologian, a moral theologian, a pastoral theologian, a spiritual theologian, biblical theologian, etc. It is indeed, a thing of joy that many African theologians are becoming experts in various theological fields. However, this is where the challenge of rupture arises: the danger of pursuing our field of specialization without attention to the whole picture, and seeing our areas of study in the narrow lenses of exclusivity. African theologies are mission theologies because they deal with the whole horizon of Christian consciousness in their engagement with history and new and unexplored horizons of cultural knowledge, cultural artifacts, and cultural arts in Africa. This means that the division into fields of specialization will have a unifying base in the Christian consciousness of Africans, which is the apprehension of Christ from an integrated socio-religious and cultural world. The African Christian's religious consciousness is a compact or a construct which has different layers, but it is held together by the personal and group embrace of the person of Christ as central to this self or group understanding.

Thus, when as a theologian I construct a Christology or an ecclesiology, I am not inventing a new truth, nor am I creating a rupture of meaning between the identity of Christ and my Christian calling to help the poor. On the contrary, I am stating how my faith as a Christian is informed by my self-understanding as belonging to a community of faith in which an answer to the questions that arise from the social context is decisive for the practice of faith and morality. Thus, the African theologian must hold these different elements in harmony without creating extraneous terms and relations, which remove the reality of faith from the social reality of practical transformation of the secular or practical life sphere. This is the kind of African theology required for the social ministry of the Church and Christians. It will account for the Christian consciousness in its diverse expressions, and from the point of view of its sources. It will draw from a total ecclesiology in which the dualism between liberation and salvation in both their secular and divine expressions are unified through an immersion in trinitarian communion.

As Bruno Forte argues so profoundly in his *Trinity as History*, recovering the history of the Trinity in the history of the world shows the dynamism of history and redemption against a static horizon of faith. This is because "the whole of Christian existence is entered into through the Trinitarian mystery—not only on the place of personal existence but also on that of ecclesial and social life. Not by accident is the exile of the Trinity from the theory and practice of Christians reflected in the 'visibilism' and juridicism which often dominate the understanding of Church and which have had consequences on the socio—political plane."[3] He argues that the return to our Trinitarian homeland is the only way in which the Church and Christians can understand the social context of history at each epoch and the role of theology in it. Quoting G. Baget-Bozzo, he writes: "The greatest ecclesial problem and the greatest task for theology is that of making the Trinity a spiritually vital thought for the believer and for theology so that faith's whole doctrine and the believer's whole existence may be thought of and lived from the viewpoint of their Trinitarian profession. Consequently, the problem is one of understanding the profession of Trinitarian faith as the permanent beginning of any criticism of ecclesiastical existence, as part of the criticism of worldly

3. Forte, *Trinity as History*, 10.

existence and of the constant proposition of the eschatological measure of history."[4] An African theology of development is aimed at giving account of the trinitarian heart of ecclesial and Christian identity
and the consequences of this for living charity in truth. It will also
deal with the removal of social sins and injustice all of which create
obstacles to trinitarian communion.

The Church's social ministry in Africa becomes the more fruitful
when it draws from trinitarian life which brings about a community
of love in our churches, ecclesial settings and the environing community. Vatican II in *Lumen Gentium* enjoins this rather strongly,
that the Church is trinitarian. The crisis of the Church at all times,
whether with regard to her self-identity or social ministry, is the crisis
of identity. This manifests itself in the conflict between charism and
truth, interior spirituality and external involvement in the secular
life, communion and autonomy, and authority and obedience. These
conflicts are resolved through a return to the source of our life and
the destiny of the Christian journey: the Holy Trinity: the Father's
universal saving creative plan, the Son's mission of salvation, and the
sanctifying mission of the Holy Spirit. A social ministry rooted in the
Trinity is a service which reflects communion, relationship, friendship, reciprocity, total availability, gratuitousness, mutual self-giving,
holiness, obedience, solidarity, self-donation, and love. These are all
perichoretic aspects of Trinitarian life. The Church and Christians in
Africa are called upon to build communion, establish relationships
between God and people and among Christians themselves and build
the kingdom of God in our communities. This can be done through
a radical and total commitment to the poor, and the marginalized
in our African communities. This is not simply by condemning the
poor living situation of the poor, or through periodic statements from
Episcopal conferences and church officials. It demands sacramentalizing this commitment by bringing succor to the poor through real and
concrete signs of the reign of God. In this regard, humble service, cou-
rageous and prophetic witnessing to the truth of the social gospel, and
unfailing commitment to charity in truth becomes a concrete sign.

Many African theologians like Agbonkhianmeghe E. Orobator
have pioneered this new way of doing a unified mission theology
which performs both critical and prophetic ministry through a prac-

---

4. Ibid., 10–11.

tical and direct appropriation of the fruits of God's kingdom in a particular social referent in Africa.[5] Other new voices in Africa include Emmanuel Katangole, Teresa Okure, Francis Oborji, Mercy Oduyoye, Emmanuel Martey, Musa Dube, Musimbi Kanyoro, J. N. K. Mugambi, among others. These voices need to be listened to and their theologies studied. This will enable the Church and Christians in Africa discover the relevant theologies and approaches to wiping away the tears from the eyes of many Africans who daily walk in the dry and deadly desert of want and suffering. We can now identify four roles that the Church in Africa can play in her service of charity in truth. A theology of African development should show how these principles could be translated from theory to praxis.

The four roles that the Church in Africa should play in the service of charity in truth are not exhaustive, but other roles could be subsumed into any of these four: *credible and prophetic lifestyle, critical function and practical acts of love, Instrumental role, and cultural and human development.* I will proceed to briefly outline what these entail and then show in the subsequent section how this could be carried out through reconciliation, justice and peace, education and cultural development, and building a civilization of love. These four roles overlap and mutually reinforce each other.

CREDIBLE AND PROPHETIC LIFE STYLE AS FIRST STEP

The Church in Africa lives in the midst of a continent which as we have shown faces myriads of problems. At the same time, it is the continent with the highest growth in new membership to the Christian faith. These new members are not simply people who were born into the faith, but many of them are converting to Christianity from African Traditional Religion and Islam. The Church in Africa is also increasingly visible in the state with its membership, its educated class of clergy and religious. Most of them are dispersed in many educational institutions, and through her social ministries in health, education, agriculture, skills development, micro-financing, resettlement of refugees, care for orphans, widows, HIV/AIDS orphans, and survivors of

5. See his revised doctoral thesis, *From Crisis to Kairos*, especially the introduction, where he outlines in a coherent and articulate manner the limitations of current African ecclesiologies.

war. What is significant to anyone who observes the history of the Christian enterprise in Africa is that the Church in Africa can be a very strong force for change and social transformation.

However, what is needed most in today's churches in Africa is credible existence. The problem of the Church in Africa today is not the absence of means, or the lack of membership, or a drop in vocation to priestly and religious life. The Church in Africa is wounded by the presence of greed and materialism, which in many instances have infested our chanceries, rectories, and convents. This is a crisis of authenticity, fidelity, and faithfulness. One can say that Africa has left the age of innocence and that the fast-paced cultural and ethical crisis in the world today has also impacted African society in a very profound manner. We find this for example in the unsustainable life styles of many church leaders, unwieldy ecclesial structures, and bureaucracy that is too expansive and expensive to maintain in poverty-stricken dioceses and parishes. There are also all kinds of acquisitive tendencies by priests, bishops, and religious. These include the kind of cars they use, the number of travels they make abroad for non-pastoral reasons, the kind of cloth they wear, the type of houses they live in, liturgical vestments, sacred vessels, the kind of churches we build among others. The canonical requirements (see canons 282, 285, and 286) that ordained ministers and religious in the Catholic Church should live simply, and should not engage in commerce and must use what they have in excess to do charity appears to have been abandoned in many instances. As Fernando Domingues puts it, today many religious and clergy believe more in the transforming power of money than in the transforming power of evangelical poverty and grace. In an environment where the new churches in Africa are pioneering and promoting, the idea of "big men of the big God," the clergy and religious of Africa must show the face of the simple man of Galilee who made himself poor for our sake so that we can become rich in God. How can bishops, priests, and religious become poor with, for, and like the poor in Africa? How can our churches in Africa show solidarity with the poor who flock to our churches, rectories and chanceries?

This is a higher calling, which every diocese and every indigenous and foreign religious order should work out with sensitivity to the social environment in which they live. The kind of life the clergy and the religious live in Africa is decisive for the credibility and continuity of the gospel message in Africa today. The critical and practical functions of the Church's social ministry begin and end with the credible lifestyle of the clergy and religious. How can the Church in Africa condemn corruption in government when she is also reeling under the weight of corruption and lack of accountability? How can the Church in Africa condemn ethnicity, paternalism, and favoritism when she is also weighed down by these unchristian ways of seeing relationship? How many dioceses and parishes in Africa give annual financial statements to the faithful? How many bishops and directors of development and peace commissions at regional, national, and diocesan levels have given public and audited accounts? When will independent auditors begin to verify our financial claims in the Church in Africa?

What we have pointed out here is to highlight the urgent need of our times. The poverty in Africa is very dire and heart-wrenching. Many of our Christians continue to flock to churches because they believe that God hears the cries of the poor. However, if what they are offered are spiritual platitudes—or if they are taken advantage of by priests and religious—then we need to examine our consciences and our own faith in the gospel we preach. The poverty in Africa today demands that the Church in Africa should embrace a vulnerable mission and be indeed a poor Church at the service of the poor of the Lord.

A vulnerable mission proceeds from an incarnational kenotic disposition. People wish to encounter the love of Christ through us, but they cannot see Christ in us unless we are like Christ indeed in sharing in the tent of the poor. A vulnerable mission identifies totally with the poverty of the people and feels that an essential dimension of the transformation of the secular sphere is to become one with those who are victims of injustice and the absence of an order of peace and righteousness. Vulnerable mission is similar to an Igbo proverb that the firewood in the neighborhood is what the inhabitants use to cook food. We do not need for instance the replication of the bureaucratic structures in Western churches to run African parishes and dioceses. There is no need to build grand basilicas in Africa, which will impose heavy financial burdens on the poor of the land in both building and maintaining them. We need simple church structures in Africa to reflect the social conditions of our people. Vulnerable mission promotes a credible lifestyle because it helps the clergy and religious to live like

Jesus, to speak the language of the people. This way, the people can see this kind of living and enter into a relationship with the clergy and religious and thus come to encounter Christ.

A vulnerable mission is also very sensitive to the vulnerability of children, women, and those on the margins of society. It goes out in search of the poor and the weak in a comforting and supportive manner. That means that Church officials should not in any way treat the poor as objects for personal agendas, but rather as subjects of divine love. These vulnerable women, young girls, children, and men who flock to our rectories and chanceries in search of help are to be protected from any kind of verbal, emotional, sexual, and physical abuse. The Church must be a safe haven where young people, women, widows, orphans, divorced persons, children and all vulnerable people can come and feel protected from the harsh weather of abuse, poverty, and injustice. It will be a tragedy if such vulnerable people are themselves taken advantage of by bishops, clergy, and religious, or development officials in Church organizations.

The danger today is that it seems the Church in Africa is gradually losing her strong moral authority. At the same time her critical prophetic voice has become muted in many countries. In my country, Nigeria, for example, many bishops and priests accept many luxury cars and huge monetary donations from corrupt government officials and people of questionable wealth. This may be applicable to other African countries where Christianity has a strong hold on the public. The question here is: Is this necessary? Must we compromise our moral and spiritual authority as religious leaders by opting to embrace politically motivated largesse which goes a long way in eroding our credibility and distancing us from the common people? What will Jesus do in these circumstances? Where is the separation of the Church and state in this kind of situation? In addition, is providing luxury jeeps and SUVs for bishops and priests part of the use to which the government should put the taxpayers' money? Should church clerics accept any kind of gifts from any kind of sources? How can the Church be independent and neutral in a political climate where priests and bishops are no longer visible moral voices or have taken sides with one political party or another because of the connection of ethnic groups, religious/denominational affinity, or because they received some gratification and occult compensation?

CRITICAL FUNCTION AND PRACTICAL ACTS OF LOVE

There are two essential dimensions of the Church's ministry in Africa with regard to charity in truth: critical and practical aspects. The critical function of the Church in Africa is that of being the prophetic voice of the voiceless; holding the government accountable, forming the conscience of the faithful as well as witnessing through concrete examples to the value of charity in truth. The churches must also offer a gospel-driven compass for critically engaging the changing faces of Africa's cultural life. This way, Christians in Africa can live in the light of Christ and bring a new Africa through their culture of hard work, honesty, commitment to sacrifice, and openness to transcending the limiting horizon of sexism, prejudice, discrimination against people of other ethnic groups among other social sins that hamper the growth and development of people in Africa.

The Church in Africa should hold governments accountable for their glaring failures to promote and protect the common good. She should be in the forefront of the fight against corruption and advocacy for democratic reforms and constitutional regime, which will lead to free and fair elections and transparency in government. This, however, cannot be possible unless the Church in Africa looks inward to discover how she can toe the path of conversion in those anti-evangelical lifestyles that have greatly diminished the prophetic stature of the Church in her critical and practical service to charity in truth. An essential part of this service of the Church is admitting the truth about the reasons for the social condition in Africa today, and our part in either changing it or eroding the moral sensitivity which should bring a better society that shows in small way the signs of God's kingdom.

Another important dimension of the Church's critical role is cultural critique. Are there aspects of African social life which are unchristian and which defeat the social mission of Christians and the Church? In this sense, the Church should seek the hidden cultural grammar in some negative attitudes and behavior which work against a culture of hard work, promote dependency, encourage some social deviancy, sexual promiscuity, marital infidelity, human rights abuse, child abuse and neglect, and violence against women. This could be done through an analysis of culture, concentrating especially on worldview analysis and symbolic intentionality hidden beyond material culture, and power-relations from inherited and acquired cultural idioms and ideologies. This is a difficult challenge, but the Church in every age and at all times is always counter-cultural and lives in tension with cultural forces represented by "powers and principalities." Cultures do not approximate to the gospel message, but may contain seeds for the gospel. Cultures are not absolute, but human realities in which the divine could be found, but they are constantly open to transcendence and transformative grace. The prophetic role of the Church will require a clear message from the Church on the truth about human life, common life in society, the ultimate human destiny, and the beauty of human life, the place of the family in the divine economy of salvation, and the civic duties of the Christian.

Today, the agency of Africans in their development can no longer be ignored either by international organizations working with and for Africa, as well as by the Church in Africa. This agency is reflected in a concrete sense through cultural knowledge, arts, and artifacts, and cultural behaviors, and through religious worldviews.

The critical role of the Church in cultural hermeneutics for doing charity in truth will begin with understanding how African cultures understand the agency of the individual in his or her self or group transcendence. What are the resources in African cultures that Africans mine for improving their conditions in life in general, and changing the course of history? Sometimes the appeal to ancestral blessings or curses, or the pervasive impact of family curse, as explanatory of the presence of evil or misfortune, and which also is used to explain people's poverty or pain is very defeatist. It breeds fear and removes the critical edge required to defeat the causes of poverty beyond the spiritually paralyzing ineluctable appeal to inexorable fate based on ancestral grammar. Every diocese or parish could seek ways of understanding how people approach the question of poverty and wealth, and their place in bringing this about in their lives. Thus a critical approach and appraisal of received and inherited worldview is very essential in valorizing the agency of African Christians for transforming the cultures and societies of Africa.

Another aspect of this cultural critique will be the way family ties are interpreted and how aid is received and applied in family life. Do our close extended family ties encourage dependency? How can charity within families lead to empowerment instead of sustaining an unbroken chain of dependency that inevitably does not create wealth and even leads to the economic downfall of the family breadwinner? This extends to the extravagance and conspicuous consumption that characterize our seasonal cultural festivities, family reunion, funeral ceremonies, Christmas and Easter celebrations, and marriage ceremonies. Another aspect of African cultural life that needs to be constantly evaluated in the light of the Church's prophetic ministry are burial rites and rites of passages. These have encouraged hedonism, false lifestyles, and the waste of money. The regenerative ethics of love, mutuality, and friendship demands that modesty should be applied to festivities and funerals. Why should someone borrow in order to bury a dead parent? Why should people borrow in order to get married? In many African communities, young African Christians marry late in life because of the lack of means to celebrate what has become customarily extravagant and expensive marriage rituals.

Pope Benedict's eco-vision is also another important aspect of the critical function of the church. The Church in Africa should adopt a "green" policy aimed at making our churches energy efficient. Simple acts like garbage and refuse disposal will give a good example to the wider society. The Church must promote a green culture that avoids all kinds of wastes. Churches in Africa could be built through the use of African architecture. They could for example adopt solar energy and wind power for ventilation among others. The increasing ecological and environmental threats to Africa's space through toxic waste dumping, emission trading, oil exploration, the dumping of inferior electronic and electrical equipment, and the importation of used vehicles and airplanes with high percentage of carbon emissions should also be among the issues addressed by the Church in Africa as well as by African Christians. Also to be condemned is the increasing carbon footprints of many politicians, and church officials who use multiple cars and SUVs in their convoys and fleets.

In addressing some aspects of African culture through the church's critical role, one must display some sensitivity to what is necessary to a people's cultural self-understanding. However, it must be stated that every culture also has some artificial accretions, which often accumulate from consistent and enduring subjective choices that now rise to the level of social sins.

The practical function is already demonstrated in the direct and immediate agency of many churches in meeting the needs of many ordinary people who are hungry, homeless, and sick. It also relates more importantly to building on the assets of ordinary Africans through pro-active evangelically driven initiatives in the areas of education, capacity-building, co-operative groups, and various support networks which empower the poor especially women and children. Jozef D. Zalot's work is the most authoritative from the practical aspect of showing how the Catholic Church in Africa has been playing a prophetic role in African development.[6] Our attempt here is not to enumerate the specific nature of the practical social ministry but to set principles which should govern them, and interpret how they are presently operating in the light of the message of *Charity in Truth*.

INSTRUMENTAL ROLE

The instrumental role of the Church is clearly set out in *CIV* 47 when Pope Benedict teaches that the role of charity in the Church as well as in the wider society is to improve the living conditions of the people so that they can take control of their lives. Poverty makes it impossible for people to take control of their lives. Development is about improving and strengthening the agency of the people to take control of their lives. Since the people cannot attain this in isolation, the Church and other social capitals and agencies support them though acts of solidarity, aid, and other forms of assistance. This is what the Church's social ministry should aspire towards. "Development programs, if they are to be adapted to individual situations, need to be flexible; and the people who benefit from them ought to be directly involved in their planning and implementation" (*CIV*, 47)

The Church in Africa has a prophetic role, which the clergy and religious embody in their work and ministry, and the laity in their engagement in the ordering of family and public life. This prophetic function is primarily directed to the service of a believing community, which is called to be prophetic. The principle of subsidiarity applies here: we cannot take away from the people what they can do for themselves. The idea of a priest or religious who is the do-gooder,

---

6. Zalot, *Church and Economic Development*.

the one who travels abroad to bring money from "his or her" friends should now be abandoned in Africa. In its place, I propose the idea of a priest or religious who helps to animate and stimulate the prophetic vocation of the local Christians to self and group transcendence. The Church's leaders in Africa should become instruments for empowering the poor and not simply creating a cycle of dependency wherein the poor and structures that promote poverty are allowed to continue to exist.

This is why a new model of charity in truth is needed in Africa. This model begins from (1) where the people are; (2) It identifies with the people's condition through immersion in their socio-cultural situation, and (3) begins to build up the poor through a mutually embraced plan and mission midwifed through the people's initiative for empowerment and animated by a Christian vision. (4) It develops participatory practices that place at the center the active involvement of the people in articulating the vision, setting out goals, and day to day implementation of the vision through solidarity. This way the success of the vision is placed on the shoulders of the people, and the sustainability of each item of development is something that is within the parameters of the participants (the facilitator, volunteers, the poor, or the subjects of the development initiatives).

The people are the agents for their own development. Valorizing their agency will demand equipping them and strengthening their capacity. It needs to be emphasized that such a model does not diminish the visibility of priests, bishops, and religious in the social ministry, but makes their role relative. In many communities and societies in Africa, the priest performs a totality of function: he is the doctor, the teacher, the investment advisor, the grassroots community development mobilizer, as well as the religious leader who has answers to every question. He alone in many places is the one who has a car or motorbike in the community and makes himself available to drive people to hospital or take their mails to the city. That this is happening in today's Africa is a sad reminder of how far our people are receding in the world development index. The comforting thing, however, is that these were the situations in which many countries in Europe found themselves many years ago. Africa has to find her own model of development and not live or understand herself in comparative terms with the rest of the world. However, in providing these social services, the priest or religious must know that he or she is only a facilitator who helps to empower the people through participatory practices. Participatory practices enable the people to address their needs through building on their assets. The Church's service to charity in truth is the development of the situation in which the poor can participate in building up wealth by helping to remove the obstacles to this participation.

The Church in Africa should abandon all pretensions of having the answer to all the social problems of the people, and embrace the poor through an intimate and personal relationship at the grassroots level. Every parish in Africa should promote a social ministry and direct wealth-creation models (agriculture, skills development, co-operative groups, micro-credit etc) which builds on the assets of the people while being sensitive to the needs of the people. In many instances, the social ministry of the Church in a particular setting will have to be interventionist for example in the outbreak of disease, natural disasters, civil war among others. However, the Church's mission is not to defeat the poverty in Africa, she should be the instrument for bringing about new structures of empowerment which will enhance and valorize the agency of the people. She should form Christians to become new people with a new vision and mission, which they bring to bear to the secular realm.

This ideal might appear far-fetched, but is rooted in the cultural world of Africans. My experience with some groups with regard to doing charity in a number of African countries has taught me one important lesson: many poor and disadvantaged people in Africa are people of faith with a strong belief in their own ability to change their condition if they are given a little push. The focus should be very limited and manageable, but the action of the Church for the poor in Africa should be aimed at making it possible for people to actualize themselves in a meaningful way and not simply feeding on their needs or "throwing money" around on the problem. The parable of the mustard seed gives us an impetus to plant seeds of love, and seeds of opportunity for people with the firm trust that the seed will bear fruit. What is worrisome is when the Church is not planting seeds or where the main focus of the social ministry begins and ends with providing services to the poor (through relief services, handouts, clothing, drugs, etc.) in terms of meeting their needs.

Another danger to be avoided is making charitable services a means for making money. Charity in truth demands more than meeting needs, nor is it a business enterprise. This challenges the Church in Africa to concrete functional acts which lead to granting the poor the inconceivable prospects "to fight their own poverty doing the works they can do with their own hands, in their own time, with their own priorities . . . and to the extent that is possible, also with the financial resources they can gather" (Fernando Domingues).

Also to be noted here is the question which many people in Africa, especially in the Church, do not wish to ask: Are the social services of the Church in Africa to be provided for solely through foreign aid from Church-run charities in Europe, Scandinavia, Canada, and the USA? When will African bishops, priests, religious, social workers stop being beggars in international forums and European and North American churches? When will we Africans stop being considered as needy people caught in a poverty trap? Is it not time for us as a church to look inward to the inner resources and generosity of our people? How do other churches, especially African Pentecostals and African Independent Churches (who have no Western sponsors), raise the money for their burgeoning charitable missions? Is the instrumental function of the Church in Africa in doing charity in truth simply the raising of funds from abroad? How can the Church in Africa raise the money and resources needed for her social mission locally? Is there a way the Church in Africa can live simply especially bishops, priests and religious, so that the poor in their parishes and dioceses can be supported to work for a better life through the excesses now made available to them. These among other questions are important in addressing the instrumental function of the Church in Africa in the service of charity in truth.

EDUCATION AND CULTURAL DEVELOPMENT

What should be the vision of the Church and African societies for the educational and cultural development of African young people in African schools? Pope Benedict calls for greater access to education as the pre-condition for international development (*CIV*, 61). However, he notes that every education must aim at the formation of the whole person. His recipe for eradication of poverty is the accumulation of the human capital through education, so that poor countries will build themselves up through their human resources and these ways guarantee an autonomous future for their children and generations yet unborn (*CIV*, 58).

The Greek poet, Pindar, once noted that the goal of education is to help us become who we are. That, incidentally, is what a world-view does; it is a mirror through which we see who we are. Thus, Africans must be concerned about the quality of education that we are giving to our children in the continent, as well as abroad. What are the values that we wish to pass on to our children? Such values will evidently define the issues of racial identity within a multicultural society, inter-ethnic harmony, the scientific and technological needs of African society, the role of the Christian religion or Islamic religion or African traditional religion, and the kind of society we are building for ourselves and our children beyond the immediate ends of today.

Education opens doors that no other process can. It gives people a way to understand their world, to develop their self-identity and skills for working productively in order to support their families and contribute to the common good. Education is an important tool in alleviating poverty and addressing the inequalities within and between countries. Education is the key to national development and the path to the survival of civilizations. Education is not a commodity for sale to the highest bidder; it is a service provided by society for the benefit of her members, especially the young people. Education (formal and informal) is an ongoing dynamic, which should be open to both the young, as well as adults who have never had an education.

However, we cannot educate the young unless we clearly understand the content and end of education. It is important that any educational process must take into consideration the cultural tradition of the people. This is what is lacking in many African countries. I contend that Western education, as practiced in African countries, must be brought into harmony with the specific challenges facing Africa today; it should, therefore, be weeded of its secular accretions and pass through the rich rarefied fields of African cultural traditions.

Writing on African education, the former Nigerian minister for education and foremost educationist, Babs Fafunwa, notes that there are seven characteristics of traditional African education, namely:

physical training, development of character, respect for elders and peers, intellectual training, vocational training, agricultural education, trades and crafts, community participation, and promotion of cultural heritage.[7] These meet the requirements of authentic educational philosophy. This is because they responded to the challenges that faced the traditional Africans at that point in time, which included establishing the preeminence of the community and social life, the intimate bond between social life and spiritual values, the multivalent character of formation to meet with diverse life situations, and the gradual and progressive development and formation of the physical, emotional, and mental faculties of the child. These should be integrated into the formulation of any philosophy of education in African schools today.

Since fundamental questions concerning the aim and nature of education are within the purview of philosophy of education, we ought to develop a philosophy of education that is native to us, receptive to other influences, yet strong enough not to lose its creativity and able to inform and form the mind of Africans. Any philosophy of education necessarily derives from a philosophy of life of the group. "A philosophy of life or worldview consists of a set of assumptions, beliefs, concepts and ideas (explicit or implicit) in terms of which one understands the world and interprets one's experience of it within that framework; and a set of values, principles and attitudes which influence how one chooses to act in it. A philosophy of life is an understanding of ultimate reality and life and one's place in it."[8]

An educational system is informed by the assumptions and beliefs on the nature of the human person, the ultimate purpose of life and human destiny, and the goal of common life among others. Two realities emerge from the foregoing excursus. The first is that every educational system has a worldview that underpins it; and the second is that those who are formed in that educational system are formed according to this worldview. The success or failure of any educational system can only be judged by its philosophy of education and the applications of this philosophy in the educational enterprise.

7. Fafunwa, *Education in Nigeria*, 20–48.

8. I am grateful to the Maryvale Institute, Birmingham, UK, for this useful insight on educational aims, which forms the guiding principle of this educational institution.

Philosophy of education is concerned with ascertaining the purpose of education and the meaning of the key terms associated with the educational process. The content and character of education are determined by what one perceives to be its aims and purpose. This is further informed by the concept we have of the human person and his or her place in life and society. All educational systems, whether Western, Islamic, Christian, or African must revolve within a philosophical cycle, evident or implied. Education is a process of transmitting cultures in terms of continuity and growth and for disseminating knowledge either to ensure social control or to guarantee rational direction of society or both.[9] Education is concerned with the formation and development of human beings, or as Jacques Maritain notes, education does not consist in adapting a potential citizen to the conditions and interactions of social life, but in *first making a man* and thus preparing a citizen.[10]

The reason for the underdevelopment of Africa is the low quality of her educational institutions. Most of us who studied abroad or who teach abroad immediately know the difference between the education in Africa and that in Canada, the USA, or Europe. The African condition plays a major role in weakening our educational institutions and African students can do better if African society and the church make quality education, cultural and human development a priority. The schools mirror the society, just as the politics and the governance of any country is a mirror into the soul of such societies.

The foremost Jewish philosopher and theologian, and the Chief Rabbi of the United Hebrew Congregations of the Commonwealth, Jonathan Sacks in his best selling book, *The Dignity of Difference*, makes some bold but interesting claims about the reason for the success of Jewish people in the world in spite of adversities. If you ask many Africans, especially Christians, why the Jews are one of the most successful races on earth, they will say that it is because Jews are God's chosen race. Sacks will agree with this, but with some qualifications. He argues that tied to the idea of covenant and being a chosen people of Yahweh, was the conscious effort since the constitution of Israel as a people to place education as the number 1 value for "Jewishness." Universal literacy is a pretty recent idea in the Western world going

9. Fafunwa, *Education in Nigeria*, 17.
10. Maritain, *Education*, 15.

back to 1870 when Britain became the first Western nation to make universal education a basic right. Sacks argues that already by 1000BC most Jews could read and write. By the third century in the Common Era, that is less than 250 years after the death of Jesus, the Jews were all dispersed in many parts of Europe, and some parts of Africa. However, the Jewish rabbis made a rule that every Jewish community that failed to establish a school was to be excommunicated. Is it any surprise to anyone that there are no Jews in the world today no matter how isolated they are from fellow Jews who do not learn to read and write the Hebrew language? Throughout the centuries, until the Enlightenment in the seventeenth and eighteenth century—when the rest of Europe was illiterate in the darkness of ignorance, wars, and diseases—the Jews maintained an educational infrastructure as their highest priority. It is no exaggeration to say that this lay at the heart of the Jewish ability to survive catastrophe, negotiate change, and flourish in difficult circumstances.[11] The Jews have taught the rest of the world, and they have proved that the basis for building a society of equal human dignity does not lie in the distribution of wealth or power, but on *equal access to education*. Education is power, and the race that does not prioritize education will forever be slaves at the foot of those races that did otherwise.

I have chosen this as one of many examples of a lack of authentic and context-sensitive education. We cannot progress as African peoples unless we dig deep into our cultural traditions and appropriate them in new ways in the identity conscious world of today. This can be applied to other aspects of life in Africa. Nigeria, for example, cannot manage her oil wealth because she does not have the manpower to do so. Why should Mobil, Shell, Chevron, and other foreign conglomerates manage African oil and transfer overseas, 37 percent of Africa's oil wealth? Why can China, India, Brazil, Venezuela, etc., be on the cutting edge of industrialization, information technology, and various scientific advances and Africa is backward in educational innovation, and scientific and technological growth?

The problem is our educational system. The statistics of Africa's educational backwardness are too grim to mention (high level of illiteracy, low productivity, drop in male enrolment, lack of priority to the education of the girl child, undue preference of stochastic drop

11. Sacks, *Dignity of Difference*, 169.

in skills or professional life, exam malpractices, etc.). Many Africans agree that human and cultural development is the goal of all authentic educational enterprise and the only path to development in any society. Most challenges in developing societies like ours can be met through integral education and the accompanying social reconstruction that is the natural consequence of education. The Church and Christian charities in Africa can play a pivotal role in the following areas:

1. *Policy Formation.* Educational aims in Africa should reflect African cultural values. This demands that the aims of education should reflect Africa's unique condition. They should integrate a liberal classical education that embodies the search for wisdom in science, technology, and arts with a religio-moral vision. Many years after independence, the curricula and syllabi of schools in Africa were written by their former colonial lords who also set educational standards for African countries. This appears to be changing in some African countries, which realize that most of these aims do not respect Africa's particular needs. The educated person in Africa is usually seen as the Westernized person and not the true African. Shortly before I left my country to study in Rome, my dad told me, "When you reach the Whiteman's land, try and know what they know but return to Africa a true Igbo African man." That explains what I mean by shaping educational policy to respect African cultural values. Africa needs to be open to the fruits of Western education, but she does not need to see Western education as the touchstone of educational orthodoxy.

2. *A Keen Sense of African History.* Every authentic education in Africa must embrace, in its totality, African histories both past and present. African history in this context includes political, cultural, scientific, technological, literary, and educational traditions. A proper understanding of Africa's past before her contact with the West, her pains under Western influence, and the ongoing identity crisis of Africa must be inculcated into young Africans. As elementary and high school student most of us spent a greater time learning Greek and European history. Little or no attempt was made to teach us African history. Schools in Africa should become centers for the recovery of the African past. The young people should be challenged to understand and appreciate their cultural identity and the sad and

glorious epochs of Africa's past. A true sense of history is often the best motivation to face the future.

3. *Context Education.* Education in Africa should respect the context of the students. This is what Thomas Groome has called "consciousness raising" because it enables people to think contextually; to analyze what is going on in their lives and in their world and why and how historical circumstances shape their lives, society, and their future. Groome proposes four important questions, which every student should answer relative to context education: (1) What is really going on here and why? (2) Who is benefiting? (3) Who is suffering? (4) What is influencing my own perspective?[12] Research and reflections in our schools and learning among the students should revolve around the specific challenges facing each African country. Unfortunately, in most African schools, what is offered is far removed from the reality of the students.

The African countries, for instance, with mineral resources, should be training their citizens to take control of their natural resources. There can be no authentic development and maximization of profit from African mineral resources if foreign companies are controlling these sectors and transferring the profit to their home. The same applies to agricultural products. Unless Africans take control of their industrial, agricultural, and mineral resources sectors they cannot make any progress economically. This is where capital is needed by the African governments. Financing industrial development is very capital intensive. However, what is most important is for the government to encourage a new kind of educational process that is contextual; there are talks about the transfer of technology from the West to Africa, but that is not realistic. What is possible is the development of basic education in the direction of local needs, the discovery of local techniques and African rationality, supplemented by the educational heritage outside Africa such that gradually there could emerge a new crop of Africans that is sufficiently empowered to take control of the resources of the continent.

There is also the need for cultural and critical education. The formation of our young people must integrate the understanding of African cultural history. Many of us who studied in Africa only started to appreciate and deepen our cultural history and African stud-

12. Groome, *Educating for Life*, 389.

ies when we left Africa. This is because it hits one like a thunderbolt that our cultures and histories are the only thing we can call forth in our encounter with people from other cultures. Authentic education within the Catholic tradition, for instance, is an integral education that will enrich African students by teaching them the richness of Christian tradition, history, morals, and values with regard to the social order, and the ultimate human destiny. It will also and more importantly teach them the values and greatness of their own histories and cultures.

The Church was the agent for the intellectual and cultural transformation of the West. Indeed, without the pioneering educational enterprise of the Church especially in the Middle Ages, the foundation of the Enlightenment or Industrial Revolution would not have been laid. The culture of reading and writing, the preservation of intellectual treasures and the arts, the invention of modern means of communication, telescope, industrial artifacts, the idea of schooling etc were all the fruits of the Church's cultural production for Western society.[13] The fulfillment of the African person, and the transformation of Africa today can only begin with the quality of education which the Church and the state and other agencies in Africa must pioneer in a renewed and deliberate manner in our times.

African students should also be given the critical framework to examine their received and imposed values, the freedom to explore uncharted territories, and the inventive skills for the flowering of the arts, the sciences and creativity in our schools.

Also to be noted here is the danger of Westernization in our schools. In many of the seminaries and centers of ministerial formation in Africa, the curriculum is still written and imposed from Rome and other Western centers of learning. The freedom of universities and schools to explore the inexhaustible range of truth should not be imperiled by ecclesial fiats that limit the possibility for new discoveries. Catholic schools are centers of evangelization, but today the challenge of evangelization has shifted from simply the transmission of gospel truth to attention to the diverse settings in which the gospel is being appropriated. Catholic education is not indoctrination but simply education that leads the student to understand himself or herself and his or her place in the world, which leads to human fulfill-

13. See Woods, *How the Catholic Church Built Western Civilization.*

ment and ultimate fulfillment at the end of life. This demands a more context-sensitive approach in both the truth to be proposed and the tools which are to be made available to the student in each case.

4. *The Quality of Teachers.* There can be no authentic transmission of knowledge and the unfurling of the latent powers of the young people of Africa without qualified and motivated teachers. Effective education requires qualified and motivated teachers, who will be role models to the students. Teachers are custodians of humanity, for they play a vital role in handing on the right kind of values and attitudes that make for a stable society. Unfortunately, teachers in African countries, are underpaid and overworked, hence, they lack enthusiasm for the work and eventually reproduce many unwholesome tendencies in their students. There are all kinds of examination malpractices, sexual harassment of students, bribery and corruption in schools and higher institutions of learning. Sometimes, students are exploited financially by their teachers, especially in universities and colleges. The teachers also lack adequate training, teaching techniques and educational resources like good libraries, computers, and internet services to help them enrich themselves as well as their students.

5. *Priority of Education.* African governments must make education, skills acquisition, and literacy their first objective. Free education should be introduced in Africa at least at the primary school level. Many African countries like Ghana, Malawi, Uganda, Lesotho, Tanzania, Madagascar, Zambia, Benin, Cameroon and Kenya have all abolished school fees. In each of these countries, school enrolment went up considerably because parents in Africa want their children to go to school but most of them cannot afford to pay their school fees. No other issue in Africa is as important as education. There are many crises in the continent, which might make this objective appear impossible, but aggressive war against illiteracy is the only way African countries can move forward in this day and age. The civilization that can stand on its own, in the world of today, is the one that has perfected the art of transmission of knowledge, from within her womb, with capillaries and arteries in other educational traditions to enrich her own native genius.

6. *A Pedagogy of Hope.* This is a subtitle of Bell Hooks work,[14] which I find appropriate for capturing the kind of formation that stu-

14. Hooks, *Teaching Community.*

dents should receive in African educational institutions. Schools in Africa should be centers for building a sense of hope, by making the students recognize the immense potential that God has implanted in them. Schools in Africa should make the students realize that they can contribute in making a change in the African society; that the future of the continent is in their hands. This is why the quality of education offered in schools in Africa is very fundamental. It should embody a sense of hope and inspire a progressive engagement of the students with the African experience and condition. It should empower the students to realize that their lives can help make a difference in Africa and that they have an infinite capacity for goodness and creativity which they can realize within their life time. Hopeful education is one that brings the students to the truth that life is worth living and dying for; that the community and the family are part of our history and demand our sacrifice, and that the future of African countries lies in their hands. Hopeful education is education that also inspires the people to work for justice, peace, and right relationship; to cultivate character; and to be purpose-driven. It also offers the students the prospect of infinite self-discovery and the encounter with history and people, which goes beyond the mere toleration of others to a healthy collaboration with them, to realize the common good of our societies and nations.

HEALTH AND HEALING

As we have pointed out in chapter three, health and healing are very essential for human fulfillment in Africa today. There are so many preventable deaths in Africa and so much suffering and sickness, which weaken the capacity of Africans to work. These diseases leave deaths, pain, and poverty in their wake. Unfortunately, there are many unscientific explanations to these deaths, which might satisfy the cultural and religious mentality but do not give a sufficient scientific or preventative guide and fail to offer help for the future health and well-being of the people. Healthcare is properly speaking the duty of the government. In many African countries, public health is provided for in annual budget and is controlled by the government. There are also private agencies that provide alternatives to government public health care. In many instances, these private hospitals, clinics, laboratories, and pharmacies provide better quality healthcare than government agencies. In most cases, the poor cannot afford these quality private healthcare services. The government healthcare services, which are poor in most cases, are not free; hence many ordinary Africans resort to traditional and herbal medicines, and native doctors and orthodox healthcare practitioners for health and healing.

The Catholic Church is very visible in healthcare services in Africa. She, of all religious groups and private agencies working in the healthcare industry in Africa, has the largest number of private hospitals and clinics providing Medicare and, in some cases, free medical treatment for HIV/AIDS, pregnant women, and people suffering from malaria. This happens even in those African countries where the Catholic Church is not a majority. In Ghana for instance, Catholics make up about 30 percent of the population but control more hospitals than any other private agency in the country. In Africa, the Church works in 16,178 health centers, including 1,074 hospitals, 5,373 out-patient clinics, 186 leper colonies, 753 homes for the elderly and physically and mentally less able brothers and sisters, 979 orphanages, 1,997 kindergartens, 1,590 marriage counseling centers, 2,947 social re-education centers and 1,279 other various centers. There are 12,496 nursery schools with 1,266,444 registered children; 33,263 primary schools with 14,061,000 pupils, and 9,838 high schools with 3,738,238 students. Some 54,362 students are enrolled in higher institutes, of which 11,011 are pursuing ecclesiastical studies. There are in Africa, fifty-three national chapters of Caritas, thirty-four national commissions of justice and peace and twelve institutes and centers promoting the Social Doctrine of the Church. This means that there are enough centers for promoting healthcare, and other aspects of the instrumental role of the church's social ministry. More could be done in this regard, but we know that the Church cannot take over the function of the state to provide healthcare.[15]

Herein lies the need for the Church and men and women of goodwill to mount a sustained effort in pressing for healthcare reform in Africa, and hold the governments of Africa accountable for the high rate of infant mortality, maternal mortality, HIV/AIDS infection, other diseases like Malaria, typhoid, meningitis, hepatitis, etc., and many infectious tropical and water borne diseases. African

15. http://www.cisanewsafrica.org/story.asp?ID=4163.

societies can no longer continue to accept the breakdown in the public health sector and glaring failure in a sector that is central to the survival of society.

The Church can also help in spreading sound message on good health practices. For example, the use of hand sanitizers, the preservation of clean water and basic water treatment to prevent infectious diseases and vectors which cause diseases, provision of clean drinking water for the people, the basic hygiene and sanitation which could help reduce infectious diseases. With regard to the spread of HIV/AIDS, there should be an aggressive education of young people and married people on the need for chastity before marriage and chastity within marriage. The ongoing sexual exploitation of young girls and women should be proactively condemned by the Church, and Christians must be taught the virtue of respect and reverence for sexuality through an appropriate theology of the body.

The question of the use of condom as prevention for HIV/AIDS is one which I have addressed in *The Face of Africa: Looking Beyond the Shadows* and do not need to be repeated here. However, the use of condom for prevention of this disease is one that demands a more comprehensive moral and ethical consideration beyond what is presently being provided by churches. It is also a question that I think should be left to individual consciences in terms of what should be done to save life and prevent deaths. However, these consciences need to be formed on the moral demands, the dangers of a condom mentality, and the obligation to protect their lives and that of their partners and spouses. The empirical reality is that there is already a condom mentality that has taken hold in some settings in Africa; there is also a resistance to the use of condom in many African societies. Thus, we need a cultural hermeneutic approach that raises the ethical questions involved within the wider concerns of promoting and maintaining healthy lifestyles in Africa. Those who call for the use of condom for therapeutic reasons in Africa and in many parts of the world need to be listened to by the Church. At the same time, we cannot abandon the future of our young people into the protection of condom, which does not guarantee 100 percent success. This was one of the messages of Pope Benedict XVI when he visited Africa in March, 2009. Unfortunately, the message was drowned in the heap of criticisms and some ideologically driven interpretations. However, the reason for the spread of HIV/AIDS in Africa goes beyond the use or lack of the use of condom. It deals with questions of the failure of the public health system, ignorance and lack of adequate education about health and sickness, cultural generalizations about health, sexuality, and diseases, family life, poverty, and the exploitation of women. At the end of the day, all issues that are related to HIV/AIDS could be reduced to a *moral* problem and not a technical one.

However, it is important that the Church also be in the forefront of helping to remove the taboos and shame associated with the disease. There are already many religious leaders who have admitted their HIV/AIDS status and have also joined in the campaign for better education and support for those who are suffering from this disease. The message should be prophetic and clear: Africa is in the grip of a terrible epidemic and everything should be done to save the continent from this pandemic. It is better to abstain from sex than to infect another, or have double infections. So even if condom will protect me, what if it doesn't when it bursts or slips in the sexual act? The Church also must concretely pursue the effort to make Anti-retroviral medication and care for AIDS patients available at free or affordable prices to sufferers. It is a shame that only about 10 percent of HIV/AIDS patients in Africa are receiving treatment and care, while the rest are left to die a slow and shameful, harrowing death watched by helpless poor families and friends. It is also worrying that in many African countries government hospitals and clinics charge people for HIV testing, and for antiretroviral medication where they are available. This shows how little premium is attached to the lives of many poor people in Africa.

The presence of so many diseases in Africa and the "sudden death" syndrome (unexplained sudden deaths) in the continent have spread so much fear and anxiety in the land. It is not surprising that the aspect of Christian faith that has grown in stature and relevance is the healing ministry. It is another aspect of the instrumental role of the Church in Africa. How can we offer holistic healing to our people? This explains why Pentecostal and Charismatic healing ministries and services have become present in all Christian denominations in Africa.

In historically examining the phenomenon of healing in African Pentecostalism, African theologians and church leaders should ask some fundamental questions: Are Pentecostal beliefs, charismatic experience, doctrines, and claims of healing logical and scientific? How do the healing ministries in African Pentecostalism reflect the African condition of suffering, poverty, and social disharmony? What are the similarities and differences between healing in African Pentecostalism and in African Traditional Religions as well as in Western medicine? How does the African undergo the charismatic experience with regard to healing, being possessed by evil spirit or by the Holy Spirit, deliverance sessions and restoration? How are sicknesses, healing, and restoration understood in African Pentecostalism? What type of philosophical inquiries and worldview analyses are used by African Pentecostals, healthcare providers, social scientists, philosophers, etc., in understanding health and healing and for proposing rational answers to fundamental questions of life (such as sickness, health, demonic attacks, witchcraft, wealth, death, love, forgiveness, etc.)? Can the African charismatic experience give expression and meaning to the cosmos as it enters a particular relationship with modern science and the wider search for ecological systems theories which address the wider common concern of humanity and the ecosystem for abundant life and sustainability?

The healing ministry offers a mirror into understanding the Pentecostal and charismatic renewal in African Christianity and reveals the urgent need for solidarity and accountability for our people's health by the Church's social ministry. It also deals with the African condition, African ontology, and worldview, the question of social change, social stability, and social integration. Thus, we need to discover the richness of healing as essential to Christian consciousness and morality in Africa with regard to how healing in today's Pentecostal and Charismatic ministries reflect the search by Africans for wholeness and abundant life. This will not only immerse the Church in the social context of Africa with regard to total ecclesiology, it will in addition use an understanding of the charismatic experience to open up Africa's map of the universe of suffering, evil, and pain and how this is both reflective of a new concern for social harmony, progress, and ethical and communal integration and reconciliation amidst the debilitating problems of social, economic, and political instability.

The socio-cultural approach in this instrumental role of the Church in the health and healing of African societies and peoples will answer two questions relevant to social change and competing claims to power: Has Pentecostal and Charismatic renewal in African Christianity valorized the agency of African Christians through a new ethical and pragmatic consciousness for procuring health and abundant life for Africans in their challenging social context? This is a question about the goal of religion as such in Africa, and the bases for legitimizing religious experience. It will highlight the power-relations between the many religious claims and counter claims in today's Africa with regard to moral, religious, and political authority in bringing about social change and progress in Africa. The second question is a question of identity: What has African Pentecostal and Charismatic renewal altered or reinforced about African religio-cultural identity in its claims to bring health, abundant life, and the struggle for power and control of the public and private domains in Africa? Answering these questions and positing them as challenges are all essential aspects of our social ministry. The questions these pose today provide data for theology in Africa and opportunities for an effective and holistic service to charity in truth.

GRASSROOTS APPROACHES TO SOCIAL MINISTRY

Charity in Truth emphasizes the importance of grassroots approaches when Pope Benedict writes; "Economic aid, in order to be true to its purpose, must not pursue secondary objectives. It must be distributed with the involvement not only of the governments of receiving countries, but also local economic agents and bearers of culture within civil society, including local churches. Aid programs must increasingly acquire the characteristics of participation and completion from the grassroots" (*CIV*, 58). The structure of our churches is an asset in the grassroots service to charity in truth. However, what should be abandoned is a top-down approach in which national and diocesan commissions on justice, peace, and development lay down principles and practices for distribution of aid without sensitivity to context. This is very evident in much of global partnership between local charities and international and national organizations. Aid and development initiatives in Africa and between African churches and Western church organizations like Caritas, Missio, Canadian Catholic Development and Peace Agency, the United States Conference of Catholic Bishops' Commission for Justice and peace have become too bureaucratized.

There are so many pieces of paperwork to be dealt with and so many forms to be filled that development facilitators in Africa have been forced to sometimes "manufacture" reports just to meet the growing demand of the donors to produce results and reports. Accountability is very important in the service to charity and truth and is a way of witnessing to the world that we are good stewards of the treasury of the Church for the poor (who are indeed the treasure of the Church). However, partnership with African churches and pastoral and social ministries should become more involved and direct and should not be limited to use of middle persons and Church officials. Vulnerable mission is also called for both for local African social and pastoral workers in the area of development, as well as Western churches and organizations. They should consider it meaningful and a great form of solidarity to visit Africa (not as tourists but as development partners), staying in the villages and hamlets and not in the protective walls of choice hotels and exclusive retreat centers. They should spend some time with the ordinary people, being immersed in the culture of the people, and building friendship and inter-cultural communications and exchanges.

This is what I learnt from my work with the Engineers Without Borders-USA, University of Illinois, Champaign-Urbana chapter. Between 2006 and 2009, more than fifteen engineering students and two professors from this group spent the average of three weeks in a local Nigerian community. Most of them spent more than three months in the community. The project they were interested in was a water project. In the first year of their visit, the local community thought that the project would be completed within two months or even two weeks since, as they thought, these were *American* engineers with all the equipment and money needed to complete the work. However, the first visit was mainly to build friendship, explore possibilities, and understand the environment and the assets of the people. The cross-cultural friendship which developed among the three stake holders to the project—the Adu Achi community, the Engineers Without Border-USA, and the Canadian Samaritans for Africa—was more decisive than the water project which was completed in 2010 over a period of five years. In addition, the influence of the female engineering students from the University of Illinois was very immediate and profound on female education in this community. Many young girls saw for the first time women engineers, exercising power over men because Maren Somers (to whom this book is dedicated), was the female director of the group, and Cheryl Wyatt was the project director. What was evident in this project was that (1) it was grassroots based; (2) the American and Canadian partners lived in the community, they ate the same food with the people, drank the same water but this time around showed how the water could be purified, they made genuine efforts to understand the culture and life of the people; they played soccer with the people and learned to dance and play their music and songs. In addition, they (3) built friendship and strengthened the people's capacity to take charge of their lives and their community projects like water, sanitation, hygiene, preventative measures for diseases like measles, HIV/AIDS, malaria, etc. There were many challenges that were overcome in this partnership, which is still ongoing. However, at the end of each visit most of the Americans and Canadians wanted to return to Nigeria and many of the Nigerians from this community were involved at different levels of participatory practices. All these strengthened their capacity to apply themselves to their environment and helped them effectively use the aid and support from both the Engineers Without Borders and the Canadian Samaritans for Africa.

Each group has to work out its own participatory practices that will be mutual, involving both the development agents and the local hosting communities. This is a model that can work also even for local priests, nuns, and community-development experts in Africa. The model is simple: it is in African small communities and villages that the birth of a new Africa will take place. There are robust local cultural networks, support systems, and economic models that are capable of taking higher responsibilities and creating wealth if they received some consistent financial and technical support from national government, church and voluntary organizations, and international donors. Small initiatives in these small communities have direct and immediate impact on poverty eradication. It is, therefore, important that social networks like women co-operatives, micro-credit unions, educational initiatives, skills development, and small businesses, as well as small agricultural loans initiatives in these small communities should be encouraged and supervised. These kinds of initiatives could be started and effectively managed by parishes and local churches independently with little help and supervision from diocesan, state, provincial and national organizations.

There is so much money lost in donor aid in Africa through bureaucracy and middlemen and women who highjack the whole development process and, in many cases, undermine the goal of charity in truth. This is particularly sad in religious and Church organizations. It is ethically wrong and defeats the whole goal of the principle of participation for a bishop, priest, nun, or NGO to seek for aid for a people without first obtaining their permission and involving them in the process. It is also ethically wrong to divert funds meant for development projects to other areas of need no matter how pressing and urgent. The intention of the donors should always be respected. This returns to our primary thesis in the foregoing analysis on principles for Church charity. Development of Africa—whether through Church, private, or governmental agencies—is primarily the responsibility of the *African* people. While I do not subscribe to Moyo's call to abolish aid to Africa, I think we need to gradually overcome an aid mentality, and the dependency cycle that have held Africa down. We need to look inwards to the material, human, and spiritual resources of Africa especially in small units and communities where there are gradual and steady growths. As a result, before seeking international aid for a diocese, parish, community, professional group, or a needy category—except in emergency or interventionist situation—the agents of development must seek first what the people can do for themselves. He or she will then work out project plans and proposals with the people's input and support.

Many scandals, which have arisen in fraudulent and phantom projects in some African church projects, arise from the lack of participatory practices wherein one person writes for projects for a people without their input. The money ends up in the person's private account and he or she can produce bogus reports at the end without any practical referent or verifications. The trust needed for international development projects and donor aid to Africa goes beyond the credibility of a development agent, a bishop, or a religious; it demands building trust with the final recipients of donor support: the ordinary people. This trust means that the people fully embrace the vision; that they agree to play their own part in the implementation, that they will contribute a significant portion of resources and financial support for the project, and will be good stewards of the project. This kind of approach is more manageable and accountable than big national programs that end up being limited and local after much waste of time and resources. However, many international organizations and Church agencies prefer to be seen as successful because of their wide national and continental outreach. Grassroots, small, and manageable development aid should be preferred to big and unmanageable national and continental projects. This is the wisdom in the internationally accepted axiom: think globally act locally.

Grassroots approaches will concentrate on the strengths and assets of the people; it will build on the energy and initiatives of intermediate agencies like parishes, churches, women's groups, age-grades, cultural groups, farmers, professional and semi-skilled artisans. It is an approach that meets the people where they are and does not impose development projects on them but builds on what they have. Grassroots approaches can operate in both rural and urban settings, because it always seeks some identifiers that can be used as platform for development. Discovering these small initiatives in Africa and strengthening them should be vital to the success of the church's social and pastoral ministries.

RECONCILIATION IN THE CHURCH IN AFRICA AND IN AFRICAN COMMUNITIES AND NATIONS

The Second African Synod's theme reflects clearly the urgent need for reconciliation in Africa.[16] There can be no justice and peace in African communities, churches, and nations unless people are reconciled to one another. Development cannot take place in an environment where people cannot work together because of ethnic differences, ancient prejudices, inter-ethnic and intra-ethnic and clannish differences. Divisions, violence, civil wars, conflicts, and chaos whether they are political, economic, religious or cultural defeat any attempt at a ser-

16. See the impressive collection of essays which I co-edited on the Second African Synod, *The Church as Salt and Light: Path to an African Ecclesiology of Abundant Life*. Also to be noted is another collection of essays edited by Agbonkhianmeghe E. Orobator, *Reconciliation, Justice, and Peace: The Second African Synod*. Both books are very practical and constructive in showing how the dreams of Africans can be realized through the agency of African Christianity and African theological reflections on social transformation through the social gospel.

vice of charity in truth. This is why the primary service of the Church in Africa should be to confront truthfully and honestly the divisions in families, communities, clans, parishes, dioceses, and provincial and state settings. Africans must learn to live and work together, and this demands a new way of seeing each other and understanding human relationship, and the goal of common life in societies.

The first step towards doing charity in truth in Africa from a practical perspective is thus the path of reconciliation, which leads to justice and peace. The Church should lead the wider African society in doing this by showing herself to be a reconciled community working for the reconciliation of all God's people. The Church in Africa needs a theology of reconciliation. "In intimate connection with Christ's mission, one can therefore sum up the church's mission, rich and complex as it is, as being her central task of reconciling people: with God, with themselves, with neighbor, with the whole of creation; and this in a permanent manner since . . . the Church is also by her nature always reconciling."[17]

An African theology of reconciliation should draw naturally from the experience of the Church in Africa and the Christians in their struggle to make sense of the present complexities of Africa's social context. Such a theology should be specific, context-sensitive, naming the experience and social context of the African Christians in its richness and ambiguity. There are two undeniable data of faith-experience in Africa today among many others: one is that African Christians have deep religious sentiments and attachment to the Lord Jesus Christ and his Church as a result of the influence of the Christian movement in Africa. The second is that the present social context of Africa influences greatly the passion and religious sentiments of African Christians. An African theology of reconciliation should, therefore, begin from these two contexts: Christology/ecclesiology and the social context. An African theology of reconciliation must draw African Christians to personal, cultural and ecclesial conversion. The call for conversion is Christoform because Christ is the source, goal, and norm for building relationship in diverse societies like Africa where the Christian message has been accepted. Christoform reconciliation is best explained in Paul when he wrote: "And for anyone who is in Christ, there is a new creation; the old creation has gone, and now

17. John Paul II, *Penance and Reconciliation*, 8.

the new one is here. It is all God's work. It was God who reconciled us to himself through Christ and gave us the work of handing on this reconciliation" (2 Cor 5:17–20). There are five important points that can be drawn from an extended reading of this passage:

(1) *Anyone in Christ Jesus has put on a new creation.* Life in Christ gives the Christian a new image, introduces the Christian into a new community, and grants him or her new hope, and a new communion. Life in Christ does not destroy our nature but changes it and give it a new meaning. Reconciliation is possible if African theologians show how our common baptism in Christ and our Christian understanding of the ultimate purpose and will of God for the salvation of all men and women embraces us all in one garment as one pilgrim people on a journey.

(2) *Reconciliation is "all God's work."* Left on our own we cannot rise above ourselves and above the limits imposed on us by our personal and cultural history. In a continent ravaged by war, violence, poverty, and ethnic conflicts and hatred, African theologies must show how God's work of reconciliation could be operative in those hidden corners where our people are hurting most. Reconciliation is a divine initiative hence we need God's grace to continue God's work of healing wounds inflicted by past and present unjust structures, of healing the rupture in relations among various ethnic and racial groups in Africa, and initiating dialogue among various religions, ethnic groups, political parties, feuding churches in order to remove the obstacles and pains that make it impossible for brothers and sisters to love and treat one another as children of one God.

(3) *Reconciliation is Christoform*: God was reconciling the world to himself *through Christ*; God has reconciled us to himself *through Christ*; we have received the ministry of reconciliation *through Christ* as his ambassadors on earth. The Church has received from Christ the ministry of reconciliation by being the instrument of communion, reconciling love, and solidarity. African theology of reconciliation will, therefore, seek to show how the life of African Christians could become deeply immersed *in Christo*. The more rooted and immersed in Christ the Christian is, the more he or she develops the mind that is in Christ (Phil 2:6), which seeks not to serve one's own interest or to promote only the good of one's friends, ethnic group, class or reference good, but to serve the other through

self-forgetting and self-forgiving love. The more Christoform the Christian life, the more universal one's vision and the more inclusive one's mission in life. The reason Christ came to earth is to unite all of us as children of God and grant us the inconceivable prospects of being children of God and members of God's happy family: "All baptized in Christ, you have all clothed yourself in Christ, and there are no more distinctions between Jew and Greek, slave and free, male and female, but all of you are one in Christ Jesus" (Gal 3:28–29). The sign of authentic Christian living in any society is the incarnation of the life of Christ and transformation of structures in the light of the gospel values of love and communion. Charity in truth begins with reconciliation, removing obstacles to relationship, and seeing the other as a friend, a brother or sister with whom I am ordained to life in God, and a sharing in the riches of God in creation.

(4) *Reconciliation involves the taking away of sin,* "for our sake God made the sinless one into sin, so that in him we might become the goodness of God" (2 Cor 6:29). The root of all division and tension, all violence and prejudice, all hatred and selfishness is sin. God reconciled the world through the Paschal mystery of the suffering, death, and resurrection of our Lord, which brought our redemption. Salvation in Christ is the overcoming of sin and evil, and the restoration of grace, peace, righteousness, right order, right relationship, and hope for sinful humanity. An African theology of reconciliation must name the sinful structures in African society and show how they have also caused serious wounds in the life of the Church and damaged the common good. It will propose the path towards conversion that will entail the admission of guilt, the firm commitment to address the causes of these sins, and determination to restore and heal the wounds these sins have caused in the Church or the wider society. The liberation of African societies from the nets of homelessness will take a long journey that will call forth the courage to truth, the courage to forgive, the courage to restore, and the humble submission to the path of ongoing reconciliation through removing the causes of division and intolerance.

(5) The final point from our passage is that *reconciliation is the good news that the Church announces as her constitutive identity and mission.* This news is not simply a proclamation or a claim; it is not simply the affirmation of the beauty of our liturgies, the majesty of our

hierarchical structure, or the solidity of our Church tradition and the antiquity and apostolicity of our dogma. The good news is the beauty of our Christian living and witnessing; that is, the authenticity and credibility of the life of the Church as Christians and the institutional Church spread the aroma of Christ. Reconciliation should be the irreducible offer that is open to every member of the Church. This demands a radical inclusivity and acceptance of any person who enters the Church, and openness and acceptance of those who do not belong to our visible ecclesial community or political or ethnic identity. The good news of reconciliation that African theologies should articulate is how the Church offers to our people the gift of salvation in Christ, and how this salvation translates into concrete life-experience such as freedom from sin, liberation from structures of sin that imprison them, and the totality of the abundant life that Christ offers to all. The Church in Africa should become the new zone where people can seek and find fresh hope, experience the refreshing reality of charity in truth, hear and follow the evangelical call for change in their conduct, and receive the fresh and boundless historical possibilities of abundant life even in the midst of uncertainties and brokenness.

It is in the Church that many Africans are looking for the realization of their dream for a better world. They flock to churches on Sundays because they believe that through the Church their relationship with Christ and with one another will be transformed to become a channel of grace and blessing and an oasis of love and compassion in a desert of wants and pain. It is in the Church that they hope to live a redeemed existence, set free from the imprisonment in one's own self-reference or group-reference. As Gregory the Great put it, through the Church, the Christian is freed from the cave because a new reality is being created "pervaded by a spirit of brotherhood and large-minded creativity, a place of reconciliation of all for all."[18] It is in the Church that men and women move from the exile of selfishness and rigid attachment to ethnic and racial caves into the ever-expanding and richly diverse communion of one body, one family in Christ. The Church as an eschatological communion, celebrating the presence of the Lord in her Eucharist and her sacramental life, and living in the joyful and hopeful expectation of the Lord's coming brings the people of God to the margins of eternity.

18. Ratzinger, *Communion*, 135–36.

This journey towards the home of our Father is what should shape the pastoral life of the Church, her liturgical life, and her prophetic ministry. In a certain sense, while the Church is at the service of culture and learns from cultural realities, she enriches different cultures by offering them the transcending truths that reveal what is in need of redemption in them. While the Church is at the service of charity in truth, she also becomes in her very life the concrete expression of charity in truth. This is why an African theology of reconciliation attempts to show how the cultural limitations and obstacles to building relations across ethnic, social, and religious divides could be overcome through a Christian understanding of communion. This was a task undertaken by the Second African Synod whose Working Document gives us some important points to consider in developing a theology of reconciliation for the Church in Africa in her service of charity in truth.

How does Second African Synod see the role of the Church in Africa in the work of reconciliation? The Working Document (hereafter *WD*) uses the images of Church as the family of God, and Christians as the salt of the earth, and light of the world, as foundation. In addition, it applies the image to the socio-cultural, socio-political, and socio-economic experience within and outside the Church. *WD* 35–39, through a brief commentary on the Sermon on the Mount, specifies those to whom the message of reconciliation, justice, and peace are addressed. The mission of the Lord and as a consequence the mission of the Church is addressed to the poor, those who mourn, the meek, those who hunger and thirst for justice, the merciful, the pure of heart, the peacemakers, and those persecuted for justice's sake. The Church is called to be the instrument of God's kingdom on earth and Christians who are salt of the earth and the light of the world have the mission of collaborating in the coming of the kingdom of God by reaching out to the hungry, the sick, the strangers, the humiliated, the naked, and the prisoner who are all the least of the Lord's brethren (Matt 25:40). The people who suffer most the absence of peace and justice in Africa, as well as those who are the pawns in the ever-revolving cycle of violence and conflicts in many African states and churches are the least of the Lord's brethren. The *WD* envisions the task of reconciliation as the Church's own way of putting the vision and mission of Christ into action.

At the individual level, the *WD* proposes that African Christians will look at how they can better be the disciples of the Lord by being actively involved in the mission of building God's kingdom of reconciliation, justice, and peace through their transformative presence as salt and light. Both images relate to the Christian identity, on one hand, and the witness of life that naturally flows from this identity, on the other. Concrete examples, considered by the Synod Fathers, of how this witness of life could be applied in African society include how the love of God could be found within the churches and how Christians can live a life of love and mutuality, showing solidarity with the poor through the fraternal service of washing each other's feet, especially those of people on the margins of society. This will challenge the limiting cultural framework of ethnicity that has become a curse to building the Church as a family of God in Africa. In addition, reconciliation in Africa through Christian witness will challenge African Christians to make rooms in their lives for forgiveness and conversion of hearts (*WD*, 40–43).

Furthermore, this has implications for the Church because "the life of an ecclesial community, which truly incarnates the Word, becomes a lamp on the threshold of society as a whole, enabling people to avoid the paths which lead to death, and take instead those which lead to life, that is to say, in following Jesus, the way, the truth, and the life (Jn 14:6)."[19] The essence of the Church is to be a reconciled family of God that lives, celebrates, proclaims, and witnesses to the inconceivable prospective of participating in the divine life of trinitarian communion. This is the Church's inner identity. This being of the Church shines through the efficacy of her sacraments especially the sacrament of reconciliation through which the ministry of divine love, mercy, and justice are administered to the faithful. This sacramental action is not only efficacious through the concrete sacramental event, it shines forth the more through the inner identity of the Church, and the external acts of her members who through their way of living and through the story that is heard about the churches show that the trinitarian communion is an offer which every Christian is participating in and which is offered to all who enter the Church.

This participation is undermined in many churches when pastors, bishops, religious men and women, and leaders at various levels

---

19. Synod of Bishops, *Working Document*, 38.

of church life display in words and deeds actions that parallel the dictatorial tendencies in many governments in Africa. WD 53, 107–10 specifically underlies the importance of looking at the way ecclesiastical authority is being exercised in many parishes and dioceses. How much unity of purpose and love exists among priests working together in the same diocese, and between them and the local ordinaries? How united are pastors with their parishioners as servants of one another, and not masters over minors, or lords over their clients? Are African bishops united among themselves, or have they become partisan, sectional, ethnocentric, and biased? How effective are the Episcopal conferences in many African countries? Do national, regional, and continental Episcopal conferences have a unity of purpose and speak with one voice?

The question of authority in the Church is, I think, a major issue that is causing division in the church in parishes, dioceses, and at the national level in many African countries. It also hampers the service of charity in truth. Sometimes sycophancy and rivalry among priests in their fight to please the bishops in return for ecclesiastical perks and gratifications have undermined unity, friendship, and mutual sharing which could have advanced the mission of Christ. In some instances, a particular circle of highly privileged priests and religious who are favored by the bishop because of ethnic, clannish, or partisan considerations control the diocese while the rest of the clergy are left on the margins, and in many cases begin to undermine the pastoral life of the diocese and gradually sow the seeds for division, conflict, and violence.

There is a crying need for a more open and honest framework for holding the clergy and hierarchy accountable in the Church in Africa. When relationships break—as they do quite frequently between bishops and their priests, or laity, and among priests or between them and their parishioners, or between superiors and their confreres—there are no adequate and open canonical frameworks to address these situations. This is because there are no specifications in the Canon Law on dealing with ethnic conflicts, caste system, priests who use African traditional religious practices for healing ministries, rejection of a bishop or priest by the people of God on ethnic or clannish grounds, or when a bishop loses the support and confidence of the clergy.[20] These are some unresolved sources of conflict that are often papered over through effete appeal to authority or to Rome, thus widening the gulf of division which imperil the mission of the Lord.

There is also the question of the increasing number of married priests and religious, or priests who have been suspended on moral or canonical grounds. The birth of the group *Married Priests Now* that is becoming visible in East and Central Africa through the influence of Archbishop Milingo[21] is a continuing challenge for reconciliation. How can the Church in Africa address the questions being raised by these groups, as well as many African men and women who have been suspended from receiving Holy Communion because they live in polygamous marriages or because their children married outside the Church? How are priests and bishops dealing with estranged Catholics who wish to return to communion in the church after brief or long time experimenting with Pentecostal and evangelical churches, or consulting *sangomas* (witch doctors), priests of African Traditional Religions, and fortune tellers in their search for answers to

---

20. Part of the reason for the absence of these frameworks in the Canon Law is that Africans and African realities with regard to conflict resolution, consensus leadership, authority, etc., were not taken into consideration in the drafting of the Code. However, the Canon Law does not resolve all the issues, questions and conflicts in the Church but its provisions are usually definitive in an extended sense in extra-canonical matters. It applies extra-canonical principles, analogies of law, jurisprudence of courts, etc. (See Canons 19, 220, 1364, 1389, 1400, 1401, 1405, etc.). The Church in Africa is challenged to propose novel and specific approaches in dealing with some of the issues raised here which were also pointed out in the Second African Synod as creating intractable conflict situations.

21. It is hoped that the interview that Archbishop Milingo gave to the Italian journalist, Michele Zanzucchi published in a book form in Italian in 2002 could be translated into English and French to be available to many Africans and non-African Catholics. In that book Milingo recounts his ordeals in Rome, his feeling of rejection, his pain and isolation at not being able to speak with the Holy Father, John Paul II when he (Milingo) was walking in the shadows of the valley of death. He also speaks of his love for God, and his agony at being misunderstood. While not an apologia for Milingo, it is important that the Church in Africa as well as the universal Church make genuine efforts to listen to the groans of many Catholics—especially estranged priests, bishops, and laity—which often lead to division and tension if not fully and openly addressed. See Zanzucchi, *Il Pesce Ripescato dal Fango*.

limit situations like death, terminal sickness, childlessness, misfortune in the family, ancestral curse, healing of family tree among others? The Church in Africa must concretely and externally show signs of being open to receiving the prodigal sons and daughters on one hand, and courageously address the internal factors and inadequacy within the Church which lead people away from the Church or alienate some clergy, religious, and laity from the Church.

WD 93–95 points out the challenges which face the Church in Africa, especially the highly clericalized notion of "church" which has led many ordinary African Christians to identify the Church in Africa only with the hierarchy. This weakens the ability of the whole Church especially the lay members of Christ's faithful to actively lead in faith-driven initiatives for reconciliation and social justice pastoral ministries to the poor and those on the margins. There is also the need for Christian families to be sufficiently supported to grow into greater communion within as domestic churches and be an example in their communities of the way to live as reconciled people in diverse settings. The divisions in many African families and between families at community level have become more evident and disturbing as economic stress and population growth continue to undermine the traditionally accepted forms of adjudicating issues that deal with land tenure and ownership, debt repayment, age-long bonds and deeds, patrimony, marriage ties, etc.

In the light of the foregoing, we can conclude that the basic ecclesiological foundation for a theology of reconciliation in African Christianity should be sought in (1) showing how the image of the Church as the family of God overcomes the limits and exclusivity which belonging to a family or a clan imposes from the African cultural perspective. In a sense, family is not an all-inclusive concept in African tradition. Belonging to one family excludes me from other families in many ways, just as belonging to a clan or an ethnic group makes me a stranger in others. WD (87–89) makes a case for this image chosen by the Synod Fathers in the First African Synod of 1994 by pointing out that the Church in Africa must seriously show how African Christians can put their differences aside. This is based on the fact that belonging to Christ brings people together as brothers and sisters in one family as sons and daughters of God. In addition, it shows how the values tied to family tradition in Africa could lead to acts of solidarity, fellowship, sharing, respect for one another, hospitality, togetherness, dialogues, etc. (2) the Church as family of God should be conceived more appropriately from the point of view of blood relationship which defines kinship ties in African cultural traditions. Christologically considered, the family of God is built on the blood of the Lamb whose sacrifice on the cross has made us a new people and a new family. The link with the blood of Christ makes a deeper connection with the cultural world of Africans especially overcoming the limiting factor of family. The bond created among Christians through the blood of Christ, sacramentally enacted through the rites of Christian initiation (especially baptism), will in this way transcend the blood ties of family, clan, or ethnicity, which in many African communities ravaged by conflicts and ancient grudges and prejudices among and between clans and ethnic groups is sometimes seen as stronger than the water of baptism.

(3) The vital participation that is realized in the Church's being as drawing from trinitarian communion is a more extensive reality for it shows the possibility of salvation and reconciliation as being built into the inner structure of the Church as well as in her mission. Thus prophetic ministry in the Church in actions for reconciliation, justice, and peace is not an add-on to the being of the Church, but rather is the Church's way of being. This reality is most evident in the Eucharist in which Christ gathers his disciples and makes them a people, the sons and daughters of God, who are reconciled and at peace with the Father and one another, so that they, in turn, can be the means of reconciliation and workers of peace and justice (*WD*, 80). The Eucharist gives the grace of healing of brokenness at personal and group levels. The Eucharist takes away sin and draws the Christians to let go of sin, selfishness, and pride which are the roots of sins. It also inspires Christians to forgive one another and to see in the life and person of Christ the very unity that is characteristic of the emergence of the kingdom of God. The Eucharist gives us the grace and model for making sacrifices for others; of how to heal brokenness and to share with one another what material and spiritual gifts we have received from God.

Above all, the Eucharist celebrates and enfolds Christians in the mystery of divine love and gives us the mandate to live charity in truth; "Since love abides here, there is no room for hate, vengeance, and injustice. Indeed, an ecclesial community built on the Eucharist becomes a genuine sacrament of unity, fellowship, and reconciliation in the midst of humanity. In this sacrament, the Lord wishes to crown with success every effort to make the world a place of glory for his Father, seeing that, according to St. Irenaeus, 'the glory of God is a man truly alive.'"[22] It is then from the heart of a reconciled church that will emerge evangelically driven initiatives in the areas of inter-Christian dialogue, and dialogue with practitioners of African Traditional Religions, Islam, and African Independent Churches (*WD* 99–102). It is through the Eucharist in which we see the face of Christ; that we see concretely and sacramentally the face of Christ in the suffering humanity. The mandate at the end of the Mass: "Go in Peace!" is a call to prophetic witnessing to go out to the whole world and share the love of Christ with a new vision of our unity in Christ from every tribe, language, people, and nation. It is an invitation to serve the poor just as Christ serves us, and to be an angel of mercy, compassion, and concrete acts of love to all those we meet. This is the message that a reconciled Church in Africa preaches by her words and above all by her witness of ecclesial love, communion, and friendship. In his Post-Synodal Apostolic Exhortation, *The Sacrament of Charity* (89–90), Pope Benedict makes the connection between the Eucharist and reconciliation, and the Eucharist and the service of charity in truth. He noted that the sacrifice of Christ which we celebrate in the Eucharist is a mystery of liberation which constantly and insistently challenges the Church and Christians to social responsibility: "The Eucharist is the sacrament of communion between brothers and sisters who allow themselves to be reconciled in Christ, who made of Jews and pagans one people, tearing down the wall of hostility dividing them (cf. Eph 2:14)."[23] He goes on to remind Christians (n.90) that the Lord Jesus, the Bread of Eternal Life, spurs us to be mindful of the situations of extreme poverty and suffering, and to denounce such degradation of the human person, and to do something about it. The Eucharist is a sacrament of charity which inspires Christians to charity: "The food of truth demands that we denounce inhumane situations in which people starve to death because of injustice and exploitation, and it

---

22. Synod of Bishops, *Working Document*, 81.

23. Benedict XVI, *Sacrament of Charity*, 88.

gives us renewed strength and courage to work tirelessly in the service of the civilization of love."[24]

BUILDING A CIVILIZATION OF LOVE IN AFRICAN FAMILIES, COMMUNITIES, AND NATIONS AND CHURCHES

Civilization of Love Defined

The whole pastoral goal of *Charity in Truth* is to show how a new ethical framework, drawing from Catholic social teaching and the Christian social gospel, could help meet the challenges of a globalized world. This ethical framework is social, political, cultural, economic, and religious and has been identified since Pope Paul VI as "a civilization of love." The term *civilization of love* was first used by Pope Paul VI, in his concluding address during the Holy Year of 1975. Civilization in this context pertains to human culture. In the words of Pope John Paul II, "Civilization belongs to human history because it answers man's spiritual and moral needs. Created in the image and likeness of God, man has received the world from the hands of the creator, together with the task of shaping it in his image and likeness. The fulfillment of this task gives rise to civilization, which in the final analysis is nothing else than the humanization of the world."[25]

The financial crisis which crippled global economy in 2008 is the result of sin: greed, selfishness, hedonism, consumerism, market forces that were allowed to run without sound ethics, and the absolute trust placed on these market forces and the laws of profit and loss, to control the global economy. It is also all about personal moral failings in matters that relate to the common good. These individual choices accumulate in deadening the system, and endangering the common good. One could argue that structures of sin are the results of the subjective rejection of the will of God that give rise to tension, rebellion, and conflict at the personal level, and then yield abundant negative fruits in communal life. It develops into concrete acts of injustice either as political systems, economic policy, and social norms that form the content of culture and thus shape human behavior and attitudes.

---

24. Ibid., 90.
25. John Paul II, *Letter to Families*, 41.

A culture of love, on the other hand, calls on humanity to understand that life is not an egoistic passion, but a gift to be accepted with gratitude; that our existence on earth is not a fortuitous and arbitrary game without any direction or moral guiding light. On the contrary, life is a project of love that is meaningful, and a vocation to be realized. Life is not a problem that is hard to resolve, but a mystery to be contemplated with humility and wonder.[26] The culture of love, which Christianity proposes, and living charity in truth which Pope Benedict makes appeal for, can penetrate all cultures, because all cultures are an effort to ponder the mystery of the world and in particular of the human person. It is a way of giving expression to the transcendental dimension of human life. The heart of every culture is its approach to the greater mystery: the mystery of God and of the human person.[27]

Every culture has at its heart the longing of men and women for love and a good life. This longing is often the basis why people wish to live together, and submit themselves to some common norms, and embrace a common meaning so as to work together in promoting the common good. A civilization of love is therefore, the realization of the regenerative ethics of friendship, love, communion, and mutuality wherein the central dynamics of living is about loving, healthy and helpful relationship, intimacy with God, with others, and the world of nature. This is the order that is required for a better world, and this order is universal and common, enabling people to participate in the life of God, the life of the world and the life of the other.

Civilization as Ubuntu and Onuru Ube

An African sense of solidarity also shows the fruits of a civilization of love. The Church in Africa is called to become the agent of this new way of living and working together in families, communities, and political institutions. It is an order in which everyone has the freedom to participate in the common life and where human fulfillment and human happiness is easily achieved through the removal of sin and evil.

This is the concept, which the *Nguni* African language calls *Ubuntu*, fraternity. This implies compassion and open-mindedness and is opposed to individualism or egotism. This concept is summarized by Desmond Tutu: "A person is a person through other persons.

26. Theological-Historical Commission 2000, *Jesus Christ*, 140.
27. Pontifical Council for Culture, *Pastoral Approach to Culture*, 1.

It is not 'I think therefore I am.' It says, rather, 'I am human because I belong; I participate, I share.' A person with *Ubuntu* is open and available to others, affirming of others, does not feel threatened that others are able and good, for he or she has a proper self-assurance that comes from knowing that he or she belongs to a greater whole and is diminished when others are humiliated or diminished, when others are tortured or oppressed, or treated as if they were less than who they are."[28] *Ubuntu* also entails forgiveness because refusal to forgive is self- and group-debasing, and it disrupts the social harmony. Indeed, for Africans life is only meaningful if it is shared in solidarity and community. There is an ancient Bantu adage which says: *umuntu ngumuntu ngabantu,* which means "mutual inter-dependence," or more literally, "we are people through other people." There is another African saying in moments of difficulty, in Hutu, which goes this way: *Ummera ummera-sha,* which means "courage, find courage and let us use your courage."

Ubuntu is today one of the most current categories from African communitarian ethics in reconciling communities, in building inter-dependent relationship, and encouraging the service of charity in truth. It is being embraced in international development discourse as a way of showing the mutuality of human living on earth, and the bond that could be established across racial, economic, political, and religious lines based on love and friendship. It is also another way of expressing the triple bottom line of people, prosperity, and planet (God + 3BL) as irreducibly inter-twined in any authentic and sustainable development praxis. It is also a force for toppling evil in society (injustice, racism, ethnocentrism, hatred, bitterness, etc.) while preserving and promoting both the individual's development as well as that of the community and the wider cosmic world.

Ubuntu underlies an African *weltanschauung,* that we are enveloped in the community of other human beings, and caught up in the bundle of life. *To be is to participate.* The *summum bonum* of African understanding of life in the light of *Ubuntu* is that to live is to share, to participate, to be related, to love and be loved, and to be inter-dependent. *Ubuntu* means humanity and is related to *umuntu,* which is the category of intelligent human force that includes spirits,

28. Tutu, *No Future,* 31.

the human dead, and the living, and to *ntu*, which is God's being as metadynamic force.[29]

Among the Igbo of Eastern Nigeria, the regenerative ethics of communion, love, mutuality, and friendship which bears result in solidarity is well phrased in the saying, *o nuru ube nwane agbakwala oso*, which means, "He who hears the cry of a neighbor should not turn the other way." *Ube* here signifies any human condition that cries for a response and a remedy; it translates as *groans* but more of *a cry that anticipates a response*. It is framed in this saying to signify that the fact of a neighbor's cry presupposes that the nearest person will hear it and respond to the immediate need. There is a pointer to the fact of common implication in the pain of others, which is founded on the relational basis of African communal life. This saying is more appropriately translated: *"I cry knowing full well that I am not alone and someone in the neighborhood would come to my aid; I groan so that my fellow men and women would come to my aid. I do not need to cry if none would come, but I cry because I believe that I am not alone in my pain and that my fellow men and women cry with me and will help lift me up."* It is this kind of cultural life that could reconcile the various groups fighting in African countries; it is the belief that should give Africans a sense of hope that together they will overcome present challenges.

In the early Medieval Age, St. Augustine had drawn the picture of the *civitas Dei* (city of God) and the *civitas terrena* (city of earth) where there is a dialectical tension between the values of the city of God incarnated in love, justice, happiness, and peace, and the vices in the city of man carried in the vessels of secular culture characterized by greed, cruelty, war, avarice, and the deadly sins. Augustine describes and anticipates a new civilization wherein the love and justice of God will reign in the hearts of all men and women: a love that he has revealed in his very nature and in the person of Jesus Christ. The civilization of love emphasizes the correct scale of values: the primacy

29. I have drawn this analysis from Michael Battle. For a good discussion of *ubuntu's* translation into a theological category for addressing Africa's social context with regard to reconciliation and apartheid see Battle, *Reconciliation*, 38–53. For a philosophical engagement of *ubuntu* in the search for justice, peace, and reconciliation in South Africa, and as an ethic for restorative justice and political and social reconstruction see Bell, *Understanding African Philosophy*, esp. 85–107.

of persons over things, of being over having; it also places emphasis on the personalist and communalist dimensions of human existence, rather than the utilitarian and individualist dimensions.

Pope Benedict shows in *CIV* that contemporary society is losing the proper sense of integral development. This loss is evident in the rejection in many nations especially in the West of the transcendental dimension of human life, and confusion in the ethical sphere about fundamental values of life, family, sexual relations, eco-ethics, and business ethics, among others. The civilization of love is a summons to a new lifestyle that involves passing from indifference to human pain to having compassion, and concern for our brothers and sisters. It is an activist solidarity with others. It makes God the central force around which our charity and social advocacy should revolve. Wars, hatred, poverty, corruption at all levels, violence, and crime—which sometimes draw the ugly calligraphy of the face of Africa—are the result of the disappearing African sense of community which sees people as brothers and sisters, and not rivals and enemies.

The civilization of love represents the whole ethical and social heritage, which Christianity offers for the liberation of any society from injustice, hatred, greed, poverty, and war, and for bringing authentic human development. It is a manifesto for social reconstruction and for building relationship in diverse communities. It is based on the belief that Jesus Christ has offered all humanity the way to be human and the way to experience the divine. He was "a man-for-the-others" (Bonhoeffer) and even though he endured suffering, he was strong to confront evil and to triumph over it through love and sacrifice. "Christ fully discloses man to himself and unfolds his noble calling."[30]

God is the source of the civilization of love and the human person is its center. In the words of St. Gregory of Nyssa, "God is above all love and the fount of love." The great St. John says, "love is of God" and "God is love" (1 John 4:7–8). The creator has impressed this character also on us. "By this all men will know that you are my disciples, if you have love for one another" (John 13:35). Therefore, if this (love) is not present, the entire image becomes disfigured.[31]

Christ reveals the face of love and the trinitarian communion of love. This love has been poured into our hearts by the Holy Spirit (Rom

---

30. Pastoral Constitution, *Gaudium et Spes*, 21.

31. Cf. Gregory of Nyssa, *De Hom Op*, 5:44, 137.

5:5). Through his Incarnation in which he showed a generous solidarity with us, and by his Paschal Mystery in which the depth of God's mercy and breadth of his love were manifested to us, Christ has put in motion an intense dynamic of intimate communion between God and the whole of humanity. Communion means that we are called to live in a union of love that mirrors the communion of love in which the three persons of the Trinity love each other in the intimate mystery of the one divine life.[32] *The civilization of love is about how the reality of God's love, incarnated in Christ, and experienced by Christians and the whole of humanity can assume reality in the world, encompassing, seizing, and possessing it. It is also concerned with Christian praxis, that is, how the experience of liberation and love could lead to action, testimony, witness, mission, and dialogue, so as to make this liberation and divine love open to all, in its spiritual and temporal dimensions and thus lead to social transformation, peace, happiness for all men and women in all states of life. Love is the only way that our world can be transformed.*

> Love must be present in and permeate every social relationship. This holds true especially for those who are responsible for the good of peoples. They "must earnestly cherish in themselves, and try to rouse in others, charity, the mistress and the queen of virtues. For the happy results we all long for must be chiefly brought about by the plenteous outpouring of charity, of that true Christian charity which is the fulfilling of the whole gospel law, which is always ready to sacrifice itself for the sake of others, and is man's surest antidote against worldly pride and immoderate self love." This love may be called "social charity" or "political charity" and must embrace the entire human race.[33]

The realization of a more humane society and just structures in Africa must begin with laying strong foundation for a civilization of love. The Church's service to charity in truth must be animated by, and lead towards a civilization of love. This is predicated on the renewal of Africa's cultural traditions through the new Christian imagination that is gradually taking root in Africa. This way, the Church can bring about the birth of a new sense of community and relationship in Africa through recovering authentic African social and ethical values. Indeed, as Eugene Uzukwu argues; "we are both the victims and

32. John Paul II, *Women*, 7.

33. Pontifical Council for Justice and Peace, *Compendium*, 581.

agents of the negation of our fundamental cultural values, which are the resources we bring in our encounter with other groups of people and which may still constitute viable resources for transformation of the continent."[34] This path will open the land of Africa for a new kind of life that is full and worthy of the human person. There are five levels of the civilization of love, which I propose for the Church in Africa and outside Africa in the service of charity in truth for African families, communities, churches, and nations:

A Culture of Love and Human Ecology

Pope Benedict (*CIV* 44) calls for respect for the dignity of human life and that any development initiative which debases human life, or removes the sacral quality, mystery, and dignity of life from conception to natural death should be rejected. Pope John Paul II was the first to use the term "human ecology" when he referred to the family as "the first and fundamental structure of human ecology" (*Centesimus Annus*, 39)."[35] Human ecology underlies the intimate connection between human beings and the rest of creation; and the preservation of the human person in this earth through right ethical and moral choices. The first and primary way of doing this is the priority of families, and a commitment to respect life, and serve the good of life at all stages.

The Church's service to charity in truth promotes a civilization of love, which upholds, preaches, and defends the dignity and right of everybody to life, especially the unborn, the weak, the sick, and the aged. The senseless killing of innocent citizens in ethnic conflicts, by state agents, or in wars within and between African countries, contradicts the ethics of this new civilization. Globally, the increase in terrorism, the sinful destruction of human lives through wars, and preventable ecological disasters are to be regretted.

Life is being arbitrarily destroyed and many lives are lost through lack of healthcare services, carelessness by medical professionals, and senseless killings in road, boat, and air accidents. The destructive forces of poverty in Africa and in many parts of the world must also be condemned. Indeed, the Church in Africa must see the debasing of

34. Uzukwu, *Listening Church*, 6.
35 Caldecott, *Social Teaching*, 43.

human life through unhealthy living conditions as an evil that contradicts the civilization of love.

There is also the need for all religious traditions to fight for the abolition of the death penalty, which is opposed to African cultural tradition of punishment and retribution. The death penalty should be expunged from the penal codes of African countries and a more humane and African way (ostracizing the criminal from the community, which in modern terms means life imprisonment) adopted for the rehabilitation and punishment of criminals. This aspect of this new civilization abhors all forms of discrimination and upholds the equality of all men and women. This applies to caste systems, which places a contagion on people because of ancient ties with deities or accidents of birth. Its needs to be emphasized again and again that every life has a value and that a boy child is not more valuable than a girl child, a way of thinking still prevalent in many African families. Indeed, everything contrary to the civilization of love is contrary to the whole truth about the human person and becomes a threat to personal fulfillment.

A Culture of Communion and Solidarity

Communion is tied to the theological category of solidarity. Beyond human and natural bonds, there is discerned in the light of faith a new model of the unity of the human race that inspires solidarity. God is love and truth in the fullness of the mutual gift of the Divine person and we should be constantly aware of our communion with Christ and with our brothers and sisters, which should propel us to the service of all in the community. This trinitarian communion impels us not only to create a church of communion, but a new world where fellow-feeling and concern for the good of others stem from our appreciation of our common origin and destiny. Solidarity is thus the fruit of the communion, which is grounded in the mystery of the triune God, and in the Son of God who took flesh and died for all. It is expressed in Christian love that seeks the good of others, especially those most in need.[36] The principle of solidarity signifies a bond of mutual concern and obligation. It is a firm commitment to the common good. Through it the fraternity of men and women becomes concrete.[37]

36. John Paul II, *Ecclesia*, 52.
37. Peschke, *Ethics*, 223.

The steps which the Church in Africa must take towards realizing solidarity in Africa through the service of charity in truth are:

- recognition of each member of society as a person
- responsibility of the strong for those who are weak
- responsibility of the weak for the weak through mutual cooperation
- power of auto-transcendence on the part of the weak
- global economic inter-dependence and mutual assistance
- putting an end to all forms of exploitation of people and nations, and
- the religious dimension of total gratuity.[38]

Solidarity in African countries should not be a vague feeling of compassion and of pity for the poor by the rich, but a firm commitment to pull down the structures that make it possible for people to be poor. It demands a tireless infusion of values into our social structures; it means being conscious of the responsibility of each for all. Solidarity does not mean throwing money to crowds at political campaign rallies, throwing parties on special occasions, giving hand-outs to political cronies, nor does it mean the unfortunate patron-client relations which sustain a prebendal framework between the elected officials and their reference or support groups. It will also entail building support networks in families and communities; wealth-creation through the promotion of local initiatives for grassroots development projects and self-help projects and programs by small businesses and co-operative movements.

Solidarity must also entail subsidiarity, that is the effort to sustain development from below and the redesigning of society in such a way that individuals are empowered in a way that they can meaningfully engage in work and so actualize their potentials.

A Culture of Dialogue and Tolerance

Africa today is not at peace mainly because of social sins. These sins, which cry out to heaven, generate violence and disrupt harmony among peoples. Indeed, injustice, selfishness, and poverty are always causes of violence. Many wars are fought today in Africa, because of

38. See John Paul II, *Solicitudo*, 38–40.

the failure of individuals and groups to rise above their narrow interests to the greater good of society. Africans must embrace once more the wisdom of the village palaver, where people gather to discuss their problems and to find ways of solving them in an atmosphere of friendship and love. The situation where African ethnic groups are constantly fighting each other or where religious groups are hostile to each other, betrays a failure of dialogue.

We need to remove the attitudes of prejudice, hostility, distrust, mutual condemnation and invectives, discrimination, and even wars and other acts of intolerance, which destroy common initiatives among Christians, Muslims, and practitioners of African traditional religion in Africa. Christians must come together with adherents of other religions to understand themselves better and articulate common insights. This is particularly important with regard to the practitioners of African Traditional Religions and Islam. The civilization of love offers the impulse for a new kind of religious experience that forges a harmony between faith and culture, the loosening of which is at the heart of the crisis of faith among many Africans. There is the need for the Church to be in the forefront in bridging the gap between love of neighbor and the desire for justice, since the love of others demands not only a sharing in their suffering, but the real action for the reconstruction of the unjust structures of society that bring suffering to people.

A Culture of Eco-Consciousness and Care

Climate change and climate variability and unpredictability are challenges already facing all African countries in different degrees based on their geography and political life. It is weakening the capacity of Africans to generate wealth; it is decreasing the GDP, and leading to migration and endangering national and international security. According to the IPCC report, *Climate Change 2007: Working Group II: Impacts, Adaption and Vulnerability*, the impacts of climate change in Africa are eightfold: water, energy, health, agriculture, ecosystems, coastal zones, settlement, industry and infrastructure, as well as tourism. In general, African countries have small chance of introducing counter-cyclical policies. They do not have enough independent means or access to loans. An increasing number of African countries are expected to go into debt crisis as a result of the financial crisis.

Poor countries risk ending up caught between decreased export incomes, falling prices for raw goods and less foreign aid at the same time as multinational companies cut production costs and demand tax reductions.

Africa is the least contributor to greenhouse gas emissions given her under-developed economy Africa contributes only 3.8 percent of greenhouse gas.[39] Unfortunately, Africa is the continent which suffers most from the effects of climate change, and will have an aggravated level of negative effects given limited mechanisms and resources in Africa to mitigate and adapt to these changes from one climactic condition to another. The 2011 famine in the Horn of Africa is a stark reminder of the devastating effects of climate change in Africa when this is added to failed political systems the poor people especially women, children and the elderly bear the brunt in unspeakable suffering and senseless deaths.

With tremendous natural resources and remarkable social and ecological diversity, the African continent reflects a close dependency of people on natural resources. This dependency and the fragile nature of African economy and national and regional politics and policies present potentially severe problems in adapting to the challenges of climate change. According to the document *Climate Change and Security in Africa*,[40] there are five factors which will severely affect African security, prosperity and well-being as a result of climate change which is worth noting at this point. *The first* is reduced water supply which will lead to changing rainfall patterns affecting agriculture and reducing food security, worsening water security and economic growth prospects, shifting temperature affecting vector diseases and more challenging hurdles in reaching the MDGs. According to the IPCC (inter-governmental panel on climate change) the cost of adaptation in Africa could be as high as 5–10 percent of Africa's GDP. The growing demand for water and scarce resources within and between African countries in some places lead to increasing competition between communities and different countries. Under certain political conditions as a result of failed or failing government, and internal ethnic divisions these competition may turn to violence and war.

39. www.ipsnews.net.
40. Carius, "Climate Change."

The second is the reduction in crop yields and increasing un-predictable weather patterns around the world, which will lead to higher prices of food and greater food insecurity and increase the stakes for control over productive land. *Third* is that changes in sea level, increased natural disasters and the reduced viability of agricultural land may cause large-scale and destabilizing population movements. *Fourth*, the cumulative impact of all these challenges on the prevalence of poverty and the ability of governments to provide services to their citizens could be a factor that tips fragile states towards socio-economic and political collapse. *Finally*, the fight for resource control among ethnic and economic groups in countries and between countries will become more violent and loud especially in the oil sector, which is fuelling conflicts in Nigeria, Chad, Sudan, Algeria, among others.

Reflecting on these realities, one is faced with a grim situation, which is that Africans are struggling to get by in the world without any clear development plan or climate change strategy. The scenario in Nigeria's Niger Delta for instance is typical of what is happening in most part of Africa. There is a drive among the ordinary Africans for what Lloyd Timberlake calls "livelihood security."[41] Unfortunately, the incorporation of sustainable rural livelihoods in the rationales of government and many international business conglomerates working in Africa has been very slow or even virtually non-existent. This has resulted in two realities among the ordinary Africans in many resource rich areas of Africa: people seek short term responses to "get by" in the midst of sweltering extreme poverty without consideration of environmental or ecological ethics. For instance, at the time when the people in the African Sahel were suffering from extreme drought, people resorted to coping strategies that offered them possibilities for survival. Thus, coping patterns as a way of responding to the increasingly volatile ecosystems of sub-Saharan Africa have been etched into

41. Timberlake argues that Africa's crisis is caused by environmental bankruptcy which is characterized by the misuse and abuse of the rich natural resources of the continent and the failure of the government, international donors and Western business interests in Africa to work towards sustainable development that leads to livelihood security. He writes; "The famine suggests a breakdown in the relationship between people and the environmental support systems that could lead Africa into a crisis of historic dimensions—one that goes far beyond short-term emergency food relief." Timberlake, *Africa in Crisis*, 10.

the everyday life of the typical African. How this coping strategies could lead to a system of living that guarantees long-term sustainability is yet to be seen. The other tendency is that the range and diversity of livelihood strategies are increasing, both in response to adversity and the widening range of choices offered by the effects of economic globalization, which have affected African societies whether in times of adversity or with regard to resource management.[42] This has been the challenge that the people of the Niger Delta face: How to cope with the adversity brought upon their land by oil exploration? How can they live healthy lives when their ecosystem is sick with pollution that has come about as a result of oil exploration? Let me conclude with a story taken from the mythical tradition of my ethnic group (Ndi Igbo) in West Africa.

My community of Adu Achi in eastern Nigeria has a stream, *Ahuruma*, where fishing is forbidden. This tradition has been as old as human memory can go. This stream was venerated until recently when many Christians started to defy some of the religious traditions, practices, and rituals surrounding the stream. The late chief priest of this stream, Nwano, told me in a conversation in 1999, when I was developing interest in cultural understanding, that the stream is like a mother to the community. Many years ago, according to him, when the whole earth was dry and there were no animals and fish, water was very scarce. People from my community were trekking great distance in search of water. Many people died from water borne diseases since they only relied on rainwater that was not well preserved and sanitized. One hot evening, Mother *Ahuruma* came down from heaven for an excursion on earth. She journeyed across many towns and villages, and after several days was very thirsty. She went from house to house begging for water from many communities and across many hills and deserts, but no one was generous enough to give her a cup of water to quench her thirst. She walked for days and weeks and was at the point of expiring when she walked into the house of another woman in Adu Achi and begged for water. This woman gave her a glass of water and also a can of water for her journey. Mother *Ahuruma* drank the water, but could have died of contamination from the water but her supernatural strength prevailed over the dirty water. She was however impressed by the generosity of this Adu Achi woman who gave from

42. Baro and Batterbury, "Land-Based Livelihoods," 65.

her scarcity. Mother *Ahuruma* then proceeded to ask God to turn her into water so that she can become clean drinkable water for this generous community.

This was how the *Ahuruma* stream was born, hence the name, *ahuruma*, which literally means "the body which turned into a long lasting gift of life for the people." It can also translate, "Observe this body, and preserve it as a memorial." The stream also gave birth to fish and green vegetation, and all kinds of other sea creatures like crocodiles, seaweeds, sea lions, etc. It was out of reverence for this stream, which is a creature from heaven, that the community decided that no one should fish in the water. Also it was forbidden for anyone to do their laundry in the stream, as the chemicals from the soap and detergent were considered unhealthy for the water and aquatic life in it. People were also punished if they stepped into the water with their shoes or slippers on as it was believed that the dirt from their footwear was wounding the stream. There are two weeks in the year when no one is allowed to fetch water from this stream. It was said that Mother *Ahuruma* decreed that twice every year, she should be given some time to rest and replenish herself.

This story, which I learnt from the chief priest more than twenty years ago, did not make much sense to me then even though I appreciated the morals of the story. However, later in my academic life, as I studied the creation stories in Genesis and the human stewardship of the earth, I came to understand at a deeper level the cultural knowledge with regard to ecology in Sub-Saharan Africa. The message is that African communities have a deep eco-consciousness and care that should be appropriated in proposing and promoting an ecological ethics both in Africa and outside Africa. Ecological consciousness and moral issues on climate change and environmental decline is a late arrival in Western societies, it was however something which was part of the welt and woof of many African societies and different religions of Asia and the East.

Also in my community, the tortoise was regarded as a sacred animal because of the mythical belief in the community that the tortoise passed on her wisdom to the community so that they can make the practical decisions required in decisive times and in times of adversity. This way, the most ancient species of African tortoise are found in Achi in eastern Nigeria. I also know numerous communities in the Igbo ethnic nation of eastern Nigeria who regard some species of snakes, birds, and animals as sacred and did not kill them and would not eat their meat. These creatures were allowed to move freely in the community, and were also respected as divine emissaries. There are many ancestral groves and fertility groves in many communities in Sub-Saharan Africa where trees are not felled. Rather, they are allowed to grow and die naturally, and even when some of them die there is a ritual of home coming for them. This is because of their link to the spirit of the living, the dead and the not-yet-born. Every being created has life, the intrinsic relationality of all things and the mutual sharing and participation in a covenant of respect and reverence for sustainability.

Today, some of these African sacred groves and streams like *Ahuruma* have been "desecrated" as traditional eco-consciousness and the law of participation of all reality in vital union have now been abandoned in many African communities as a result of industrialization, westernization, and increasingly scarcity of means. One of the key reasons for this abandonment is poverty, which has seen many people in Africa being pushed to the point of desperation to kill some of these protected species for food and meat. In many cases, the protected animals like tortoise, elephants, are seen as having supernatural powers and are used for ritual sacrifices, and to make amulets and charms. Some of the sacred groves and trees have been destroyed by road construction, and urban or rural development. In a few instances, some religious avant-gardes have also led the campaign to break these practices, which they consider as fetish and pagan.

What is at issue here for me is the worldview behind these practices. There is much to be said about how these practices fit into Christian understanding and how they can be interpreted in the light of the received faith traditions that now dominate Africa over the inherited African Traditional Religions. However, one cannot fail to appreciate the ecological spirituality and morality behind these practices. It reveals a world in which the human and the non-human life forms have a mutual relationship that is mimetic of the divine. There is an intimate bond in African traditional thinking between the world of nature and the human world, and the participation of nature and the human in a common web of life. It shows that nature is inherently divine and that the divine is not something removed from the natural ordering of the forces and energies of creation. It also underlies that the survival of the human race is predicated on the survival of the rest of the created world. In addition, African traditional eco-spirituality and morality holds that human activity are governed by certain natural laws all of which work together for the good of all creations of which the human is only a very tiny though important member. Indeed, the infinite majesty of creation is underlined by the truth within African mythical tradition in various ethnic groups of the late arrival of the human into an infinite and sacred universe. He or she does not define the world process but is defined by the mysterious sacred hand and vital forces, which hold everything in care. Thus, holding creation in care is a reciprocal act of gratitude from the human person. African ecological spirituality will see the present climate change as evil. It is an evil because it is not an inevitable phase in an evolutionary process, but rather because it is caused by failed human choices and the failure of the human race to become a good participant in the global process that should be governed by a regenerative partici-patory ethics of communion, solidarity, friendship, mutuality, and care. African ecological morality thus will agree with the consensus among scientists that climate changes are human-induced or anthropogenic, which will disrupt every ecosystem and impose catastrophic hardships on many parts of the world. Ecological ethics is seen within African traditional thinking as essential for the vitality and fecundity of the human in his or her orientation to being a participant in creation (not a Lord of the Manor). Thus, it is also somewhat "selfish" on the part of the human person because he or she will suffer and even die if he or she fails to do so.

On a recent visit to the *Ahuruma* stream, I was shocked at her gradual death. The Engineers Without Borders-USA who visited the stream with me and helped with the Canadian Samaritans for Africa to provide a comprehensive water project for my community at-tributed the drying of *Ahuruma* to climate change. For many in my community who do not understand the logic and science of climate change, the dying and inevitable death of *Ahuruma* is a sign of the ter-rible things that could come upon humanity if we continue to violate the sacredness of the earth. If we do not preserve the earth, the earth will not preserve us. We must embrace a common *civis* of nature and the human, and all creation. Christians must play an important role in articulating and living an eco-spirituality that respects the integrity of creation and the rights of all creation to flourish.

The distinctive African contribution to the discourse of moral issues in climate change and environmental decline is the wisdom of Mother *Ahuruma*, which is a new narrative of the civilization of love for environmental ethics. We can see the need for this wisdom when we look at the ecological crisis and environmental disaster in Nigeria's oil rich Niger Delta caused by oil spillage and gas flaring or the devastation of the BP Gulf oil spillage. However, the worst form of ecological disaster caused by oil exploration in Nigeria is gas flaring. Nigeria flares more gas than any other country in the world: approximately 75 percent of total gas production in Nigeria is flared, and about 95 percent of the "associated gas" which is produced as a by-product of crude oil extraction from reservoirs in which oil and gas are mixed.[43] Flaring in Nigeria contributes a measurable percentage of the world's total emissions of greenhouse gases; due to the low efficiency of many of the flares much of the gas is released as methane (which has a high warming potential), rather than carbon dioxide. At the same time, the low-lying Niger Delta is particularly vulnerable to the potential effects of sea levels rising. Many communities in the Niger Delta believe that local gas flares cause acid rains which corrodes the metal sheets used for roofing. A study done by Augustine O. Isichei shows that the air, leaf and soil temperatures were increased eighty percent or one hundred meters from the stack, and species composition of vegetation was affected in the same area.[44] Gas flaring in this region has led to many health problems for the indigenous population. Some of the common diseases in the area are respiratory illness, hearing loss, birth defects, asthma, bronchitis, and myriads of skin problems.

Some of the dangers of the absence of the wisdom of *Ahuruma* are the rising pollution and waste crises in many African cities, the squalor and unhealthy living conditions of many African rural, city, and slum dwellers. The poor water and sanitation in African communities has increased the rate of infectious diseases and water borne diseases. According to the All African Conference of Churches (AACC) statement in 2007 issued in Entebbe Uganda (21–25 May 2007, "Churches

43. The World Bank estimates that Nigerian gas flaring releases some 35 million tonnes of carbon dioxide annually. This represents 0.2 percent of total global man-made carbon dioxide emissions; of which the rest of Africa contributed 2.8 percent; Europe 14.8 percent; the USA 21.8 percent and the rest of the world 60.4 percent. See SPDC, *Nigeria Brief*; World Bank, *Environmental*, 162.

44. Isichei and Sanford, "Waste Gas Flares," 177–87.

for Water in Africa"), in rural Africa 65 percent of the population still lack access to adequate water supply. It is estimated by the IPCC on its Special Report on Emission Scenarios (SRES) that by 2020 between 350 million and 600 million Africans will have no access to clean water as a result of climate change. Presently about 73 percent has no access to adequate sanitation. The AACC statement states: "We are deeply troubled by the aggravating impact of climate change which threatens to further alter the water patterns in Africa. Climate change is already causing unpredictable rainfall, prolonged droughts, devastating floods, desertification and drying up of water sources. The existence and future of millions of Africans is jeopardized. We urge the industrialized countries to take their responsibility, and together with industrializing countries to start immediately to cut the emission of carbon dioxide, to put advanced alternative energy technology at the disposal of Africa and to assure funding for mitigation and adaptation measures in Africa, as well as in other affected regions of the Global South."[45]

The same cries were heard from the African delegates to the Copenhagen conference in the African Climate Justice Manifesto when they bemoaned as follows: "The effects of climate change are real, we are seeing the consequences; but they are not of our making. For over two centuries the industrialized world became wealthy by drenching the atmosphere in carbon. They plundered resources from every region of the world. On the mountains of coal and oil, they built cities of plenty. In great buildings they constructed while triggering the climate crisis they shelter from its effects. Those left outside are now told to seek another path to prosperity, while the sun beats down, or a perfect storm, not of their making, gathers in the horizon."[46]

Many Africans continue to wonder why Western companies, in collusion with some unscrupulous African businessmen and politicians, dump toxic wastes and hazardous electronics and chemicals in Africa and the dangerous prospects of carbon emission trading between Africa and the Rest. Indeed all across the African continent, the landscape is changing: the snowy caps of Mount Kilimanjaro, Mount Kenya, and Elgon are melting. The shorelines of Lake Chad, River Nile, and River Niger as well as lakes Victoria and Tanganyika are receding at a very frightening speed. Lake Chad, for instance, has receded to

45. All African Conference of Churches (AACC), "Churches for Water."
46. African Climate Justice Manifesto.

about one twentieth of its size thirty-five years ago. Some other ecological threats in Africa which challenge African ecological ethics are:
the Sahara desert encroachment into Northern Nigeria, Chad, Niger,
and Sudan; many Africans are worried about the random locust invasion in African Sahel, as well as the intermittent drought in the Horn
of Africa, and in Kenya and Tanzania, and the erosion disasters and
constant landslides in eastern Nigeria to mention only a few.

Many scientists agree that Africa's best course of action is not
to blame but to adapt, before the changing environmental crisis
destroys Africa. One of the most visible strategies is the Climate
Change Adaptation in Africa (CCAA) initiative jointly funded by
the Canadian International Development Research Center and the
United Kingdom's Department for International Development. The
program will document the experience of various communities,
especially smallholder farmers, looking at the vulnerability of their
farms to changes in rainfall, and how communities have acclimatized
to those changes. The program will focus especially on learning from
the local level those farming practices that have proven resilient and
sustainable for instance the earth-keepers initiative of the African
Independent Churches in Zimbabwe and some of the climate change
mitigation and adaptation practices being developed in Tanzania, the
Greater Horn of Africa (Eritrea, Ethiopia, Kenya, and Sudan) by a
team based at Sokoine University of Agriculture in Tanzania.[47] Some
of the practices will include climate predictions and dispersal of information. This means that the tools for general circulation models
(GCMs) should be applied in Africa to help Africans to understand
the variable nature of the climate change, predict the impact of such
changes, and project future climate change. Adaptation and mitigation can be effective in Africa if there are good GCMs that are capable
of tracking the primary data of a largely non-existent climate observ-
ing system in Africa.

There is the need to apply strongly the clean development mechanism that prioritizes eco-sensitivity and environmental sustainability
in development policies and practices. The developed countries according to the *African Climate Justice Manifesto*, must also honor two-
fold climate debts to Africa: (1) They must acknowledge that they have
used more than a fair and sustainable share of the earth's atmospheric

---

47. See "Lasting Impacts."

space. They must repay their debt through deep domestic emission reductions and by transferring the technology and finance required to enable Africa to follow a less polluting pathway, without compromising African development. (2) The developed countries must compensate Africa for the adverse effect of their excessive historical and current per-person emissions, which are burdening Africa with rising climate-related cost and damages. This is a matter of justice and social ethics. However, African and global response to climate change must integrate the wisdom and *civis* of *Ahuruma,* a shared sense of responsibility and a regenerative ethics of care, solidarity, mutuality, friendship and an appreciation of our common destiny in a common planet.

Conclusion

An African Story of the World

CHARITY IN TRUTH IS the only way in which God's plan for the world can be realized. As Christians we believe that God has given us the grace and the mission through our moral choices to make the world to conform to God's plan. Hope is built on our God-given capacity as humans to rise above the limitations of our humanity to live and act towards one another and towards creation with a sense of love and care. Hope springs from God's life in us, which draws us to rise above our limitations and stretches our vision beyond the human horizon to the margins and perspectives of God. Hope also draws us to light a candle instead of cursing the darkness, and to embrace God's will at all times so that we can in that light become sensitive to the presence of evil, injustice, poverty, and suffering in our world. The radical nature of human suffering, in many instances, calls for radical options. These determine the urgency and the ways and means of confronting and eradicating these evils often lurking secretly in human hearts and in human structures. Healing our society through authentic Christian charity and human love; restoring the scale of justice which has condemned many in Africa to a life of endless pain and poverty; and building relationships on the basis of equality and mutual respect, are tasks which can no longer be postponed.

God has a plan for the world in which Africans have a special place, because God chooses the weak and the poor to lift them up. Since God has a plan for the world (Jer 29:10–11; Gal 4:4), we are assured of the definitive coming of God's kingdom, which has already begun. We should, therefore, prepare for this kingdom by daily commitments founded on faith, hope, and love. This commitment should be extended not only to individuals but also to our communities, in particular social contexts and in world history. It is a hope founded on the promise of the Lord to remain with us even to the end of the world (Matt 28:20). We can, no doubt, break the iron cage of structures of sin that hold us down as a people. There is always the danger of despair when one looks at the magnitude of the problems that social sins have created in African society.

However, the Church in Africa must pioneer a new and hopeful way of living that looks beyond the shadows of the present moment. All religious men and women in Africa must become moral leaders through active prophetic witnessing. This is why charitable and aid initiatives need to be well organized in such a way that it procures a better life for the millions who are praying everyday for divine intervention. Fortunately, God uses our human instruments and resources to reach out to those on the margins. Religious groups in Africa must also see it as their duty to infuse hope in the weary hearts of Africans by presenting the message of hope and action. They must show how we as a people, and the international community can bring about the fruits of the hope that we are praying for in a concrete sense.

In the final analysis, the end of poverty and human suffering in Africa will begin with the collapse of the attitude of hopelessness and desperation in the hearts of many Africans, who are afraid of tomorrow. There are many Africans who are losing hope in a better tomorrow because they think that African nations are on the certain and irremediable path of perdition. The social reconstruction, which we have proposed here through the service of charity in truth, can be realized through African people, especially those who gird the loins of hope, toe the path of interior transformation, and practice charity without limits or distinctions. No one is too insignificant in the reweaving of the contoured socio-political and economic geography of our wonderful continent. As Socrates warned the Greeks many years ago: The brilliant statesman had enriched and embellished the city; had created protective walls around it; had built ports and dockyards; had launched navies; had eternalized the glory of the city by the temples of undying grandeur and beauty; has multiplied in Attica the feasts of arts and reason; but he did not occupy himself with the problem of how to make Athenians better men and women. As a result his work has remained incomplete and his creation cadulous. Creating a better

Africa will demand creating better Africans, and hopeful Africans in a hopeful and helpful world.

Hope for a better future is above all rooted in Christ. Christians believe that Christ is alive. God is not dead but alive and active in a dynamic way. The celebration of the victory of Christ over death is what is marked at Easter. I believe that the Easter event has significance for the world and Africa. Easter opens a principle of hope in a radical way. Easter celebrates the possibility of a new beginning for all men and women of good will. This new beginning of life is the vitality of God which we all receive every day when we wake up. Life does not consist of the satisfaction of present needs only, but in the creative existence which springs from a purpose-driven longing that arises in the depths of a soul that is saved. Easter celebrates the triumph of Christ over the forces of evil and death; it also celebrates the possibility of our own triumph over the negative forces that weigh us down. Easter casts a long gaze beyond the shadows of present difficulties. It also opens the horizon of present transformation. By his Resurrection, Jesus has shown that he has power over the whole universe and its elements. There is nothing impossible for God; even the power of death could not defeat his eternal, divine plan. If we see things through the eyes of God and in the light of the events in Christ's life, we can never lose hope in the possibility of the conquest of freedom and poverty among individuals and groups.

In the same way, for all believing Christians and all men and women of good will throughout the world, there is the hope of victory against the *dead ends* of our lives as individuals and groups. The Resurrection of Jesus produced faith and hope in the disciples: men and women who were afraid to witness to Christ at his trial publicly stood up for Christ. Hope is borne of faith not in our abilities but in the power that we have received which precedes us and is above us. Easter celebrates the gift of liberation and salvation that God has granted to the world in Christ. Many people struggle with personal difficulties; others have health problems; and some are crippled by fear about the future. There are many who are caught in the intractable chain of poverty and frustration. These pains are felt in Africa at the personal and communal levels. There is hope for those who do not lose heart in the face of evil or wince against the structures of sin and those who sustain them.

The world today is gripped in the fear of terrorism. There are many people the world over who are condemned to a colorless life because of their personal histories or by unjust situations in society. We do not need to look too far to see that around us there are signs of hope; even in our inner self where our human fragility meets the power of God's grace. We hear of news of wars, sexual abuse (especially against women and children), hate crimes, poverty, and natural disasters. Particularly, I think of the fate of *Mama Africa;* which appears to be in trouble. Africans and non-Africans have become weary of the bad news in and from Africa.

Africa has become the continent of tombs, but unlike the tomb of Jesus, the tombs of Africa are not empty. They are now filled with bleaching bones of the dead who have been killed in innumerable civil wars in the continent. These tombs are in a certain sense the tomb of the Risen Lord, who is the archetypical man whose face we see even in the most wrinkled or sad faces of the suffering sea of the least of our brethren. The tomb of Jesus is filled with the millions of Africans who are dying of HIV/AIDS and malaria. The tomb of Jesus has become the gathering place of many poor and hungry children of Africa who are orphaned, and the lost generations of Africa whose lives have become the tale of agony and sorrow. However, in the midst of these man-made difficulties—most of which are caused by bad government and the exploitation of the poor religious masses by many political and religious elites—there is still hope in the eyes of many young people. The Lord's victory is the sign that we too will overcome our own difficulties. Jesus has the power to change our human condition. *This liberation from the nets of sin, suffering, death, hatred, poverty, injustice, and the fear of what is to come and fear of each other is the meaning of Easter.* It offers strength for today and hope for tomorrow. Africans should dare to believe and to hope and act with fresh and renewed strength inspired by the presence and power of the God of hope in their personal and group history. Writing on God as the principle of hope, Jürgen Moltmann states:

> The God of hope is the God of freedom. In him no boundaries are set nor does he set any. He breaks through defences of anxiety and the walls of care. He breaks through boundaries which we ourselves have set in order to distinguish ourselves from other men and to affirm ourselves. He breaks into the boundary of our solitude in which we have hidden so that no

one will come near us. He steps over the boundary of race, in which man loathes man, and the boundaries of class and strata in society. He despises difference between black and white, poor and rich, educated and uneducated; for he seeks men-poor, suffering, hating and ugly, cramped and stunted men-and accepts them as they are. That knowledge makes us free and is a source of support. We can hope in him-the God of freedom.[1]

The African story is the story of the world. It speaks of a world with so much wealth, but poor in using it. It speaks of a world with abundant gifts, but poor in developing them. The African story is also the story of a continent that has so much blessing, but is bogged down in many instances by man-made factors. I will like to close this book with a very interesting story that I learnt from my village elders as a boy growing up in Adu Achi. It is the story of our world. It is a story of what happens when we love and what happens when we fail to love. It speaks of the danger of greed, as well as the threat of exploiting the earth without limit. It is a story about the needed new way of living that I have termed a regenerative ethics of love, friendship, solidarity, mutuality, sustainability, care, and reciprocity:

Once upon a time, there was a severe famine in the animal kingdom; there was no rain for many years, and a prolonged dry season. Everywhere was dry, without any vegetation and without any food. People were dying in great numbers, and there was adversity in the land. The tortoise was a very wise animal, and he thought to himself, "What are we going to do to save the planet because if nothing urgent was done, all the living things will all perish?" The tortoise then went in search of food to eat. As he walked along the dry land he found a palm kernel after a long search. He brought the kernel home to break it and share with his family and perhaps die. As he was cracking the kernel, it fell off the stone platform into a deep hole.

The tortoise was so angry and went in search of the kernel. He got his equipment and started to dig the hole into which the kernel fell. He dug for a very long time and the hole led him to the land of the spirits. When he got to the spirit world he found a spirit eating his palm kernel. The tortoise was furious and told the spirit to return the kernel to him immediately. When the spirit refused, both of them started

---

1. Moltmann, *Gospel of Liberation*, 27.

struggling for the kernel. As they fought for the kernel, their noise drew the attention of the king of the spirit world who was sleeping.

The king now told tortoise that he was going to give him a magical drum filled with food. He instructed him, that whenever he beats the drum food will start coming out. He counselled the tortoise to share the food with other animals. The tortoise was so happy that he took the drum home with joy. When he got home, he beat the drum, then food started coming out, so he invited his wife and children and they ate so much until their stomachs started to hurt. The tortoise took the drum to the village square and invited all the living things in the land for dinner. They all started beating the drum and food poured out mysteriously from the magical drum. All the animals ate to their fill and were all satiated. In their drunken spirit and uncontrolled passion for food and drink they continued to beat the drum even when they have had enough food and drink. They became disordered and careless with the handling of the drum that they broke it and the food stopped flowing out from the drum. The animals appealed to the tortoise to go back to the king of the spirit world to beg him for another magical drum.

The tortoise again left for the spirit world. When he got there he appealed to the king of the spirits to give him a bigger magical drum which will bring more food that will last for a long time because the famine and drought had become unrelenting. The king now realized that tortoise and his community were greedy people they did not share the food with other people, they also were eating more than what they needed, and were foolish not to store food for the future. They wanted to eat up what they could have stocked up. The king of the spirits then decided to punish the tortoise and his community. He gave the tortoise a very big evil drum and told him that it will be better for him to wait until he gets home before beating the drum. The curiosity of the tortoise wouldn't let him wait until he got home, so along the way he started beating the drum and a very big demon came out and flogged him until he fainted. When he woke up, he thought to himself, "Since other animals enjoyed with me at the time of merriment, they will also suffer with me too." He took the drum home and invited all the animals to the village square and left them with the evil drum. They started beating the drum and different demons of all sizes and shapes came out instead of food and spanked all the animals for their selfishness and greed until all the animals passed out. The tortoise brought so much good to the animal world, but he also brought so much misery to the animals. This is a parable but it is a pointer to how much each person can do to make the world a better place. There is so much good we all can do to make the world a better place for everyone. We are indeed the hope we are praying for. It all depends on the choices we make.

Appendix

Ten Commandments for Christian Charities and Non-Governmental Organisations Working in Africa

- Thou shall not judge Africa, African reality, and African people using your limited cultural lenses.
- Thou shall not impose development projects and development plans on Africans. Development projects and aid initiatives work best in Africa when you identify with what African communities, groups, and social capitals are doing already.
- Thou shall not make Africans mere consumers of finished products or a dumping ground for inferior or used products, toxic waste, or carbon emissions. Africans wish to be producers and inventors. The poor should never be the dumping ground of our unused and unusable products, goods, toys, cloths, and sub-standard materials.
- Thou shall not undertake any projects in Africa based on a project proposal submitted to you by one person or through African middlemen and women. Africans are community-oriented and every project or development initiative must emerge from the community in order to succeed and be sustainable. Go to Africa to discover the aid and development initiatives you can support.
- Thou shall listen to Africans to know what they want and how they think you should help. Do not decide on any development and aid initiatives in Africa without first doing an evaluation on how participatory practices will be an integral process in these projects. African agency and resources should be preferred to other external considerations through joint visioning, strategy,

planning, implementation, and supervision as well as maintenance for sustainability.

- Thou shall make a distinction between humanitarian emergencies and development projects: the first is crisis-response and is short term; the second demands partnership and is long-term and community based.

- Thou shall make a distinction between addressing needs and prioritizing the assets of Africans. Actualizing the assets of Africans and the resources in Africa should be a basic orientation of all development initiatives in Africa. Tapping into the assets of Africans will lead to capacity building, ownership, responsibility, and grass root development of African communities.

- Thou shall remember always that Africans need solidarity and not sympathy. Remember that there are so many positive things happening in Africa that you can support. Do not cry for Africa; support Africans to solve their own problems, using their own resources, industry, energy, cultural traditions, and their own plans.

- Thou shall not project African and African societies in negative light in order to draw the sympathy of non-Africans to support emergency response or development projects. Always respect people's privacy and develop sensitivity to other people's culture through slow but steady cultural proficiency. Always seek permission from Africans, just as you do in any other culture before taking their pictures or hearing their stories. It is a violation of their rights to privacy to use their pictures or stories in movies and documentaries, and on websites and other media outlets without seeking and obtaining their consent. Some of these pictures and stories are less than ideal for their dignity and respect.

- Remember that charity in truth begins from our experience of divine love. Charity should proceed as a vulnerable mission in which we connect to the greater things which lie beyond us and the grace of the greater things which hold us together.

Bibliography

Acta Apostolicae Sedis XCVIII (6 January 2006) 40–53.

Africa Institute of South Africa. *Africa's Development Thinking Since Independence: A Reader.* Pretoria: Africa Institute of South Africa, 2002.

African Climate Justice Manifesto, "Draft of the Official Document of the African Delegation to the Copenhagen Conference on Climate Change."

Ake, Claude. *Democracy and Development in Africa.* Washington DC: The Brookings Institution, 1996.

Alegre, Marco. "Extreme Poverty in a Wealthy World: What Justice Demands Today." In *Freedom From Poverty as a Human Right: Who Owes What to the Very Poor?,* edited by Thomas Pogge, 237–54. Oxford: Oxford University Press, 2007.

All African Conference of Churches (AACC). "Conference Report: 'Churches for Water in Africa', 21–25 May, 2007, Entebbe, Uganda." Geneva: WCC Publications, 2007.

Allen, John L., Jr. "African Bishops Examine 'Practice of Power, Authority.'" *National Catholic Reporter* (8 October 2009). Online: http://ncronline.org/news/african-bishops-examine-practice-power-authority.

Allen, Prudence. *The Concept of Woman.* Vol. 1. Grand Rapids: Eerdmans, 1997.

———. "Integral Sex Complementarity and the Theology of Communion." In *Communio* 17:4 (1990) 251–362.

Anya, Anya O. *Re-inventing Nigeria for the 21st Century.* Lagos: Obafemi Awolowo Foundation, 1996.

Appiah, Kwame Anthony. *In My Father's House: Africa in the Philosophy of Culture.* Oxford: Oxford University Press, 1992.

Aquinas, Thomas. *Summa Contra Gentiles: Book One: God.* Translated by Anton C. Pegis. Notre Dame, IN: University of Notre Dame Press, 2005.

———. *Summa Theologiae.* Translated by Fathers of the English Dominican Province. Allen, TX: Christian Classics, 1981.

Ashley, Benedict M. "Introduction." In *The Common Things: Essays on Thomism and Education,* edited by Daniel McInerny, 1–18. Mishawaka, IN: American Maritain Association, 1999.

Assefa, Taye et al. "Introduction." In *Globalization, Democracy and Development in Africa: Challenges and Prospects,* edited by Taye Assefa et al., v–xv. Addis Ababa: Organization for Social Science Research in Eastern and Southern Africa (OSSREA), 2001.

Augustine. *Confessions.* Translated by Henry Chadwick. Oxford: Oxford University Press, 1998.

————. *De Libero Arbitrio (On the Free Will)*. Translated by Anna S. Benjamin and A. H. Hackstaff. New York: Bobbs-Merrill, 1964.

————. *The Works of St. Augustine, A Translation for the 21st Century: The Trinity*. Translated by Edmund Hill. New York: New City, 1991.

Ayittey, George B. N. *African Unchained: The Blueprint for Africa's Future*. New York: Palgrave Macmillan, 2005.

Bahnsen, Greg L. *Theonomy in Christian Ethics*. Nutley, NJ: Craig, 1973.

Baro, Mamodou, and Simon Batterbury. "Land—Based Livelihoods." In *Towards a New Map of Africa*, edited by Ben Wisner et al., 53–69. London: Earthscan, 2005.

Battle, Michael. *Reconciliation: The Ubuntu Theology of Desmond Tutu*. Cleveland, OH: Pilgrim, 1997.

Bell, Richard H. *Understanding African Philosophy: A Cross-Cultural Approach to Classical and Contemporary Issues*. New York: Routledge, 2002.

Benedict XVI. *Charity in Truth*. Boston: Pauline, 2009.

————. "Fighting Poverty to Build Peace." Message for the Celebration of the World Day of Peace, 1 January 2009. Vatican: Libreria Editrice Vaticana, 2008.

————. *God is Love*. Boston: Pauline, 2006.

————. "The Human Family, A Community of Peace." Message for the Celebration of the World Day of Peace, 1 January 2008. Vatican: Libreria Editrice Vaticana, 2007.

————. "A Proper Hermeneutic for the Second Vatican Council." In *Vatican II: Renewal Within Tradition*, edited by Matthew Lamb and Matthew Levering, ix–xv. Oxford: Oxford University Press, 2008.

————. *The Sacrament of Charity: Sacramentum Caritatis*. Ijamsville, MD: The Word Among Us, 2007.

Bonino, Serge Thomas. "'Nature and Grace' in the Encyclical *Deus Caritas Est*." *Nova et Vetera* 5.2 (2007) 231–48.

Botterweck, G. J., and Ringgren Helmer, eds. *Theological Dictionary of the Old Testament*. Vol. 1. Grand Rapids: Eerdmans, 1974.

Bujo, Benezet. *African Theology in its Social Context*. Translated by John O'Donohue. New York: Orbis, 1992.

Caldecott, Stratford. *Catholic Social Teaching: A Way In*. London: Catholic Truth Society, 2001.

Calderisi, Robert. *The Trouble with Africa: Why Foreign Aid Isn't Working*. New York: Palgrave Macmillan, 2007.

Carius, Alexander. "Climate Change and Security in Africa: Challenges and Internal Policy Context. United Nations Office of the Special Adviser on Africa (OSAA), Berlin, December 2009", Online: http://www.un.org/africa/osaa/reports/climate_change_security_2009.pdf

The Catechism of the Catholic Church. Nairobi: Paulines Publications Africa, 1998.

Coleman, John A. "Catholic Human Rights Theory: Four Challenges to an Intellectual Tradition." *Journal of Law and Religion* 2 (1984) 349–55.

Collins, Carol. "Jubilee 2000 Debt Relief Campaign Targets G8 Leaders." *African Recovery* 12.1 (1998) 1.

Congregation for the Doctrine of Faith. *Instruction on Christian Freedom and Liberation*. Vatican: Libreria Editrice Vaticana, 1999.

Curtis, Edward. "Image of God (OT)." In *The Anchor Bible Dictionary*, vol. 3, edited by David Freedman, 389–91. New York: Doubleday, 1992.

Dawson, Christopher. "The Failure of Liberalism." In *The Wisdom of Catholicism*, edited by Anton C. Pegis, 862–73. New York: Random House, 1949.

DeLancey, Virginia. "The Economies of Africa." In *Understanding Contemporary Africa*, 4th ed., edited by April A. Gordon and Donald L. Gordon, 109–54. London: Rienner, 2007.

De Zeeuw, Maarten, and Mwangala Mubita. "Dr. Moyo's Proposal to Abolish Development Aid." *JCTR Bulletin* 80:2 (2009). Online: http://www.jctr.org.zm/bulletins/bull8oabolishAid.html

Di Noia, Augustine. "Imago Dei-Imago Christi: The Theological Foundations of Christian Humanism." *Nova et Vetera*, 2 (2004) 267–78.

Donnelly, Jack. "Human Rights and Human Dignity: An Analytic Critique of Non-Western Conception of Human Rights." *The American Political Science Review* 76.2 (1982) 303–16.

Dorr, Donal. *Option for the Poor: A Hundred Years of Vatican Social Teaching.* Dublin: Gill and Macmillan, 1985.

Dougherty, Richard J. "Natural Law." In *Augustine Through the Ages*, edited by Allan D. Fitzgerald, 582–84. Grand Rapids: Eerdmans, 1999.

Duchrow, Ulrich. *Alternatives to Global Capitalism.* Heidelberg: Kairos Europe, 1995.

Dulles, Avery. *Church and Society: The Laurence J. McGinley Lectures, 1988–2007.* New York: Fordham University Press, 2008.

———. *The Reshaping of Catholicism: Current Challenges in the Theology of Church.* New York: Harper and Row, 1988.

Easterly, William. *The White Man's Burden: Why the West's Efforts to Aid the Rest Have Done So Much Ill and So Little Good.* New York: Penguin, 2006.

Ela, Jean-Marc. *African Cry.* New York: Orbis, 1986.

Elbadawi, Ibrahim, and Alan Geleb. "Financing Africa's Development: Towards a Business Plan." In *Beyond Structural Adjustment: The Institutional Context of African Development*, edited by Nicolas Van De Walle et al., 35–75. New York: Palgrave Macmillan, 2003.

Elshtain, Jean Bethke. *Who are We?: Critical Reflections and Hopeful Possibilities.* Grand Rapids: Eerdmans, 1999.

Fafunwa, A. Babs. *History of Education in Nigeria.* London: Allen and Unwin, 1974.

Fergin, D. "Birth of a Buzzword." *Newsweek*, 15 February, 1999. Online: http://www.newsweek.com/1999/02/14/birth-of-a-buzzword.html

Filibeck, Giorgio. *The Theme of Violence: Texts of John Paul II, October 1978—October 1985.* Vatican City: Pontifical Commission, 1986.

Finnis, John. *Natural Law and Natural Rights.* Oxford: Clarendon, 1980.

Forte, Bruno. *The Church: The Icon of the Trinity, A Brief Study.* Translated by Robert Paolucci. Boston: Daughters of St Paul, 1991.

———. *Trinity as History: Saga of the Christian God.* Translated by Paul Rotondi. New York: Alba House, 1996.

French, William. "Common Ground and Common Skies: Natural Law and Ecological Responsibility." *Journal of Ecumenical Studies* 42.3 (2007) 373–88.

Friedman, Thomas L. *The World is Flat: A Brief History of The Twentieth Century.* New York: Farrar, Straus, and Giroux, 2005.

Gallagher, Donald, ed. *A Maritain Reader.* New York: Image, 1964.

George, Susan. *A Fate Worse Than Debt.* London: Penguin, 1988.

———, and Fabrizio Sabelli. *Faith and Credit: The World Bank's Secular Empire.* London: Penguin, 1994.

Gordon, April A. "Population, Urbanisation, and AIDS." In *Understanding Contemporary Africa*, 4th ed., April A. Gordon and Donald L. Gordon, 223–30. London: Rienner, 2007.

Gregory of Nyssa, *De Hom Op.* J.P. Migne Patrologiae Graeco-Latinae. Ridgewood, NJ: Gregg, 1965.

Gremillion, Joseph. "Justice and Peace." In *Modern Catholicism: Vatican II and After*, edited by Adrian Hastings, 188–93. New York: Oxford University Press, 1991.

Groome, Thomas. *Educating for Life.* New York: Crossroad, 1998.

Gutierrez, Gustavo. *A Theology of Hope.* New York: Orbis, 1973.

Guyer, Jane I., et al., eds. *Money Struggles and City Life.* Ibadan: Center for Social Science Research and Development, 2003.

Hallman, David G. *Ecotheology: Voices from South and North.* Geneva: World Council of Churches, 1994.

Hegel, G. W. F. *The Philosophy of History.* Translated by J. Sibree. New York: Dover, 1956.

Hertz, Noreena. *The Debt Threat: How Debt is Destroying the Developing World.* Toronto: Harper Collins, 2004.

Hollenbach, David. *Claims in Conflict.* New York: Pauline, 1979.

Hooks, Bell. *Teaching Community: A Pedagogy of Hope.* New York: Routledge, 2003.

"Human Development Report Documents Catastrophic Impact of AIDS in Africa." Online: http://hdr.org/2004.

Ignatieff, Michael. *The Right Revolution.* Toronto: House of Anansi, 2004.

Ike, Obiora ed. *Globalization and African Self-Determination: What is Our Future?* Enugu, Nigeria: CIDJAP, 2004.

Ilo, Stan Chu, et al. ed, *The Church as Salt and Light: Path To an African Ecclesiology of Abundant Life.* Eugene, Oregon: Pickwick Publications, 2011.

Ilo, Stan Chu. *The Face of Africa: Looking Beyond the Shadows.* Bloomington, IN: Author House, 2006. (Reprint: Ibadan, Nigeria: Spectrum, 2008.)

———. "Partnering for Eco-Justice in Africa." Paper presented at the 12 International Conference of the International Society for Third Sector Research, Israeli Center for Third Sector Research, Ben Gurion University, Negev, 17 March, 2009.

International Theological Commission. "Communion and Stewardship: Human Persons Created in the Image and Likeness of God." Vatican: Libreria Editrice Vaticana, 2004. Online: http://www.vatican.va/roman_curia/congregations/cfaith/cti_documents/rc_con_cfaith_doc_20040723_communion-stewardship_en.html

———. "Proposition on the Dignity and Rights of the Human Person." In *International Theological Commission: Texts and Documents 1969–1985*, vol. 1, edited by Michael Sharkey, 251–66. San Francisco: Ignatius, 2009.

Isichei, Augustine O., and William W. Sanford. "The Effects of Waste Gas Flares on the Surrounding Vegetation in South-Eastern Nigeria." *Journal of Applied Ecology* 13 (1976) 177–87.

Jacobs, Jill. *There Shall be No Needy: Pursuing Social Justice through Jewish Law and Tradition.* Woodstock, VT: Jewish Lights, 2009.

John Paul II. *The Church in America.* Boston: Pauline, 1999.

———. *Dignity and Vocation of Women.* Kampala: St Paul, 1989.

———. *Ecclesia In America.* Boston: Pauline, 1999.

———. *Letter to Families.* Vatican: Libreria Editrice Vaticana, 1994.

———. "Peace with all Creation." In *Origins* 19.28 (1989) 465–68.

————. *Reconciliation and Penance.* Nairobi: Paulines Africa, 1994.

————. *Solicitudo Rei Socialis.* Nairobi: Paulines Africa, 1983.

Johnson, Elizabeth A. "Losing and Finding Creation in the Christian Tradition." In *Christianity and Ecology,* edited by Dieter T. Hessel and Rosemary Radford Ruether, 3–23. Cambridge: Harvard University Press, 2000.

Joseph, Richard, and Alexandra Gillies, eds. *Smart Aid for African Development.* Boulder, CO: Rienner, 2009.

Kagan, Robert. *Of Paradise and Power: America and Europe in the New World Order.* New York: Vintage, 2004.

Kavanaugh, John F. "Intrinsic Value, Persons, and Stewardship." In *The Challenge of Global Stewardship: Roman Catholic Responses,* edited by Maura A. Ryan and Todd David Whitmore, 67–81. Notre Dame, IN: University of Notre Dame Press, 1997.

Kennedy, Leonard, et al., eds. *Images of the Human: The Philosophy of the Human Person in a Religious Context.* Chicago: Loyola, 1995.

Kerber, Mary. "Globalization: The Challenge for Africa." In *Structures of Sin, Seeds of Liberation,* edited by Patrick Ryan, 51–60. Nairobi: Paulines Africa, 1998.

Kobia, Samuel. *The Courage to Hope.* Geneva: World Council of Churches Publications, 2003.

Kooy, V. H. "Image." In *The Interpreter's Dictionary of the Bible, Volume 2,* edited by George Arthur Buttrick, 681–82. Nashville: Abingdon, 1981.

"Lasting Impacts: How IDRC-Funded Research has Improved Lives in the Developed World." Online: http://www.idrc.ca/en/ev-149607-201-1-DO_TOPIC.html

Lewis, Stephen. *Race Against Time.* Toronto: Anansi, 2005.

Lifton, Robert Jay. *Super Power Syndrome.* New York: Thunder's Mouth, 2003.

Long, Steven A. "Natural Law or Autonomous Practical Reason: Problems for the New Natural Law Theory." In *St. Thomas Aquinas and the Natural Law Tradition: Contemporary Perspectives,* edited by John Goyette et al., 165–93 Washington DC: The Catholic University of America Press, 2004.

Magesa, Laurenti. *The Church and Liberation in Africa.* Eldoret, Kenya: Gaba, 1976.

Maritain, Jacques. *Education at the Crossroads.* New Haven: Yale University Press, 1971.

————. *Man and the State.* Chicago: The University of Chicago Press, 1951.

————. *The Rights of Man and Natural Law.* San Francisco: Ignatius, 1986.

Martey, Emmanuel. *African Theology: Inculturation and Liberation.* Maryknoll, NY: Orbis, 1993.

Mbaku, John Mukum. "Ideologies and the Failure of Economic Development in Africa." In *Africa: Contemporary Africa,* vol. 5, edited by Toyin Falola, 391–416, Durham, NC: Carolina Academic Press, 2003.

McDonagh, Sean. *The Greening of the Church.* Maryknoll, NY: Orbis, 1990.

McGarry, Cecil, and Patrick Ryan. *Inculturating the Church in Africa: Theological and Practical Perspectives.* Nairobi: Paulines Africa, 2001.

Meredith, Martin. *The Fate of Africa from the Hopes of Freedom to the Heart of Despair.* New York: Publish Affairs, 2005.

Middleton, J. Richard. *The Liberating Image: The Imago Dei in Genesis 1.* Grand Rapids: Brazos, 2005.

Moltmann, Jürgen. *The Gospel of Liberation.* Translated by H. Wayne Pipkin. Waco, TX: Word, 1973.

———. *The Way of Jesus Christ.* Translated by Margaret Kohl. Minneapolis: Augsburg Fortress, 1993.

Moyo, Dambisa. *Dead Aid: Why Aid Is Not Working and How There Is a Better Way for Africa.* New York: Farrar, Straus, and Giroux, 2009.

Mudimbe, V. Y. *The Invention of Africa: Gnosis, Philosophy, and the Order of Knowledge.* Bloomington, IN: Indiana University Press, 1988.

Mugambi, J. N. K., and Mika Vahakangas, eds. *Christian Theology and Environmental Responsibility.* Nairobi: Acton, 2001.

Muyebe, Stanislaus, and Alex Muyebe. *The African Bishops on Human Rights: A Resource Book.* Nairobi: Paulines Africa, 2002.

Nagel, Thomas. "Poverty and Food: Why Charity is Not Enough." In *Global Justice: Seminal Essays,* edited by Thomas Pogge and Darrel Moellendorf, 49–60. St Paul, MN: Paragon House, 2008.

Nash, James, A. "Seeking Moral Norms in Nature: Natural Law and Ecological Responsibility." In *Christianity and Ecology,* edited by Dieter T. Hessel and Rosemary Radford Ruether, 227–50. Cambridge: Harvard University Press, 2000.

The New Encyclopedia Britannica. Chicago: Encyclopedia Britannica, 1983.

Newland, George. *Christ and Human Rights: The Transformative Engagement.* Aldershot, UK: Ashgate, 2006.

Newswatch Magazine 8.9 (1988) 18.

North, Gary. *The Dominion Covenant: Genesis.* Tyler, TX: Institute for Christian Economics, 1982.

Novogratz, Jacqueline. *The Blue Sweater: Bridging the Gap between the Rich and Poor In an Interconnected World.* New York: Rodale, 2009.

Nyamiti, Charles. *Studies in African Christian Theology: Some Contemporary Models of African Ecclesiology: A Critical Assessment in the Light of Biblical and Church Teaching.* Vol. 3. Nairobi: CUEA, 2007.

Oberman, Heiko A. *The Harvest of Medieval Theology.* Grand Rapids: Baker Academic, 2000.

O'Brien, David J., and Thomas A. Shannon, eds. *Catholic Social Thought: The Documentary Heritage.* Maryknoll, NY: Orbis, 1992.

O'Brien, Robert, and Marc, Williams. *Global Political Economy: Evolution and Dynamics.* New York: Palgrave Macmillan, 2004.

O'Callaghan, John P. "Imago Dei: A Test Case for St. Thomas's Augustinianism." In *Aquinas the Augustinian,* edited by Michael Dauphinais, et al., 100–144. Washington, DC: The Catholic University of America Press, 2007.

Orobator, Agbonkhianmeghe, ed. *Reconciliation, Justice, and Peace: The Second African Synod.* Maryknoll,NY: Orbis Books, 2011.

Orobator, Agbonkhianmeghe E. *From Crisis to Kairos: The Mission of the Church in the Time of HIV/AIDS, Refugees and Poverty.* Nariboi: Paulines Africa, 2005.

———. *Theology Brewed in an African Pot.* Maryknoll, NY: Orbis, 2009.

Osborn, Eric. *Irenaeus of Lyons.* Cambridge: Cambridge University Press, 2001.

Ostrom, E., et al. "Aid Incentives and Sustainability: An Institutional Analysis of Development Co-Operation." Sida Evaluation Study, No. 02/01. Stockholm: Sida, 2002.

The Pastoral Constitution on the Church in the Modern World. Gaudium et Spes, Second Vatican Council, Vatican Collection. Vol. 1. Edited by Austin Flannery. Dublin: Dominican, 1990.

Paul VI. *Constitutiones, Decreta, Declarationes*. Typis Polyglottis Vaticanis, 1966.
————. *Populorum Pregressio* 64. Nairobi: Paulines Africa, 1998.
Peet, Richard. *Unholy Trinity*. London: Zed, 2003.
Peschke, R. H. *Christian Ethics* II. Bangalore: Theological Publications In India, 1993.
Pogge, Thomas. "Severe Poverty as Human Rights Violation." In *Freedom from Poverty as a Human Right: Who Owes What to the Very Poor?*, edited by Thomas Pogge, 11–53. Oxford: Oxford University Press, 2007.
Pontifical Council for Culture. *Towards a Pastoral Approach to Culture*. Vatican: Libreria Editrice Vaticana, 1999.
Pontifical Council for Justice and Peace. *Compendium of the Social Doctrine of the Church*. Vatican: Libreria Editrice Vaticana, 2005.
The Pope Speaks 8.4 (1964).
Radcliffe, Timothy. "'Glorify God in your Bodies': 1 Corinthians 6, 12–20 as a Sexual Ethic." *New Blackfriars* 67 (1986) 306–14.
Ratzinger, Joseph. *Called to Communion: Understanding the Church Today*. Translated by Adrian Walker. San Francisco: Ignatius, 1996.
Riddell, Roger C. *Does Foreign Aid Really Work*. Oxford: Oxford University Press, 2007.
Rourke, Thomas R. "Contemporary Globalization: An Ethical and Anthropological Evaluation." In *Communio* 27.3 (2000) 1–8.
Sachs, Jeffrey D. *Common Wealth: Economics for a Crowded Planet*. New York: Penguin, 2008.
————. *The End of Poverty*. New York: Penguin, 2005.
————, ed. *Investing In Development a Practical Plan to Achieve the Millennium Development Goals*. New York: UN Development Group, 2005.
Sacks, Jonathan. *The Dignity of Difference*. London: Continuum, 2003.
Sacred Congregation on Clergy. *General Directory for Catechesis*. Nairobi: Paulines Africa, 1998.
Salih, M. A. Mohamed. "Globalization and Human Insecurity in Africa." In *Globalization, Democracy and Development in Africa: Challenges and Prospects*, edited by Taye Assefa et al., 61–81. Addis Ababa: Organization for Social Science Research in Eastern and Southern Africa, 2001.
Schonbom, Christoph. "Fides, Ratio, Scientia: The Debate About Evolution." In *Creation and Evolution: A Conference with Pope Benedict XVI in Castel Gandolfo*, translated by Michael J. Miller and edited by Stephen Otto Horn and Siegfried Wiedenhofer, 84–106. San Francisco: Ignatius, 2008.
————. *From Death to Life: The Christian Journey*. Translated by Brian McNeil. San Francisco: Ignatius, 1975.
————. *God's Human Face: The Christ-Icon*. Translated by Lothar Krauth. San Francisco: Ignatius, 1994.
Sen, Amatyr. *Development as Freedom*. New York: Anchor, 1999.
Singer, Peter. *The Life You Can Save: Acting to End World Poverty*. New York: Random House, 2009.
Skard, Torid. *Continent of Mothers, Continent of Hope*. London: Zen, 2003.
SPDC. *Nigeria Brief: Harnessing Gas*. Lagos: SPDC, 1996.
Stackhouse, Max L. "The Fifth Social Gospel and the Global Mission of the Church." In *The Social Gospel Today*, edited by Christopher H. Evans, 146–59. Louisville: Westminster/John Knox, 2001.

————. "Globalization, Public Theology and the New Means of Grace." Santa Clara Lectures. Santa Clara University, 2003. Online: http://www.scu.edu/bannancenter/eventsandconferences/lecturs/archives/stackhouse.cfm.

Synod of Bishops. *The Church in Africa in the Service of Reconciliation, Justice, and Peace: Instrumentum Laboris, Working Document.* Vatican: Libreria Editrice Vaticana, 2009.

Taiwo, Olufemi. "Exorcising Hegel's Ghost: Africa's Challenge to Philosophy." In *African Studies Quarterly: The Online Journal for African Studies.* No pages. Online: www.africa.ufl.edu/asq/vl/4/2.htm.

Tesha, John A. "Reminiscences and Personal Reflections: Development Initiatives for Africa." In *Africa's Development Thinking Since Independence: A Reader,* edited by Eddy Maloka, 9–17. Pretoria: Africa Institute of South Africa, 2002.

Theological-Historical Commission for the Great Jubilee of the Year 2000. *Jesus Christ Word of the Father.* Vatican: Vatican, 1997.

Tillard, J. M. R. *Flesh of the Church, Flesh of Christ: A Source of the Ecclesiology of Communion.* Collegeville, MN: Liturgical, 2001.

Timberlake, Lloyd. *Africa in Crisis: The Causes, the Cures of Environmental Bankruptcy.* Philadelphia: New Society, 1986.

TransAfrican Forum Globalization Monitor 1.11 (2003).

Tutu, Desmond. *No Future Without Forgiveness.* New York: Image, 2000.

UNAIDS. *The Global Economic Crisis and HIV Prevention and Treatment Programs: Vulnerabilities and Impact.* Geneva: The World Bank Global HIV/AIDS Program, 2009.

————. *2008 Report on the Global AIDS Epidemic: Executive Summary.* Geneva: UNAIDS, 2008.

UNICEF. *Africa's Orphaned Generations.* New York: United Nations Children's Fund, 2003.

UN Development Group. *Investing in Development: A Practical Plan to Achieve the Millennium Development Goals.* New York: Untied Nations Development Program, 2005.

UN General Assembly. *New Partnership for Africa's Development: Progress in Implementation and International Support: Secretary-General's Report.* A/63/130, 4.

United States Conference of Catholic Bishops. "Renewing the Earth: An Invitation to Reflection and Action on Environment in Light of Catholic Social Teaching. A Pastoral Statement of the United States Catholic Conference. November 14, 1991". Washington: NCCB/USCC, 1991.

Uzukwu, E. Eugene. *A Listening Church.* New York: Orbis, 1996.

Van De Walle, Nicolas, et al., eds. *Beyond Structural Adjustment: The Institutional Context of African Development.* New York: Palgrave Macmillan, 2003.

Villa-Vicencio, Charles. *A Theology of Reconstruction: Nation-Building and Human Rights.* Cambridge: Cambridge University Press, 1992.

Von Rad, Gerhard. *Old Testament Theology.* Vol. 2. New York: Harper and Row, 1965.

Vorgrimler, H., ed. *Commentary on the Documents of Vatican II.* Vol. 5. New York: Herder and Herder, 1975.

Walsh, William J., and John P. Langan. "Patristic Social Consciousness—The Church and the Poor." In *The Faith That Does Justice: Examining the Christian Sources for Social Change,* edited by John C. Haughey, 113–51. New York: Paulist, 1977.

Wawrykow, Joseph P. *The Westminster Handbook to Thomas Aquinas.* Louisville, KY: Westminster/John Knox, 2002.

Weigel, George. *The Truth of Catholicism: Inside the Essential Teachings and Controversies of the Church Today.* New York: HarperCollins, 2002.

Welch, Lawrence. "Gaudium et Spes, the Divine Image, and the Synthesis of Veritatis Splendor." In *Communio* 24.4 (1997) 794–814.

Wisner, Ben, et al., eds. *Towards a New Map of Africa.* London: EarthScan, 2005.

Wiwa, Ken. "Money for Nothing-and the Debt is for Free." *Globe and Mail.* May 22, 2004, A19.Woods, Thomas E. *How the Catholic Church Built Western Civilization.* Washington DC: Regnery, 2005.

World Bank/Industry and Energy Operations Division West Central Africa. *Defining an Environmental Development Strategy for the Niger Delta. May, 25, 1995. Volume 1. Online: http://www-wds.worldbank.org/external/default/WDSContentServer/WDSP/IB/2000/11/10/000094946_00082605382641/Rendered/PDF/multi_page.pdf.*

Yunus, Muhammad. *Banker to the Poor: Micro-Lending and the Battle against World Poverty.* New York: Public Affairs, 2003.

Zalot, Jozef D. *The Roman Catholic Church and Economic Development in Sub-Saharan Africa.* New York: University Press of America, 2002.

Zanzucchi, Michele. *Il Pesce Ripescato dal Fango* (The Fish Rescued from the Mud). Milan: Edizioni San Paolo, 2002.

Zuckert, Michael. *Natural Rights and the New Republicanism.* Princeton, NJ: Princeton University Press, 1994.

Index

- Charity in Truth - POPE BENEDICT
74 - STABLE → SUPPLY & DEMAND.
93 - OVERUSE (CUTTING CONSUMPTING)